Pasos
Spanish

Rosa María Martín
and Martyn Ellis

HODDER
EDUCATION
AN HACHETTE UK COMPANY

Orders: Please contact Bookpoint Ltd, 130 Milton Park, Abingdon, Oxon OX14 4SB.
Telephone: (44) 01235 827720, Fax: (44) 01235 400454. Lines are open from 9.00 to 5.00,
Monday to Saturday, with a 24-hour message answering service. You can also order through
our website www.hoddereducation.co.uk

British Library Cataloguing in Publication Data
A catalogue record for this title is available from the British Library.

ISBN: 978 1444 116 007

First published   2011
Impression number   10 9 8 7 6 5 4 3 2
Year   2014 2013 2012 2011 2011

Hachette UK's policy is to use papers that are natural, renewable and recyclable products
and made from wood grown in sustainable forests. The logging and manufacturing processes
are expected to conform to the environmental regulations of the country of origin.

Cover illustration © John McCabe – Fotolia
Typeset by Servis Filmsetting Ltd, Stockport, Cheshire
Printed in Great Britain for Hodder Education, An Hachette UK Company, 338 Euston
Road, London NW1 3BH by CPI Group (UK) Ltd, Croydon, CR0 4YY.

Contents

Introduction

Pasos Spanish Practical Grammar is a reference and grammar practice book containing clear, accessible grammar explanations with examples in both Spanish and English. It can be used alongside *Pasos Spanish Beginner's Course*, or as a general grammar for the independent learner. Grammar is explained in a practical way, with easy-to-understand examples at different levels. Grammatical items are first presented at a level suitable for basic users or those just starting out learning Spanish and then at a more complex level, aimed at the more competent student or independent user. This two-step approach enables you to study the basics before moving on to more advanced uses and forms, at a pace that suits you best. Both the main section and these *Más allá* sections are accompanied by practice exercises, with an answer key at the end of the book.

In summary, the aims of the book are as follows:

- to provide simple, clear and useful explanations of grammar forms and use
- to compare and contrast grammatical forms in order to highlight differences and establish meaning
- to provide opportunities to practise each grammatical category through varied tasks
- to extend and expand your knowledge of grammar in use through coverage of less common uses of grammatical items
- to show English equivalents of all samples of language in use so that learners can increase their lexical range as they study the grammar

As a general rule, the presentation and practice of each grammar point follows a standard pattern which allows you to find your way easily through each category. The pattern is as follows:

1. *¿Qué es?* A brief description of the item and its use, ideal for quick reference.
2. *Form* An explanation of how each grammatical item is formed, for example verb endings, position of adjectives, table of personal pronouns.
3. *Use* An explanation of when and how the grammar item is used. Some chapters offer *En breve* summaries enabling you to see at a glance what you have studied in detail.
4. *Gramática práctica* A set of practice exercises for each grammar item, with a key so that you can check your accuracy.
5. The *Más allá* section, providing a description and an explanation of more complex or advanced uses of a grammar point, which allows you to further explore the language.
6. *Más práctica* More practice exercises at the higher level.

The example sentences that appear throughout the book aim to show each grammar point in use, and these are accompanied by their English translation or equivalent. This will enable you to see exactly how the grammar item works in everyday Spanish.

Pasos Spanish Practical Grammar includes a glossary of terms, a detailed section on pronunciation and spelling including the study of accents, and an index for easy reference.

1 Glossary of grammatical terms

This glossary is intended to help you if you are not familiar with the grammatical terminology used in this book or if you need the occasional reference point. Each item is accompanied by an example to show how it is used in practice and the number of the relevant section in which the item is analysed appears in brackets.

ACTIVA (active) (44) This is also known as **voz activa** (*active voice*) and is, in general terms, the form of the verb used when the action of the sentence is carried out by the subject:

Mi madre compró una falda.	*My mother bought a dress.*

Contrast this with the passive voice (PASIVA) (44).

La falda fue comprada por mi madre.	*The dress was bought by my mother.*

ADJETIVO (adjective) (6, 11, 12) This is a word like 'old', 'happy', 'this' or 'my'. Adjectives are words which qualify or determine a noun. Adjectives in Spanish agree in number (singular and plural) and gender (masculine and feminine) with the nouns they refer to:

el coche gris	*the grey car*
los parques grandes	*the big parks*
estos parques	*these parks*

There are a number of different kinds of adjective:

ADJETIVO CALIFICATIVO (qualifying adjective) (6)
This describes the quality or the state of an object or person. They usually follow the noun.

cansado	*tired*
contento	*happy*
grande	*big.*

ADJETIVO DEMOSTRATIVO (demonstrative adjective) (11)
This is used to indicate something or someone:

este chico	*this boy*
aquel bolso	*that bag*

ADJETIVO POSESIVO (possessive adjective) (12)
This is an adjective which indicates possession:

mi casa	*my house*
su maleta	*his suitcase*
su coche	*their car*

Possessive adjectives agree in number (singular and plural) with the object to which they relate:

sus libros	*his books / their books*
mis padres	*my parents*

ADVERBIO (adverb) (18)
A word which changes or gives extra information about a verb. Many of these end in **-mente**:

Anda lentamente.	*He walks slowly.*
Generalmente como a las dos.	*Generally I have lunch at two.*

ADVERBIO DE TIEMPO (adverb of time) (18)
There are different types of adverbs; one type is the adverb of time.

These refer to the time or the length of time when something takes place.
They include the following:

aún	*still / yet*
El niño duerme aún.	*The child is still sleeping.*
Aún no he terminado.	*I haven't finished yet.*
mientras	*while*
Terminé mis deberes mientras mi madre preparó la cena.	*I finished my homework while my mother cooked dinner.*
nunca	*never*
Nunca va al gimnasio.	*He never goes to the gym.*

ARTÍCULO (article) (4, 5)
There are two kinds of article:

ARTÍCULO DEFINIDO (definite article) (4)
el, la, los, las, the equivalent of 'the' in English:

el chico	*the boy*
las chicas	*the girls*

ARTÍCULO INDEFINIDO (indefinite article) (5)
un, una, unos, unas, the equivalent of 'a' or 'some' in English:

una bicicleta	*a bicycle*
unos libros	*some books*

COMPARATIVO (comparative) (8)
This is used to compare two things in terms of size, quality, speed, etc. They are formed by adding **más** to the adjective, as in these examples:

más grande	*bigger*
más interesante	*more interesting*
más rápido	*faster*

CONDICIONAL (conditional) (32)
The conditional tense is the equivalent of 'would' or 'could', and the forms end in **-ría, -rías**, etc.:

Yo compraría esta chaqueta.	*I would buy this jacket.*

Conditional sentences are used to express a condition. They usually follow **si** (*if*):

Si hace buen tiempo, iremos a la playa.	*If the weather is good we'll go to the beach.*
Si él fuera más simpático, tendría más amigos.	*If he were friendlier, he would have more friends.*

CONJUGACIÓN (conjugation) / CONJUGAR (conjugate)

To conjugate a verb, we show it in all its persons and tenses:

yo hablo	*I speak*
tú hablas	*you speak*
él hablaba	*he was speaking*
nosotros hablamos	*we speak*
vosotros hablaréis	*you will speak*
ellos hablaron	*they spoke*

CONJUNCIÓN (conjunction) (21)

Conjunctions are words that link sentences or parts of sentences:

Pedro trabaja y Juan estudia.	*Pedro works <u>and</u> Juan studies.*
Ana trabaja en Madrid pero vive	*Ana works in Madrid <u>but</u> she lives*
en las afueras.	*in the suburbs.*

CONSONANTE (consonant) (2)

Consonants are all the letters in the alphabet that are not a vowel (VOCAL): i.e. all the letters except 'a', 'e', 'i', 'o', 'u'. See also VOCAL.

DIMINUTIVO (diminutive) (7)

This describes words formed by adding a suffix (see SUFIJO) to a word to indicate its small size:

pequeño	*small*
pequeñito	*very small, tiny*
casa	*house*
casita	*little house*

DIPTONGO (diphthong)

A diphthong is formed when two unstressed vowels occur together and are pronounced as one syllable:

bueno	*good*
baile	*dance*

ESTILO INDIRECTO (indirect speech)

A way of describing what someone says without quoting them directly:

Dijo que vendría.	*He said he would come.*

Direct speech is known as ESTILO DIRECTO.

EXCLAMACIÓN (exclamation) (15)

This describes a sentence in the form of an exclamation, which often begins with **qué**:

¡Qué calor hace!	*It's so hot!*
¡Qué emocionante!	*It's so exciting!*

FEMENINO (feminine)

One of the two grammatical genders, the other being MASCULINO (masculine).

la niña	*the girl*
la casa	*the house*

There is also a NEUTRO (neuter): **lo, esto, eso**, etc.

See also GÉNERO (gender).

FUTURO (future) (28)
The tense used to express the future:

Terminaré el sábado.	*I'll finish on Saturday.*
Los dos hermanos irán a la misma universidad.	*The two brothers will go to the same university.*

FUTURO ANTERIOR (Future Perfect) (36)
This is used to speculate about an event or an action at around the time of speaking:

Habrán llegado.	*They will have arrived (by now).*

GÉNERO (gender) (3)
Almost all Spanish nouns are either MASCULINO (masculine) or FEMENINO (feminine).

Other grammatical categories (e.g. adjectives) may also have a grammatical gender.

There is also a **género neutro** (*neuter*): **eso, aquello**, etc.

GERUNDIO (gerund) (34)
This is the same as the **-ing** form in English. It is formed by adding **-ando** to **-ar** verbs and **-iendo** to **-er** and **-ir** verbs, as in these examples:

está trabajando	*he's working*
estoy comiendo	*I'm eating*
Estamos viviendo en el centro.	*We are living in the centre.*

It is normally used with the verb **estar** (*to be*) to describe an activity that is continuing at or around the moment of speaking.

IMPERATIVO (imperative) (37)
This is the form of a verb used to give an order, a warning or a piece of advice:

Ven aquí.	*Come here.*
No hagas eso.	*Don't do that.*
Cuídate.	*Look after yourself.*

IMPERFECTO (imperfect) See PRETÉRITO IMPERFECTO

INDEFINIDO (PRETÉRITO) See PRETÉRITO INDEFINIDO

INDICATIVO (indicative)
This is called the **'Modo' Indicativo**. It means the 'mood' of the verb.

Any phrase which introduces a real event or state, or a question or order, takes the indicative form as opposed to the SUBJUNTIVO (subjunctive) (38, 39).

An example of the indicative:

Empezamos la clase cuando el profesor <u>llega</u>.	*We start the class when the teacher arrives.*

Contrast this with an example of the subjunctive:

Empezaremos la clase cuando el profesor <u>llegue</u>.	*We'll start the class when the teacher arrives.*

INFINITIVO (infinitive) (33)
This is the basic unconjugated form of the verb, the same as the 'to' form in English. There are three forms of verb:

-ar trabajar	*to work*
-er comer	*to eat*
-ir vivir	*to live*

INTERROGATIVO (interrogative) (14)
Questions can be formed by using question words, such as:

¿Qué? (*What?*), **¿Cuándo?** (*When?*), **¿Dónde?** (*Where?*)

¿Qué vas a hacer?	*What are you going to do?*
¿Dónde está Segovia?	*Where is Segovia?*

In addition, questions can be formed by changing the stress and intonation of an affirmative sentence:

¿Tienes dinero?	*Do you have any money?*

IR + A + INFINITIVO ('going to' future form) (28, 42)
This is used to express either an intention or something that is certain to happen:

Voy a visitar a mis abuelos.	*I'm going to visit my grandparents.*
Va a llover.	*It's going to rain.*

MASCULINO (masculine) (3)
One of the genders used in Spanish to describe all objects, people or concepts. Nouns in Spanish are either masculine or feminine.

NOMBRE (noun: also called SUSTANTIVO) (3)
The name given to an object: **un coche** *a car*

or a concept: **la sociedad** *society*

OBJETO (object) (9)
The object or person affected by the action of a verb. This could be a noun or a pronoun:

María fue a <u>la playa.</u>	*Maria went to the beach.*

Sometimes a sentence can have two objects:

Manuel dio el libro a Javier.	*Manuel gave the book to Javier.*

'El libro' is the object which is directly affected by the verb and so this is called the OBJETO DIRECTO (direct object).

'Javier' is the object (or in this case the person) indirectly affected. This is called the OBJETO INDIRECTO (the indirect object).

PARTICIPIO PASADO (past participle) (31, 35)
This is the form of the verb used as part of the perfect tense (PRETÉRITO PERFECTO) and also as part of the passive:

Ha llegado.	*He has arrived.*
Fue construido.	*It was built.*

PASADO (past) (29, 30, 31)
This is the term used for any form of a verb used to talk about the past.

The most common forms are the PRETÉRITO INDEFINIDO (Simple Past):

Fui al cine.   *I went to the cinema.*

and the IMPERFECTO (Imperfect):

Íbamos al cine todos los sábados.
We used to go to the cinema every Saturday.

The PRETÉRITO PERFECTO (Present Perfect) is also used to refer to the past, usually the recent past:

Han estado en Francia.   *They've been in France.*

PASIVA (passive) (44)
Also **voz pasiva**. This is the form of the verb which indicates that the subject is the recipient of the action, not the doer:

La casa fue construida por mi tío.   *The house was built by my uncle.*

In this sentence the person that carried out the action is **mi tío**, but the subject is **la casa**, which receives the action.

PASIVA REFLEJA (Passive with **se**) (44)
This is used for the equivalent of the English 'to be (done)':

La casa se construyó.   *The house was built.*

It consists of the verb in the active form preceded by **se**.

PERFECTO (Perfect) See PRETÉRITO PERFECTO (Present Perfect) (31)

PLURAL (plural) (3)
The plural form indicates that there are more than one of an item.

Tengo tres hermanos.   *I have three brothers.*

See also SINGULAR (singular) (3).
NOMBRES (nouns), ADJETIVOS (adjectives), ARTÍCULOS (articles), and VERBOS (verbs) can all appear in the plural.

PLUSCUAMPERFECTO See PRETÉRITO PLUSCUAMPERFECTO

POSESIVO (possessive) (12)
This indicates possession and can have a number of forms:

    PRONOMBRE POSESIVO (possessive pronoun)
    mío (*mine*), **tuyo** (*yours*), **suyo** (*his, hers, yours* (formal)), etc.

    ADJETIVO POSESIVO (possessive adjective):

    mi coche   *my car*
    sus hijos   *his children*

PREFIJO (prefix) (7)
This is added to the beginning of an existing word to modify its meaning, often creating an opposite:

posible   *possible*
imposible   *impossible*

A prefix may also be used to modify a word in many other ways:

llenar	*to fill (a bottle)*
rellenar	*to fill in a form, to refill*

PREPOSICIÓN (preposition) (20)

A word which describes the relation between things or people and other things or people: Examples are: **a** (*to*), **de** (*of / from*), **desde** (*since / from*), **con** (*with*), etc.

PRESENTE (present tense)

The form of a verb used to talk about the present.

The present tense can be PRESENTE (Present Simple) (24):

Vamos al mercado los sábados.	*We go to the market on Saturdays*

or PRESENTE CONTINUO (Present Continuous) (34)

Mi padre está trabajando mucho.	*My father is working a lot.*

PRETÉRITO (preterite)

This refers to the past; it appears in the names of the different past tenses in Spanish: **pretérito indefinido** (*simple past*), **pretérito imperfecto** (*imperfect*), **pretérito perfecto** (*present perfect*), **pretérito pluscuamperfecto** (*past perfect*).

PRETÉRITO IMPERFECTO (30)

This is the tense used to describe something that used to happen over an extended period of time in the past, as in:

Los domingos jugaba al tenis.	*On Sundays I used to play tennis.*

It is also used to describe what something was like in the past, for example:

La casa era muy grande.	*The house was very big.*

PRETÉRITO INDEFINIDO (29)

This tense expresses a single action that took place in the past:

Fui a Madrid.	*I went to Madrid.*

PRETÉRITO PERFECTO (31)

This tense is used to describe events happening at an unspecified time in the past and in the recent past. It is formed with the auxiliary verb **haber** plus the past participle of the main verb:

He estado en Madrid.	*I've been to Madrid.*
Hemos comprado muchas cosas.	*We've bought a lot of things.*
He trabajado mucho esta semana.	*I've worked very hard this week.*

PRETÉRITO PLUSCUAMPERFECTO (36)

This tense expresses 'the past of the past'; it refers to events or an event taking place before the time being referred to in a sequence of speech, for example:

La policía llegó a la casa pero los ladrones habían escapado.	*The police arrived at the house but the thieves had escaped.*

PRONOMBRE (pronoun) (9, 10, 11)
This is used as a substitute for the NOMBRE (or SUSTANTIVO) (noun).

Juan está aquí / Él está aquí.   *Juan is here / He is here.*

(**él** is the pronoun.)

Other examples are: **éste** (*this one*), **ése** (*that one*), etc.

PRONOMBRE INDEFINIDO (indefinite pronoun) (16)
These are words like **alguien** (*someone*), **ninguno** (*none*), etc.

PRONOMBRE PERSONAL (personal pronoun) (9)
These can be subject pronouns, such as **yo** (*I*), **tú** (*you*), **nosotros** (*we*):

Yo estudio español.   *I study Spanish.*

Or object pronouns, e.g.: **me** (*me*), **te** (*you*), **le, la, lo** (*him, her, it*), **nos** (*us*), **os** (*you*) etc.:

Te invito a la cena.   *I'll treat you to dinner.*
Juan la vio ayer.   *Juan saw her yesterday.*

PRONOMBRE RELATIVO (relative pronoun) (13)
A pronoun which is used to refer to something or someone previously mentioned and also to relate two phrases to each other:

El hombre que vino ayer.   *The man who came yesterday.*

REFLEXIVO (reflexive) (10, 25)
Some verbs are normally conjugated in the reflexive form, with the reflexive pronouns **me, te, se, nos, os, se**.

Me levanto a las siete.   *I get (myself) up at seven.*
Te vistes muy mal.   *You dress (yourself) very badly.*
Los niños se bañan.   *The children bathe (themselves).*

RELATIVO (relative pronoun) See PRONOMBRE RELATIVO

SINGULAR (singular) (3)
The form of a word which indicates one person or one object:

mesa   *table*
él   *he*
es   *is*

It also indicates that an action is done by one person:

Yo escribo   *I write*

SUBJUNTIVO (subjunctive) (38, 39)
This is also called MODO SUBJUNTIVO. It means the 'mood' of the verb which is used in expressions of possibility, doubt, hope, wishes, etc.

Es posible que venga.   *It's possible that he will come.*

In Spanish, the subjunctive is also used in conditional sentences after **si** (*if*):

Si tuviera tiempo, iría de compras.   *If I had time I would go shopping.*

SUFIJO (suffix) (6)
The name we give to additions to the end of words to modify their meaning, for example converting a word into a diminutive:

pequeñito   *tiny*

SUJETO (subject)
The word or phrase which indicates who or what is performing an action:

María hace los deberes.   *María does her homework.*

(María is the subject.)

The subject is normally placed before the verb, except in a question, when it is often placed after the verb.

SUPERLATIVO (superlative) (8)
The form of the adjective used to indicate the best, worst, biggest, etc. of more than two items:

el mejor   *the best*
el más interesante   *the most interesting*

SUSTANTIVO See **NOMBRE**

TIEMPO (tense)
This refers to the time a verb is describing: PRESENTE, PERFECTO, FUTURO, IMPERFECTO, PASADO, etc.

VERBO (verb) (23)
A word which describes an action or state:

ir   *to go*
tener   *to have*

VERBO AUXILIAR (auxiliary verb) (36)
This is a verb used to form compound tenses such as the PRETÉRITO PERFECTO (present perfect) or PLUSCUAMPERFECTO (past perfect). In both these cases the auxiliary verb is **haber** (*to have*):

Juan ha viajado mucho este año.   *Juan has travelled a lot this year.*
Había olvidado la llave.   *He had forgotten the key.*

VERBO PRONOMINAL (pronominal verb) (41)
This is a verb which uses reflexive pronouns, such as **me, te, se**, etc., even though the pronoun has no literal meaning:

irse   *to go*
dormirse   *to sleep*
callarse   *to shut up*

VERBO REFLEXIVO (reflexive verb) See **REFLEXIVO**

VOCAL (vowel) (2)
The alphabet is divided into consonants (CONSONANTES) and vowels (VOCALES). The vowels are 'a', 'e', 'i', 'o', 'u'.

VOZ ACTIVA (active voice) See **ACTIVA**

VOZ PASIVA (passive voice) See **PASIVA**

2 Pronunciation and spelling
Pronunciación y ortografía

1 The Spanish alphabet

The Spanish alphabet consists of the following 27 letters. Here they are with their names.

a a	h hache	ñ eñe	u u
b be	i i	o o	v uve
c ce	j jota	p pe	w uve doble
d de	k ka	q cu	x equis
e e	l ele	r erre	y i griega
f efe	m eme	s ese	z zeta
g ge	n ene	t te	

When we talk about letters of the alphabet, they are all feminine in gender:
la a, la be, la hache, etc.

La 'a' de 'casa'.   *The 'a' of 'casa'.*

2 Pronunciation and spelling

In Spanish, most words are written exactly as they are pronounced, with very few exceptions.

2.1 Las vocales *Vowels*

Spanish has five vowels: 'a', 'e', 'i', 'o', 'u'. They are short and clear and completely consistent in the way they sound. They are always pronounced, and always in the same way.

2.2 Las consonantes *Consonants*

Generally, in Spanish one sound corresponds to one letter. Consequently there are few difficulties in the pronunciation of consonants. The following letters and combinations are pronounced in their own unique way in Spanish.

2.2.1 'b' and 'v'

These are both pronounced rather like the English 'b', as in 'big'. If it appears in the middle of a word it has a slightly softer sound:

'b', 'v' = [b]
beber (*to drink*), **volver** (*to return*) as in 'big'
'b', 'v' = [v]
cabeza (*head*), **cerveza** (*beer*)   as in 'tribal'

2.2.2 'c' and 'z'

'c' + 'e', 'i' = [th]

centro (*centre*), **cine** (*cinema*)	as in 't<u>h</u>eatre'

'c' + 'a', 'o', 'u' = [k]

carta (*letter*), **coche** (*car*), **cuando** (*when*)	as in '<u>k</u>oala'

'z' + 'a', 'o', 'u' = [th]

zapatos (*shoes*), **zorro** (*fox*), **zumo** (*juice*)	as in 't<u>h</u>eatre'

Note:

In Spanish-speaking Latin American countries, and also in parts of the south of Spain, 'ce', 'ci' and 'z' are pronounced more like the 's' sound: so 'cebra' sounds like '<u>s</u>ebra', 'cine', sounds like '<u>s</u>ine'; 'vez' sounds like 've<u>s</u>'.

2.2.3 'h'

'h' is never pronounced but it must be written:

hablar (*to speak*), **hermano** (*brother*), **¡hola!** (*hello*), **hilo** (*thread*)

2.2.4 'k' and 'q'

'k' is only found in words that did not originate in Spanish and have been borrowed or adapted from other languages, e.g. **kilómetro**. The sound [k] before 'e' and 'i' is formed by using 'qu'.

'q' is always followed by 'u' but the 'u' is not sounded (unlike in English):

'qu' + 'e', 'i', = [k]

queso (*cheese*), **quince** (*fifteen*)

If we want to sound the 'u', then the letter combination is 'c' + 'u', not 'q' and 'u'.

¿<u>Cu</u>ánto <u>cu</u>esta?	*How much is it?*

Compare this with:

Quiero queso.	*I want cheese.*

in which the 'u' is not pronounced.

2.2.5 'j' and 'g'

'j' is pronounced at the back of the throat. The nearest equivalent is an emphasised 'h' sound in '<u>h</u>am':

jamón (*ham*), **joven** (*young*)

'g' has the same pronunciation as 'j' if it is placed before 'e' or 'i':

gente (*people*), **Ginebra** (*Geneva*)

'ge', 'gi' and 'je', 'ji' are pronounced the same and are easily confused when writing. But most Spanish words with this sound begin with 'ge', 'gi'.

'g' + 'a', 'o', 'u' is pronounced the same as in English 'go', 'gas':

Galicia, **gota** (*drop*), **guapo** (*good-looking*)

'gue', 'gui' are pronounced like the English 'g' in 'go'. The 'u' between the 'g' and 'e' or 'i' is never pronounced:

guerra (*war*), **guisante** (*pea*)

However, there are some words in Spanish which sound like [gwe], and these are written 'güe', 'güi'; with what is known as a diaeresis: ü:

bilingüe (*bilingual*), **pingüino** (*penguin*)

2.2.6 'ñ'

'ñ' is pronounced as the 'ny' sound in 'ca<u>ny</u>on':

mañana (*tomorrow*), **castaño** (*chestnut (colour)*)

2.2.7 'r'

'r' is pronounced differently depending on its position in the word.
At the beginning of a word, and after 'l', 'n' or 's', the 'r' is strong and is rolled rather like a Scottish 'r':

robo (*robbery*), **rojo** (*red*), **alrededor** (*surrounding*), **sonreír** (*to smile*), **Israel**

If the same sound is to be obtained between vowels then it is doubled in the written form and appears as 'rr':

perro (*dog*), **carro** (*cart*)

This is because, if we require a softer 'r' sound, more like the English 'r' sound, only one 'r' appears between the vowels:

pero (*but*), **caro** (*expensive*)

2.2.8 's'

In parts of southern Spain and Latin America an 's' placed at the end of a word is not pronounced. The plural and singular may therefore be confused in pronunciation: 'las casas' sounds like [la casa].

3 Stress

In Spanish only one syllable in each word is stressed. The stress is free, which means it can be on any syllable, but there are simple rules which indicate where the stress falls.

3.1 Words ending in a vowel

For these, or with the consonants 'n' or 's', the stress falls on the penultimate syllable:

<u>ca</u>ma (*bed*), **<u>ca</u>sas** (*houses*), **<u>co</u>men** (*they eat*)

3.2 Words ending in a consonant other than 'n' or 's'

For these, the stress falls on the last syllable:

be<u>ber</u> (*to drink*), **sa<u>lud</u>** (*health*)

3.3 Accents

3.3.1

An accent is required when the stress falls on the last syllable of a word ending in a vowel or 'n' or 's'. The accent is added to the last vowel:

sa<u>lí</u> (*I went out*), **visita<u>ré</u>** (*I will visit*), **pea<u>tón</u>** (*pedestrian*), **sa<u>lís</u>** (*you leave*)

3.3.2

An accent is required when the stress falls on the penultimate syllable in a word ending in a consonant other than 'n' or 's':

fácil (*easy*), **difí**cil (*difficult*), **Gonzá**lez

If the stress falls on the antepenultimate syllable (two syllables from the end), this syllable always has an accent:

bolígrafo (*ballpoint pen*), **lás**tima (*pity*), **fantás**tico (*fantastic*)

3.3.3

Words of one syllable never carry a written accent:

pie (*foot*), **diez** (*ten*), **ya** (*already / now*)

except when two words have the same form but a different meaning:

de	*of*	**dé**	subjunctive form of **dar**
el	*the*	**él**	*he*
mi	*my*	**mí**	*me* (after preposition)
si	*if*	**sí**	*yes*

3.4 Capital letters

Spanish uses capital letters less frequently than English. They are used at the beginning of a sentence and after a full stop:

Juan volvió a su trabajo. Entró.   *Juan returned to work. He went in.*

Unlike English, capital letters are <u>not</u> used for:

(a) months, seasons and days of the week:

septiembre (*September*), **domingo** (*Sunday*)

(b) languages and nationalities:

Hablo español.   *I speak Spanish.*
Soy francés.   *I am French.*

3.5 Question and exclamation mark

There are two symbols for a question mark: '¿' placed at the beginning of the sentence and '?' at the end.

The same occurs with the exclamation mark: '¡' at the beginning and '!' at the end:

¿Quieres ir al parque conmigo   *Would you like to go to the park with*
**   esta tarde?**   *me this afternoon?*
¡Qué frío!   *It's so cold!*

3 Nouns *El nombre o sustantivo*

1 ¿Qué es?

Nouns (**nombres, sustantivos**) are words used to name people, animals, places, things and also feelings, concepts and ideas.
They are words such as: *woman, dog, chair, family, happiness* or *duty*.

Common nouns (**nombres comunes**) refer to everything and everybody:

hombre (*man*), **padre** (*father*), **perro** (*dog*), **casa** (*house*), **coche** (*car*), **felicidad** (*happiness*), **sueño** (*dream, sleep*), etc.

Proper nouns (**nombres propios**) are used to name individual people, animals, places, or other things such as institutions, positions or special holidays. In these cases the first letter is always upper case.

- names and surnames of people: **María Martínez**
- countries, towns, rivers, mountains and similar: **España, Sevilla, Pirineos**
- institutions, companies, departments: **Parlamento, Director**
- special holidays: **Navidad** (*Christmas*)**, Pascua** (*Easter*)
- forms of address: **Sr. (Señor), Sra. (Señora), Srta. (Señorita), Don, Doña**

2 Gender (masculine and feminine) *Género (masculino y femenino)*

> **En breve**
> All Spanish nouns have a gender: masculine or feminine.
> This can be natural gender: masculine = male and feminine = female:
> **niño** (*male child*), **niña** (*female child*)
> or grammatical gender, which is arbitrary:
> **cuchillo** (*knife*), **cuchara** (*spoon*)
> In general, if a word ends in **-o** it is masculine and if it ends in **-a** it is feminine:
> **centro** (m), **plaza** (f)
> but there are many other endings and rules (see below).

In Spanish all nouns are either feminine or masculine. This is called gender. The most common indicators are the endings of words (**-o** or **-a**), but gender can also be identified by the use of the definite article (*the*): masculine **el**, feminine **la**.

 See Unit 4.

Words ending in other vowels or consonants may be masculine or feminine and have to be learnt. In dictionaries, the gender is indicated after each noun: **hombre** (m), **mujer** (f). In some cases there are simple rules to follow, but in general the easiest way to remember nouns is to learn every word with the article: **el** hombre, **la** mujer.

2.1 Natural gender

As we have seen, this refers to people and animals. We can apply some common rules, as follows:

2.1.1 Forms and rules

	Masculine	**Feminine**
Change ending: -o > -a	niñ**o**	niñ**a**
Add ending: -consonant + -a	doctor	doctor**a**
Same word: -e = -e	estudiante	estudiante
Different word (less common):	hombre padre yerno (*son-in-law*) padrino (*godfather*)	mujer madre nuera (*daughter-in-law*) madrina (*godmother*)

2.1.2 People

- first names: **Antonio, Antonia; Luis, Luisa; Rafael, Rafaela; Juan, Juana**
- forms of address: **señor, señora, señorita; don, doña**
- family, relations, friends: **hermano** (*brother*), **hermana** (*sister*); **amigo, amiga** (*friend*); **vecino, vecina** (*neighbour*)
- jobs and professions, occupations and positions: **camarero** (*waiter*), **camarera** (*waitress*); **director, directora; intérprete**
- nationalities: **americano, americana; español, española**

 See Unit 6 Adjectives for more on nationalities.

2.1.3 ¡Es diferente!

2.1.3.1 el recepcionista / la recepcionista

Words ending in **-a, -ta, -ista**:
Although nouns ending in **-a** are normally feminine, some words that finish in **-ista** can be either masculine or feminine. The only way to tell is from the article, **el** or **la**.

Most of these words refer to professions: **el periodista, la periodista** (*journalist*); **el recepcionista, la recepcionista**.

A few words that finish in **-a** and **-ta** can also be masculine or feminine: **el / la guía**, (*guide*); **el / la colega** (*colleague*); **el / la atleta; el / la astronauta**.

2.1.3.2 el cliente > la clienta

Words that finish in **-e** are normally masculine and some change to **-a** in the feminine form: **el cliente, la clienta; el dependiente, la dependienta** (*shop assistant*); **el jefe, la jefa** (*boss*); **el presidente, la presidenta**.

2.1.3.3 el modelo / la modelo

Some words that finish in **-o** (for professions or activities) are used both for masculine and feminine: **el / la piloto; el / la modelo; el / la soprano; el / la testigo** (*witness*).

2.1.3.4 el médico / la médico/a?

Some words are less clear and change as society changes and more women do jobs that were formerly considered mainly masculine. The word for *doctor* is a case in point; the masculine form is **médico** but the feminine is variously seen as **la médico** or **la médica**, the latter being used much more in recent years.

2.1.3.5 el actor / la actriz

Special endings: some nouns don't follow any of the rules described above and form the feminine with special endings:
el príncipe (*prince*) / **la princesa** (*princess*); **el rey** (*king*) / **la reina** (*queen*)

2.1.3.6 el bebé, la persona

Some nouns that have only one form, either feminine or masculine, apply to both males and females:

la persona (*person*), **el bebé** (*baby*), **el personaje** (*character*), **el genio** (*genius*), **la estrella** (*star*), **la víctima** (*victim*), **el ángel** (*angel*), **el ser** (*being*)

2.1.3.7 Words ending in -í, -ú

These are the same for masculine and feminine. There are only a few of these and they are mainly nationalities: **el marroquí / la marroquí; el pakistaní / la pakistaní; el hindú / la hindú**.

2.1.4 Animals

Most domestic animals and pets and some wild animals follow the rules above:

- **-o / -a**: **perro, perra** (*dog*), **gato, gata** (*cat*), **mono, mona** (*monkey*);
- consonant + **-a**: **león, leona** (*lion*) (note that the accent disappears in the feminine: see Unit 2 Section 3.3 page 12)
- **-e**: **elefante** (m / f)
- **-í**: **jabalí** (m / f) (*wild boar*)
- different word: **caballo, yegua** (*horse, mare*); **toro, vaca** (*bull, cow*)
- special endings: **tigre, tigresa** (*tiger*)

2.2 Grammatical gender

Nouns that refer to objects, ideas, and feelings also have their own gender. They may be either masculine or feminine.

2.2.1 Forms and rules

The same rules and forms apply as for natural gender. Most words that end in

Ending	Gender	Example
-o	masculine	el libr**o**
-a	feminine	la cas**a**
-e	arbitrary	el coch**e**, la call**e**
-consonant	arbitrary	el cami**ón**, la ciud**ad**

-o are masculine and most that end in **-a** are feminine. The rest can be either, and so the best way to learn them is with the article: **el, la** (*the*).

Also, the very few words ending in **-í** and **-ú** can be either gender: **el maniquí, el tabú.**

2.2.2 Para recordar: ¡Es lógico!

Here are some easy extra rules to help you remember:

Always masculine:

- numbers: the Spanish for *number* is **el número**, a masculine noun, so logically, all numbers are masculine: **el (número) cinco, el ocho, el treinta**
- colours: the Spanish for *colour* is **el color**, so all colours are masculine: **el (color) rojo, el azul, el verde**
- days: the Spanish for *day* is **el día**, even though it ends in **-a**, so all days are masculine: **el (día) lunes, el martes, el miércoles** etc.
- months: the Spanish for *month* is **el mes**, a masculine noun, so although Spanish months do not use the article, they are masculine: **el (mes de) noviembre, abril, mayo**
- languages: the Spanish for *language* is **el idioma**, so we have: **el español, el italiano, el inglés**, etc.

Always feminine:

- letters of the alphabet: **la (letra) 'a', la 'b', la 'o', la 'm'.**

2.2.3 ¡Es diferente!

There are a few exceptions to the rules above.

- We have seen that **día**, although ending in **-a**, is a masculine noun and so we say **Buenos días** for *Good morning*.
- Other masculine nouns ending in **-a** are: **el mapa, el sofá, el planeta, el tranvía** (*tram*); also some names of colours: **el rosa, el naranja**
- Many words ending in **-ma** are also masculine: **el pijama, el clima, el programa, el problema, el tema, el crucigrama** (*crossword*), **el sistema, el fantasma** (*ghost*), **el poema**; but not: **la cama** (*bed*) or **la crema**.

- Feminine words that end in **-o**: **la mano** (*hand*)
- Some nouns that are an abbreviation of the full word are also feminine: **la moto (la motocicleta), la foto (la fotografía), la radio (la radiodifusión/ radiofonía)**
- The gender of foreign words is generally masculine: **el camping, el champán, el pub, el poster, el chalet, el software**; unless they are associated with a feminine Spanish word: **la web (la red)**.

3 Number *Número: Singular & Plural*

To form the plural we simply add **-s** or **-es** to the end of the word: **-s** to the end of nouns ending in a vowel; **-es** to the end of nouns ending in a consonant.

vowel + s: **hermano, hermanos**
consonant + es: **señor, señores**

The plural form of the article is used with the plural of the noun: **los, las** (*the*): **los hijos** (*the children*), **las hermanas** (*the sisters*).

 For more about articles, see Unit 4.

3.1 ¡Es diferente!

3.1.1

If a noun ends in **-s** and either has one syllable or is stressed on the last syllable, we add **-es**: **el país, los países** (*countries*); **el autobús, los autobuses**.
Nouns ending in **-s** preceded by a non-stressed vowel do not change for the plural: **el lunes, los lunes; el jueves, los jueves**.

3.1.2

Some words are always used in the plural: **las gafas** (*glasses*), **los pantalones** (*trousers*; although we can also say **el pantalón**).

3.1.3

Spelling changes occur from singular to plural in the following cases:

 See also Unit 2 Section 2 and 3 pp 10–13.

- Words ending in **-z** change to **-c** in the plural: **una vez** (*once*), **dos veces** (*twice*)
- Words ending in **-án, -én, -ín, -ón, -ión** and **-és** lose the accent: **el alemán, los alemanes; el inglés, los ingleses; la ración, las raciones** (*portions*); **el andén, los andenes** (*platforms*)
- Words ending in **-en** add an accent to the preceding syllable to keep the stress in the same place: **el joven, los jóvenes**.

3.1.4 *Mixed gender groups*

When two or more masculine or feminine nouns are in a mixed group, the masculine plural is used: **el padre** (*father*) + **la madre** (*mother*) = **los padres**; **el hijo** (*son*) + **las hijas** (*daughters*) = **los hijos**.

4 Gramática práctica

3.4.1 Write the feminine of the following words.

el abuelo, el tío, el compañero, el padre, el hermano, el vecino, el hombre, el señor, el primo, el yerno, el amigo, el español, el colombiano, el nicaragüense, el pakistaní

3.4.2 Give the other gender form of each job.

1. Pepe es camionero.	Pepita es
2. Ángel es taxista.	Ángela es
3. Enrique es intérprete.	Enriqueta es
4. Manuel es traductor.	Manuela es
5. Víctor es farmacéutico.	Victoria es
6. Antonia es cocinera.	Antonio es
7. Francisca es periodista.	Francisco es
8. Rafaela es dependienta.	Rafael es
9. Aurelia es profesora.	Aurelio es
10. Pabla es fontanera.	Pablo es

3.4.3 Write '-o' or '-a' at the end of each word. What do they mean?

el libr-   la mes-   el cuadern-   el bolígraf-   la carter-   la ventan-
el clim-   el gimnasi-   la taz-   el vas-   el teléfon-   la radi-
la naranj-   el ros-   el sof-   la mot-   la tortill-

3.4.4 Put the following words in the plural and add the article. What do they mean?

chocolate, fresa, lunes, pastel, galleta, ensalada, queso, pan, árbol, camión, bar, tía, marido, madre, ciudad, martes.

3.4.5 Write sentences like the one in the example using the words in the box.

Example: una cerveza > Quiero dos cervezas. (*I'd like two beers*)

> un helado, un café, una hamburguesa, un refresco, un zumo, un vino, un té, una tortilla, un bocadillo, un pastel

5 Más allá

5.1 Gender *Género*

5.1.1 Natural gender

¿La rana: macho o hembra?

The words for many animals are either masculine or feminine, no matter whether the actual animal is male or female. For example, **el cocodrilo** is a male or female crocodile; **la rana** is a female or male frog.

More examples: **la jirafa** (*giraffe*), **el delfín** (*dolphin*), **el jabalí** (*wild boar*), **el pulpo** (*octopus*), **el tiburón** (*shark*), **el ratón** (*mouse*), **el gorila** (*gorilla*), **la tortuga** (*tortoise*), **la serpiente** (*snake*), **la ballena** (*whale*), **la rata** (*rat*), **la cebra** (*zebra*), **la gaviota** (*seagull*).
To distinguish them, we can say: **el cocodrilo macho** (*male*), **el cocodrilo hembra** (*female*).

5.1.2 Grammatical gender

Although we said earlier that the gender of many nouns simply has to be learned, we can make this easier for ourselves by identifying patterns amongst groups of nouns.

Masculine nouns:

- Mountains, rivers and seas are usually masculine, from **el monte**, **el rió**, **el mar**: **el Collarada** (mountain in the Pyrenees), **el Ebro** (river in the north east of Spain), **el Mediterráneo**.
- Some countries (sometimes used with the article) are masculine: **El Salvador, (el) Uruguay, (el) Japón, (el) Brasil**.
- Compound nouns (formed by two words) are masculine: **el paraguas** (*umbrella* – **parar aguas**, *to stop the water*), **el sacacorchos** (*corkscrew* – **sacar corchos**, *to take out corks*), **el abrelatas** (*can opener* – **abrir latas**, *to open cans*).

Feminine nouns:

- Most nouns ending in **-d**, **-z** and **-l** are feminine: **la ciudad** (*city*), **la voz** (*voice*), **la cárcel** (*prison*).
- Most nouns ending in **-ción** and **-sión** are feminine: **la canción** (*song*), **la profesión** (*profession*).
- Islands and regions: **Las (islas) Canarias, la (región / comunidad de) Andalucía**.
- Some countries (sometimes used with the article): **(la) China; (la) Argentina**.

Note:

- Fruit trees are masculine: **el naranjo** (*orange tree*), fruit is feminine: **la naranja** (*orange*)
- Some nouns that are feminine take a masculine article: **el agua, el aula, el águila**. This is because the initial 'a' is stressed and not easy to say after a preceding 'a'.

See also Unit 4.

5.2 Number *Número: singular & plural*

5.2.1

Words that finish in **-á, -ó** or **-ú** (last vowel stressed) usually add **-s**: **esquí, esquís; champú, champús; menú, menús.**

A few add **-es**: **maniquíes, tabúes** (although many people nowadays just add **-s**).

5.2.2

Words ending in **-ay, -ey, -oy** add **-es**: **rey, reyes.**

5.2.3

Words ending in **-sis, -tis** and **-us** don't change: **la crisis, las crisis; la faringitis, las faringitis; el virus, los virus.**

5.2.4

Names of consonants add **-s**: **la b, las bes; la efe, las efes; la k, las kas.** But vowels add **-es** in the plural: **la a, las aes; la i, las íes; la o, las oes; la u, las úes** (but **la e, las es**).

5.2.5

Foreign words usually add an **-s**: **el jersey, los jerseys; el bistec, los bistecs; el pub, los pubs; el club, los clubs.**

5.2.6

Surnames or family names don't change: **el señor García, los señores García** (*los García*).

6 Más práctica

3.6.1 Put these words into the following categories: MS (masculine singular), FS (feminine singular), MPL (masculine plural), FPL (feminine plural). Some might correspond to two categories; if so, write them in both.

paraguas agua jabalí crema menús días rey princesa ratones patatas vecinos amigas fotos viernes madre primos mujeres nuera abuelo padres motos pijama sofás crisis ciudad jirafas mono pakistaní radio programa mano

3.6.2 Read the dialogue on the following page and underline the nouns. Give their gender and say whether they are singular or plural.

El apartamento

Mujer:	Buenas tardes, le llamo para preguntarle por el apartamento del anuncio. ¿Cómo es?
Hombre:	Pues es grande, tiene un salón muy bonito, tiene cocina, comedor, cuatro dormitorios, dos terrazas, tiene televisión, lavadora y lavavajillas.
Mujer:	¿Es para cuatro personas?
Hombre:	Pues. . .sí. . .claro, es muy grande y los muebles son completamente nuevos.
Mujer:	¿Está cerca de la playa?
Hombre:	A unos quince minutos de la playa en coche.
Mujer:	¿Tiene piscina?
Hombre:	Sí, claro, tiene piscina y jardines.

4 The definite article *El artículo definido (o determinado)*

1 ¿Qué es?

A definite article is a word that accompanies a noun. It always appears immediately before the noun and is used to specify or define the noun it refers to: *house* becomes *the house* so that we know which house we are talking about.

In Spanish, the article generally tells us whether a noun is feminine or masculine, which is not always clear from the endings:

el recepcionista (*the male receptionist*), **la recepcionista** (*the female receptionist*); **el pastel** (*the cake*), **la tortilla** (*the omelette*).

 See Unit 3 Sections 2, 5.

2 Forms

2.1 The definite article

In English there is only one word for the definite article: *the*. But in Spanish there are four, depending on gender (masculine or feminine) or number (singular or plural):

	Masculine	**Feminine**	**(English)**
Singular	el	la	= the
Plural	los	las	= the

El hotel es bueno.	*The hotel is good.*
La casa es grande.	*The house is big.*
Los camareros son eficientes.	*The waiters are efficient.*
Las niñas son simpáticas.	*The girls are nice.*

2.2 ¡Es diferente!

2.2.1 *Feminine nouns with a stressed 'a' or 'ha' as their first letter(s) take* el *as the definite article:*

El agua está fría.	*The water is cold.*
El área donde estamos es bonita.	*The area we are in is pretty.*
El aula está a la derecha.	*The classroom is on the right.*
El hambre es mala.	*Hunger is bad.*

Note this doesn't happen in the plural: **las aguas, las aulas**.

Las aulas son nuevas.   *The classrooms are new.*

2.2.2 Contracted forms: al and del

When the article **el** is preceded by the preposition **a** it produces a contracted form: **al**.

When the article **el** is preceded by the preposition **de** it produces a contracted form: **del**.

Note that these are the only contracted words in Spanish.

Voy al banco.   *I'm going to the bank.*
El cine está a la derecha del   *The cinema is to the right of the*
   hotel.   *hotel.*
El salón está al final del   *The lounge is at the end of the*
   pasillo.   *corridor.*

3 Uses of the definite article

3.1 Cases in which the article is used

3.1.1 Before names of family members

El abuelo es muy simpático.   *Grandad is very nice.*
La tía no está en casa.   *Auntie is not at home.*

But it is not used with **mamá** and **papá**:

Mamá está en casa, pero papá   *Mum is at home but dad*
   está en la oficina.   *is in the office.*

3.1.2 Before titles

When we talk about a person, using their title, we include the article:

El señor García va a la reunión.   *Mr García is going to the meeting.*
La señora González trabaja aquí.   *Mrs González works here.*
El doctor Martín viene ahora.   *Doctor Martín is coming now.*

But it is not used when we address the people directly, using their titles:

Mucho gusto, señor García.   *Pleased to meet you, Mr García.*
Señora González, ¿cómo está usted?   *Mrs González, how are you?*

3.1.3 With days of the week

El lunes tengo clase de español.   *On Monday I have a Spanish class.*
Los sábados voy de compras.   *On Saturdays I go shopping.*

But it is not used with days in dates:

Hoy es lunes, cinco de junio.   *Today is Monday 5th June.*

3.1.4 With dates

When we give the date of an event, the article is equivalent to *on the*:

Mi cumpleaños es el treinta de diciembre.	*My birthday is on the 30th December.*

It is also used with words like **hoy** (*today*), **mañana** (*tomorrow*) when followed by the date:

Hoy es el ocho de marzo.	*Today is the 8th March.*

But it is not used when we write the current date in a document, a diary for example.

3.1.5 With time expressions and before numerals

Es la una y media.	*It's half past one.*
Son las siete de la tarde.	*It's seven in the evening.*
Es el número siete.	*It's number seven.*
¿Vives en el octavo piso?	*Do you live on the eighth floor?*
No, vivo en el noveno.	*No, I live on the ninth.*

3.1.6 When expressing measurements and weights

Son diez euros el kilo.	*It's ten euros per kilo.*

3.1.7 With seasons

La primavera es una estación muy bonita.	*Spring is a beautiful season.*
El verano es época de vacaciones en España.	*Summer is holiday time in Spain.*

But not usually after the preposition **en**:

Tengo exámenes en primavera.	*I have exams in the spring.*

3.1.8 With parts of the body and clothes

When the possessive adjective is used in English, especially after **doler** (*to hurt / ache*):

Me duele la cabeza.	*My head aches.*
Ponte los guantes.	*Put your gloves on.*

But not in: **Tengo dolor de cabeza**. (*I have a headache.*)

3.1.9 With some countries and places

Often when these form part of the name itself, e.g.

El Salvador, La Habana, La Rioja, los Pirineos, el (mar) Mediterráneo, las (islas) Canarias.

 See Unit 3 Section 5.

3.1.10 Some common phrases of place

a / en la escuela, la universidad, la cárcel, el hospital, la iglesia, el trabajo.

Voy a la escuela.	*I'm going to school.*
Estoy en la universidad.	*I'm at university.*
Estoy en el trabajo.	*I'm at work.*
Voy al hospital.	*I'm going to the hospital.*

3.1.11 *With names of sports teams*

El Sevilla es un buen equipo.	*Sevilla is a good team.*
El Barcelona juega este domingo.	*Barcelona are playing this Sunday.*

3.1.12 *With leisure activities*

Juego al tenis.	*I play tennis.*
Voy al cine.	*I'm going to the cinema.*
Practico la natación.	*I go swimming.*
Veo el partido de fútbol.	*I'm watching the football match.*

3.1.13 *After the verb gustar*

The definite article is always used with **gustar** and verbs which work in a similar way (**encantar, interesar, apetecer**, etc.):

Me gusta la carne pero no me gusta el pescado.	*I like meat but I don't like fish.*

3.1.14 *Before names of languages*

El español es un idioma muy útil.	*Spanish is a very useful language.*

But it is not used after the verbs **hablar, aprender, estudiar, saber**:

Hablo inglés.	*I speak English.*
Aprendo francés.	*I learn French.*
Sé chino.	*I know Chinese.*

Neither is it used after the preposition **en**:

Está hablando en español.	*He is speaking in Spanish.*

 See point 5.1 below.

3.1.15 *With generic nouns that belong to a certain group or category*

el vino, el alcohol, el ejercicio, la gente, la mujer, el hombre, la familia, etc.

These can be in the singular:

La gente de este pueblo es muy simpática.	*People in this town are very friendly.*
El vino español es excelente.	*Spanish wine is excellent.*
El ejercicio es bueno para la salud.	*Exercise is good for your health.*
La mujer ocupa un lugar importante en la política.	*Women occupy an important place in politics.*

Or in the plural:

las personas, los niños, los españoles, los periódicos, etc.

Los españoles son muy acogedores.	*Spaniards are very welcoming.*
Los niños comen mucho en la actualidad.	*Children eat a lot nowadays.*
Los periódicos son caros.	*Newspapers are expensive.*

But

Tienes que hacer ejercicio.	*You have to do exercise.*
No debes beber alcohol.	*You shouldn't drink alcohol.*
Lee periódicos.	*He/she reads newspapers.*
Compra libros.	*He/she buys books.*

 See section 5 below.

3.1.16 *The noun* casa

This has two meanings: *house* and *home*. The article is used when it means *house*.

Llegó a la casa y llamó a la puerta.	*He arrived at the house and knocked on the door.*

But when it means *home* the article is not used:

Voy a casa.	*I'm going home.*

Note: In Latin America the article may be used:

Latin America: Vamos a la casa. = *Let's go home.*
Spain: Vamos a casa.

3.1.17 *With abstract nouns*

la sociedad (*society*), la naturaleza (*nature*), la educación (*education*), la belleza (*beauty*), el amor (*love*), la esperanza (*hope*), la felicidad (*happiness*).

La sociedad está cambiando.	*Society is changing.*
La naturaleza está en peligro.	*Nature is in danger.*
La educación es esencial.	*Education is essential.*

3.2 Cases in which the article is not used

3.2.1 *Before the name of a person:* María, Juan

3.2.2 *After* tener

No tiene niños.	*She has no children.*
Tengo esperanza.	*I have hope.*

3.2.3 *After* hay*

Hay café y té para beber.	*There's coffee and tea to drink.*
Hay paella para comer.	*There's paella to eat.*
No hay entradas.	*There aren't any tickets.*

But remember: to say whether something exists:

Hay <u>un</u> restaurante en el pueblo.	*There is a restaurant in the village.*

3.2.4 *After* ser *followed by a profession*

Es médico.	*He's a doctor.*

But:

Es el médico del pueblo.	*He is the village doctor.*

3.2.5 *With ordinal numbers in titles for kings, queens or popes*

Juan Carlos primero	*Juan Carlos the First*

3.3 Use of the article combined with other grammatical categories before the noun

3.3.1 *with* otro/a/os/as *(other)*

No quiero este jersey, quiero el otro.	*I don't want this sweater, I want the other one.*
Deme los otros pantalones.	*Give me the other trousers.*

3.3.2 *with* todo/a/os/as *(all)*

El niño quiere todo el pastel.	*The little boy wants all of the cake.*
Tengo todas las cosas preparadas.	*I have everything prepared.*

3.3.3 *With numerals (see also point 3.1.5 above)*

Quiero ver a los dos niños.	*I want to see the two children.*
Las tres hermanas viven juntas.	*The three sisters live together.*

Note: **los dos**: *both*:

Quiero los dos.	*I want both.*

3.4 An article used with an adjective, with no noun appearing

This makes the adjective behave like a noun:

Prefiero el coche nuevo.	*I prefer the new car.*
Prefiero el nuevo.	*I prefer the new one.*

4 Gramática práctica

4.4.1 Write the correct articles for these words.

aceite, huevos, vinagre, sal, queso, jamón, patatas fritas, pastel, pan, tomates, sardinas, paquete, cajas

4.4.2 Complete the sentences with the correct articles.

1. _____ agua es buena para _____ salud.
2. _____ área donde vivo es muy bonita.
3. _____ teatro está a _____ derecha.
4. _____ camión ha tenido un accidente con _____ moto.
5. _____ lunes tengo clase de español.
6. _____ domingos voy a _____ iglesia.
7. _____ hermano de Ana está en _____ oficina.
8. _____ camareros de _____ restaurante son buenos.
9. No me gusta _____ carne, prefiero _____ pescado.
10. Tienes que ponerte _____ guantes porque hace frío.

4.4.3 Put the article in the correct place, if it is needed. (Some capital letters will need to change to lower case.)

1. Señora Martín es profesora.
2. Me duele cabeza.
3. Gente de esta ciudad es muy agradable.
4. Abuelo es muy bueno.
5. Hermana de Luis está en casa.
6. Voy a casa de padres de mi amigo Luis.
7. Madrid jugará contra Barcelona.
8. Papá está en casa.
9. Padre de Luis vive en Valencia.
10. Quiero hablar con señor Pérez.
11. Señor Pérez, venga aquí, por favor.
12. Doctor Collado viene ahora.
13. Hoy es lunes, cinco de enero.
14. Niño va a escuela.
15. Estudio en universidad.
16. Español es un idioma muy útil.

5 Más allá

5.1 Uses of the article

5.1.1

Important: the article is mostly used in cases when the noun is the subject in the sentence:

El vino es caro.	*The wine is expensive.*
El médico es bueno.	*The doctor is good.*
La música es excelente.	*The music is excellent.*

5.1.2

But: when the noun is an object in the sentence the article is frequently not used:

Quiero vino.	*I'd like some wine.*
Juan es médico.	*Juan is a doctor.*
Escucho música.	*I listen to music.*

If the article is added, it is to specify:

Juan es el médico del pueblo.	*Juan is the village doctor.*

This explains the cases in 3.1.14 and 3.1.15 above.

Contrast

El español es fácil.	*Spanish is easy.*
El ejercicio es bueno para la salud.	*Exercise is good for your health.*

with

Estudio español.	*I study Spanish.*
Hago ejercicio.	*I do exercise.*

5.1.3 Exceptions

With nouns that express leisure activities and also after verbs like **gustar**; in these cases the article is used (see points 3.1.12 and 3.1.13 above):

Juego al fútbol.	*I play football.*
Me gusta la televisión.	*I like television.*

5.1.4

This also explains why the article is not used after the verb **tener**:

Para postre tenemos fruta y helado.	*For dessert we have fruit and ice cream.*

except when the noun is described or explained by another word:

No tengo abrigo.	*I don't have an overcoat.*
No tengo el abrigo negro.	*I don't have the black overcoat.*

5.1.5

Note that with abstract nouns the article is also used when the noun acts as an object in the sentence:
Compare

La sociedad está cambiando.	*Society is changing.*
La naturaleza está en peligro.	*Nature is in danger.*

with

No comprendo la sociedad actual.	*I don't understand modern society.*
Amo la naturaleza.	*I love nature.*

5.2 Use of the article combined with other grammatical categories before the noun:

See point 3.3 above. It is also used with **los demás** and **las demás** (in the plural):

Ahora vienen los demás invitados.

The rest of the guests are coming now.

5.3 With names

la Tierra (*the Earth*), **el Rey** (*the King*), **el Primer Ministro** (*the Prime Minister*), **el Papa** (*the Pope*).

5.4 *lo (neutral form)*

This is used before an adjective in the following expressions:

lo + bueno, lo + malo, lo + mejor, lo + peor and **lo + de** (e.g. **lo de ayer**).

The adjective becomes an abstract noun. In English it is often translated as *things*.

Lo bueno de mi ciudad es la gente, lo malo es el tráfico.

The good thing about my city is the people, the bad thing is the traffic.

6 Más práctica

4.6.1 Add the article to these sentences if necessary.

1. cerveza es barata
   quiero cerveza

2. médico viene ahora
   Pedro es médico

3. me encanta música
   escucho música

4. idiomas son útiles
   estudio idiomas

5. hago ejercicio
   me encanta ejercicio

6. no tengo dinero
   no tengo dinero que me diste

7. tenemos pollo para comer
   pollo está bueno

8. comemos fruta para postre
   nos gusta mucho fruta.

4.6.2 Translate into Spanish.

1. Paella is the national dish in Spain.
2. Family is important for children.
3. Spanish wine is good.
4. Exercise is good for your health.
5. Spanish society is different now.
6. Nature is in danger.
7. Education is important.
8. University is expensive.
9. Alcohol can be bad for your health.
10. Breakfast is included in the price.

5 The indefinite article
El artículo indefinido (o indeterminado)

1 ¿Qué es?

Indefinite articles are words that go before nouns in the same way as definite articles. For example:

a house   (*a* = indefinite article)
the house   (*the* = definite article)

The indefinite article is used to accompany nouns that are unknown or are not important to the speaker.

Juan compró una casa.	*Juan bought a house. (general concept)*
Juan compró la casa.	*Juan bought the house. (we know which one)*
Quiero un bolígrafo.	*I want a pen. (any pen)*
Quiero el bolígrafo.	*I want the pen. (referring to a specific pen)*
Tengo un bolígrafo.	*I have a pen. (it doesn't matter which pen it is)*

2 Forms

2.1 Four forms of the indefinite article

The indefinite article has four forms depending on the gender and the number of the noun it refers to. The equivalent in English is *a* (or *an*) for the singular forms and *some, any* for the plural forms.

	Masculine	**Feminine**	**(English)**
Singular	un	una	= a, an
Plural	unos	unas	= some, any

Ana tiene un apartamento.	*Ana has an apartment.*
Pedro quiere una casa grande.	*Pedro wants a big house.*
Quiero unos plátanos.	*I would like some bananas.*
¿Tienes unas cervezas?	*Do you have any beers?*

2.2 ¡Es diferente!

2.2.1 *Feminine nouns with a stressed 'a' or 'ha' as their first letter(s)*

These take **un** as the indefinite article:

Quiero un agua mineral.	*I'd like a mineral water.*
Ésta es un área turística.	*This is a tourist area.*
Tenemos un aula pequeña.	*We have a small classroom.*
¡Tengo un hambre . . .!	*I'm so hungry . . .!*
	(lit. I have such hunger . . .!)

Note that this doesn't happen in the plural: **unas aguas, unas áreas, unas aulas**.

Estas áreas son muy industriales.	*These areas are very industrial.*
Las aguas de los ríos están contaminadas.	*The waters of the rivers are polluted.*

3 Uses of the indefinite article: un / una

3.1 Uses of the singular form of the article, un / una:

3.1.1

It is mostly used in the same way as **a / an** in English.

¿Tienes un lápiz?	*Have you got a pencil?*
Un hombre pregunta por ti.	*A man is asking for you.*
Quiero una cerveza y un zumo	*I'd like a beer and an*
de naranja.	*orange juice.*

3.1.2 *When we talk about something unknown or for the first time, as an introduction*

Note that after the item is introduced it is then referred to with the definite article:

1

Juan: **Estoy leyendo un libro.**	*I'm reading a book.*
Pedro: **¿De qué trata el libro?**	*What is the book about?*
Juan: **El libro trata de un rey famoso.**	*The book is about a famous king.*

2

Juan: **Pepe tiene un amigo en España.**	*Pepe has a friend in Spain.*
Pedro: **¿De qué ciudad es el amigo**	*What city is Pepe's*
de Pepe?	*friend from?*
Juan: **El amigo de Pepe es de Barcelona.**	*Pepe's friend is from Barcelona.*

3.1.3 *After hay*

En la ciudad hay un hospital y una catedral
In the city there is a hospital and a cathedral.

3.1.4 To help distinguish nouns from adjectives

Juan es español. (adjective)	*Juan is Spanish.*
Un mexicano (noun) trabaja en esta oficina.	*A Mexican works in this office.*

3.1.5 To add emphasis

¡Juan es tonto!	*Juan is silly!*
¡Juan es un tonto!	*Juan is a (really) silly person.*

3.1.6 To indicate possession with *doler*

Me duele un dedo.	*My finger aches.*
Me duele una muela.	*My tooth aches.*

3.1.7 Used before an adjective without the noun it refers to

It transforms the adjective into a noun. In English the word **one** is added in this case.

Compra una nueva.	*Buy a new one.*
Trae uno grande.	*Bring a big one.*

3.2 ¡Es diferente!

The following are cases in which the indefinite article is generally used in English but not in Spanish.

3.2.1 Nouns indicating professions, nationality, beliefs or religions

Juan es profesor.	*Juan is a teacher.*
Ana es ingeniera.	*Ana is an engineer.*
Pedro es español.	*Pedro is Spanish.*
Susana es socialista.	*Susana is a Socialist.*
Marcos es católico.	*Marcos is a Catholic.*

3.2.1.1

But it <u>is</u> used if the profession / nationality / belief / religion is followed by an adjective or a qualifying phrase:

Juan es un profesor muy bueno.	*Juan is very good teacher.*
Es una ingeniera excelente.	*She is an excellent engineer.*

3.2.2 In exclamations after words like ¡qué ! (what a. . .!)

¡Qué libro tan interesante!	*What an interesting book!*

3.2.3

It is not used before **medio/a** (*half*): **medio kilo, medio litro, media docena**:

Quiero medio kilo de salchichón.	*I would like half a kilo of salami.*

3.2.4 *Before the numbers* cien *(a hundred),* mil *(a thousand)*

Isabel tiene mil dólares en el banco.	*Isabel has a thousand dollars in the bank*
Necesito cien euros.	*I need a hundred euros.*

3.2.5 *Before* otro

Quiero otro café.	*I would like another coffee.*

4 The plural forms: **unos / unas**

The plural forms of the article, **unos / unas**, are used in the following cases.

4.1 Meaning *some* or *a few*

¿Quieres unas patatas fritas?	*Would you like some chips (crisps)?*
¿Quieres unas galletas?	*Would you like some biscuits?*
¿Quieres unas galletas para los niños?	*Would you like a few biscuits for the children?*
Leí unas revistas en el avión.	*I read some / a few magazines on the plane.*
Voy a invitar a unos amigos.	*I'm going to invite some / a few friends*

4.2 Meaning *any, a few* or *a pair of*

¿Tienes unas tapas?	*Do you have any (or a few) tapas?*
¿Tienes unos pasteles?	*Have you got any (or a few) cakes?*

But we can also say:

¿Tienes tapas? *or* **¿Tienes pasteles?**	*Have you got any snacks (or cakes)?*
¿Tienes unos pantalones?	*Do you have any / a pair of trousers?*
Voy a comprar unos pantalones.	*Im going to buy some / a pair of trousers.*
¿Tienes unas tijeras?	*Do you have any / a pair of scissors?*
Necesito unas gafas de sol.	*I need a pair of sunglasses.*

4.3 Meaning *approximately, about*

Fernando gana unos mil euros al mes.
Fernando earns about a thousand euros a month.

5 Gramática práctica

5.5.1 Write the correct indefinite article (**un / una / unos / unas**) in the following sentences.

1. Quiero _____cerveza.
2. Póngame _____ café con leche, por favor.
3. Deme _____ zumo de naranja.
4. Póngame _____ naranjada, por favor.
5. Quiero _____ tapas, por favor.
6. Quiero _____vino tinto, por favor.
7. _____ té con limón, por favor.
8. Póngame _____ patatas fritas.
9. Quiero _____ zumo de naranja.
10. _____ calamares, por favor.
11. Quiero _____ chocolate caliente, por favor.
12. Póngame _____ churros con el café.

5.5.2 Transform the sentences using words from the box with the corresponding article, if one is needed.

Example: Quiero atún. > Quiero una lata de atún.

bote botella caja cuarto docena kilo lata litro medio media paquete

1. Quiero atún.
2. Quiero galletas.
3. Quiero agua mineral.
4. Quiero huevos.
5. Póngame queso.
6. Deme patatas fritas.
7. Quiero mermelada.
8. Deme vino blanco.
9. Quiero pasteles.
10. Póngame tomates.
11. Quiero sardinas.
12. Deme aceite.

6 Más allá

Here are some more cases when the indefinite article is not used in Spanish but necessary in English.

6.1 After the following verbs:

llevar (*to wear*), **buscar** (*to look for*), **encontrar** (*to find*), **comprar** (*to buy*) and **usar** (*to use*)

Juan siempre lleva traje en el trabajo.   *Juan always wears a suit at work.*
Elena busca trabajo.   *Elena is looking for a job.*
María no encuentra billete para ir a Londres.
María cannot find a ticket to go to London.

Note: The indefinite article is used if the noun in the sentence is followed by an adjective:

Juan siempre lleva un traje negro en el trabajo.
Juan always wears a black suit at work.

Elena busca un trabajo interesante.   *Elena is looking for an interesting job.*
María no encuentra un billete barato para ir a Londres.
María cannot find a cheap ticket to go to London.

6.2 In exclamatory expressions

¡Es mentira!   *It's a lie!*

6.3 After expressions with **sin** (*without*) or **como** (*as*)

No puedes comer esto sin cuchillo.   *You cannot eat this without a knife.*
Elena trabaja como enfermera, pero   *Elena works as a nurse. but she is*
   es médica.   *a doctor.*

7 Más práctica

5.7.1 Write the correct article (if needed) in the right place.

1. Andalucía es comunidad de España.
2. La Sagrada Familia es iglesia muy famosa.
3. Antonio Gaudí es arquitecto.
4. Picasso es pintor muy famoso.
5. El Barrio Gótico es zona muy antigua.
6. Las Ramblas son avenidas muy famosas.
7. El Camp Nou es estadio de fútbol.
8. Pedro es colombiano y es futbolista.

5.7.2 Translate the sentences into English.

1. ¡Qué falda tan bonita!
2. Quiero medio kilo de jamón.
3. ¡Es mentira!
4. Es estudiante.
5. ¿Eres colombiano?
6. Estudia para hacerse profesor.
7. Ali es musulmán.
8. Quiero media docena de huevos.
9. ¡Qué pena!
10. Juan está buscando trabajo.
11. María no encuentra trabajo.
12. No debes salir sin paraguas.
13. No tiene coche, tiene moto.
14. Ana siempre lleva pantalones.
15. ¡Qué casualidad!

6 Qualifying adjectives
Adjetivos calificativos

1 ¿Qué es?

Qualifying adjectives say something about a noun; they tell us what the noun is like by adding a quality to it.

bonito	*pretty*
feo	*ugly*
grande	*big*
pequeño	*small*

2 Form and position of qualifying adjectives

Adjectives in Spanish agree with the noun they describe in number (singular or plural) and in gender (masculine and feminine).

Their form is dependent on the nouns they qualify.

las chicas simpáticas	*the nice girls*

2.1 Number

The rule for forming the plural of adjectives is the same as for nouns:

2.1.1

Adjectives ending in a vowel add **-s** and those ending in a consonant ('d', 'l', 'n', 'r') add **-es**.

el bolso rojo	*the red bag*
los bolsos rojos	*the red bags*
la casa grande	*the big house*
las casas grandes	*the big houses*
el jersey azul	*the blue sweater*
los jerseys azules	*the blue sweaters*

2.1.2

Some adjectives need to add or remove an accent when they form the plural to follow orthographic rules: **joven > jóvenes; marrón > marrones**.

 See Unit 2.

2.1.3 *¡Es diferente!*

Some nationalities ending in **-í** or **-ú** in the singular form add **-es** to form the plural:

marroquí, marroquíes; israelí, israelíes; hindú, hindúes.

Note that these forms are the same for the masculine and the feminine.

2.2 Gender

2.2.1 *The rules for gender changes*

These are similar to those for nouns, but there are some differences.

-o / -a	fantástico (m) / fantástica (f) (*fantastic*)
-e / -e (no change)	verde (*green*), grande (*big*), caliente (*hot*), interesante (*interesting*)
-consonant (l, n, r, z) -consonant (no change)	azul (*blue*), marrón (*brown*), feliz (*happy*)

un amigo simpático	*a nice (male) friend*
una amiga simpática	*a nice (female) friend*
un coche verde	*a green car*
una bicicleta verde	*a green bike*
un coche gris	*a grey car*
una bicicleta gris	*a grey bike*

Remember: nouns add **-a** to a consonant: **el profesor / la profesora**.

2.2.2 *¡Es diferente!*

2.2.2.1 *Adjectives expressing nationality and ending in a consonant*

These change like nouns (as they can also be nouns). Remember they don't have capitals: **español, española; inglés, inglesa**.

2.2.2.2 *Adjectives derived from nouns ending in -dor, -tor, -sor*

These also add an **-a**:

conservador / conservadora	*conservative*
receptor / receptora	*receiving*
precursor / precursora	*preceding*

2.2.2.3

A few adjectives ending in **-a** do not change (like the nouns):

optimista	*optimistic*
pesimista	*pessimistic*
egoísta	*selfish*

Colours which are originally nouns fall into this category:

naranja (el color naranja)	*orange*
rosa (el color rosa)	*pink*
violeta (el color violeta)	*violet*

2.2.3

If we want to describe two nouns with the same adjective, and one of the nouns is masculine and the other feminine, the adjective always takes the masculine form:

Son amigos y amigas simpáticos.   *They are nice friends.*

3 Position

3.1 After the noun

Most adjectives occur immediately after the noun.

un coche grande	*a big car*
vino tinto	*red wine*
agua fresca	*fresh water*

3.2 Before the noun

A few can occur before the noun. In this case their masculine form is shortened as follows*: **primero > primer, tercero > tercer**.

Vivo en el primer piso.	*I live on the first floor.*
Mi hermana vive en el tercer piso.	*My sister lives on the third floor.*

 * For more see Más allá, Section 6 below.

3.3 After the verb **ser** (*to be*)

La mujer es alta.   *The woman is tall.*

3.4 In any order

If two adjectives are required to describe or qualify a noun, and they are of equal importance, they can appear in any order and have **y** (*and*) between them.

un bolso grande y negro	*a big black bag*
un bolso negro y grande	

4 Use

4.1

Adjectives modify the noun. They add extra information to the noun:

un coche (*a car*) > **un coche grande** (*a big car*)

4.2

Adjectives can be accompanied (and changed) by adverbs:

| **muy bueno** | *very good* |
| **bastante malo** | *quite bad* |

4.3 El rojo, el grande

Adjectives accompanied by the definite article become a noun, so that the noun is not repeated. In English we use the word <u>one</u> to achieve this effect.

| **A: ¿Qué bolso quieres?** | *Which bag do you want?* |
| **B: El marrón.** | *The brown one.* |

5 Gramática práctica

6.5.1 Sort the adjectives from the box into the following categories:

M (masculine), F (feminine), M/F (masculine or feminine).

---

verde delgado baja alto azul naranja grande simpática pequeña alta
feo malo rubia conservador bonito delgada guapo moreno guapa
marrón circular gris optimista débil cosmopolita

6.5.2 Now make the above adjectives plural.

Example: verde > verdes

6.5.3 Rewrite these sentences to give the nationality.

Example: Mi amiga Julia es de Colombia > Mi amiga Julia es colombiana.

1. Mi amiga Carol es de Irlanda.
2. Mi amigo Ali es de Egipto.
3. Mi amigo Ernesto es de Perú.
4. Mi amiga María es de Bolivia.
5. Mi amiga Isabel es de Guatemala.
6. Mi amiga Hiroko es de Japón.
7. Mi amigo Arturo es de México.
8. Mi amiga Fátima es de Marruecos.
9. Mi amigo Kris es de Grecia.
10. Mi amiga Elena es de Brasil.
11. Mi amigo Héctor es de Uruguay.
12. Mi amiga Susana es de Ecuador.

6 Más allá

6.1 Shorter masculine forms

Other adjectives can occur before the noun with shorter masculine forms:

bueno > buen, grande > gran, malo > mal.

 see Section 3.2 above for **primer** and **tercer**.

6.1.1 The feminine form

This does not change: **buena, mala, primera, tercera**:

una chica buena > una buena chica:

Except for **grande**: **una casa grande > una gran casa**.

6.1.2

Their meaning can change when they appear before the noun:

una casa grande	*a big house*
una gran casa	*a grand house*
una mujer grande	*a large woman*
una gran mujer	*a great woman*

6.2 Change of meaning

There are some adjectives which change their meaning, depending on whether they are placed before or after the noun, e.g.: **antiguo, pobre, viejo**:

mi antiguo piso	*my old flat (the flat I used to live in even if it was new)*
mi piso antiguo	*my old flat (the flat I live in that is old)*
un hombre pobre	*a poor man (lacking money)*
un pobre hombre	*a poor man (I feel sorry for him)*
un amigo viejo	*an old friend (friend who is old)*
un viejo amigo	*an old friend (I've known him for years)*

6.3 Emphasis

Some other adjectives can be placed before the noun to add emphasis:

es un problema grave	*it's a serious problem*
es un grave problema	

6.4 Combined colours

When we combine two words to describe a colour they don't change: **azul marino, azul claro, rojo oscuro**.

un jersey azul marino	*a dark blue sweater*
una chaqueta (color) rojo oscuro	*a dark red jacket*

6.5

In English you can put two nouns together with one of them acting as an adjective: **a Spanish teacher, a tennis court.** This does not occur in Spanish, where **de** is used instead:

un profesor de español	*a Spanish teacher*
una pista de tenis	*a tennis court*

 See Unit 22, Word order.

7 Más práctica

6.7.1 María's family and friends keep losing things. Say what they have lost, making any necessary changes.

Example: I Mi padre ha perdido una bufanda roja, muy larga, de lana.

Persona	Objeto	Color	Tamaño	Material
padre	1 bufanda	rojo	muy largo	lana
primo	2 cartera	marrón	mediano	piel
hermana	3 bolso	transparente	grande	plástico
abuela	4 gafas de sol	dorado	grande	metal dorado
prima	5 pulsera		pequeño	plata
hermano	6 bolsa	negro	muy grande	tela
tía	7 guantes	azul marino	pequeño	piel
madre	8 pendientes		largo	oro

6.7.2 Give the Spanish for the following.

Chicken soup
Tomato juice
Lamb chop
Fish soup
Strawberry ice-cream

House wine
Cheese cake
Veal stew
Apple tart
Tomato sauce

7 Word formation

1 ¿Qué es?

Words can be changed by adding different endings or 'bits' which modify their meaning. These are called suffixes. We can also add 'bits' to the beginning of the words. These are called prefixes. The rules are not consistent and not all words can be modified. It often depends on the intentions and the feelings of the speaker. For example, **pequeño** already means *small*, but for emphasis or to express affection we add **-ito**:

Es pequeño, pequeñito.	*It's small, really small.*
Oye, niñito, ven aquí	*Hey, little one, come here.*
Hola chiquitita.	*Hi, little one.*

2 Suffixes

2.1 Form

There are different kinds of suffixes:

2.1.1 Augmentatives: (big/great, very, extremely. . .)

These have endings like:

-ón / -ona

un chico grandullón	*a boy who is large for his age*

-azo / -aza

un perrazo	*a big dog*

-ote /-ota

grandote	*very big*

-ísimo / -ísima

carísimo	*very expensive*

 For **-ísimo** as a superlative, see Unit 8 Section 7.2.

2.1.2 *Diminutives: (*little, small, nice, cute*)*

These have endings like:

-ito / -ita

el perrito	*the little dog*
la mesita	*the small table (bedside table)*
pequeñito	*small*

-ín / -ina

chiquitín	*little / small*
poquitín	*a little bit*

-illo / -illa

cucharilla	*teaspoon*
feíllo	*unattractive*

-ico / -ica (this has a more regional use)

sillica	*little chair*

2.2 Use

Suffixes give a special meaning to the word that often implies size, but may also reflect our feelings, emotion, affection and intensity.

2.2.1 *To modify nouns*

perrito	*little dog*
perrazo	*large dog*
perrucho	*not a very nice dog*

2.2.2 *To modify adjectives*

un coche grandote	*a really big car*
un chico pequeñajo	*a small boy*
un hotel pequeñito	*a small hotel*

2.2.3 *To modify some adverbs*

Es un poquito grande.	*It's a little bit big.*
Habla despacito.	*Speak a bit slower.*

2.2.4 *To understate issues*

Tengo un problemita.	*I have a little problem.*
¿Puedo hacerte una preguntita?	*Can I ask you a little question?*

2.2.5 Used as a pejorative

To describe something that's not very nice:

-ajo / -aja
Es un pueblo pequeñajo.   *It's a nasty little town.*

-ucho / -ucha

Es un pueblucho.   *It's a horrible town.*
Viven en una casucha.   *They live in a terrible house.*

2.2.6 Word endings or suffixes indicating profession or occupation

carnicero   *butcher*
pastelero   *cake maker*
panadero   *baker*

2.2.7 Places of work

pastelería   *cake shop*
panadería   *baker's shop*
carnicería   *butcher's shop*

2.2.8 Words of endearment

pequeñito   *little one*
chiquitita   *little one*
abuelita   *Gran*

2.2.9 Names and colours

These can take diminutives (**-ito**):

Names: **Pedrito, Juanito, Anita**
Colours: **rojito, azulito, verdecito**

2.2.10

Some words add an extra bit between the word and the suffix:

verdecito; pueblecito (can also be **pueblito**, especially in Latin America)

2.2.11

Some words become 'proper' words with a different meaning from the original ones:

palo	*stick*	**plato**	*plate*
palillo	*toothpick*	**platillo**	*saucer*
pan	*bread*	**silla**	*chair*
panecillo	*bun*	**sillón**	*armchair*
cuchara	*spoon*		
cucharilla	*teaspoon*		

3 Prefixes

These go before the word and give extra meaning to it. The most common ones are: **anti, super, contra, auto, hiper, bi / tri**. They can be added to nouns, adjectives and verbs:

la política **anti**nuclear	*antinuclear politics*
un niño **super**dotado	*an extremely gifted child*
un **contra**ataque	*a counter-attack*
anteayer	*the day before yesterday*
bilingüe	*bilingual*
autodisciplina	*self-discipline*
hiperactivo	*hyperactive*

 ***For uses of super as a superlative, see Unit 8 Section 10.1.9.**

4 Gramática práctica

7.4.1 What words do these come from?

> verdecito fuertecito pueblecito cochecito balconcito calentito malito
> guapito grandecito puentecito calorcito cielito amorcito

7.4.2 Give the diminutives of the following words:

> pequeño azul despacio lento blando redondo cuadrado blanco pobre
> viejo pronto deprisa cuidado fresco

7.4.3 Join the word parts from each list to give the equivalents of:

little house, big house, little book, big book, horrible house, big dog, little dog, little window, horrible town, little table, teaspoon, little child, big man.

Lista A	Lista B
cas	ita
cuchar	ona
grand	ote
perr	ito
libr	azo
mes	ucha
niñ	illa
puebl	ucho
ventan	

8 Comparatives and superlatives
Comparativos y superlativos

1 ¿Qué es?

Comparative and superlative forms are used to express degrees of intensity, quantity or quality. They are:

más / menos . . . que	*more / less than*
tan / tanto como	*as . . . as*
el más (grande) de	*the most . . . of*

Comparatives and superlatives are used with adjectives, nouns, adverbs and verbs.

2 Comparatives of adjectives

Adjectives of quality can express different grades of comparison.

2.1 Forms

The comparative is formed by using:
más (*more*), **menos** (*less*) followed by **que** (*than*)

or

tan (*as*) before the adjective followed by **como** (*as*).

más grande que	*bigger than*
menos interesante que	*less interesting than*
tan emocionante como	*as exciting as*

Note: There is no equivalent of the English *-er* ending, as in *cheaper, faster* etc.

El tren es más rápido que el autobús.	*The train is faster than the bus.*
El tren es más cómodo que el autobús.	*The train is more comfortable than the bus.*
El autobús es menos caro que el tren.	*The bus is less expensive than the train.*
El bus es menos cómodo que el tren	*The bus is less comfortable than the train.*
Javier es más alto que Francisco.	*Javier is taller than Francisco.*
El cine es menos caro que el teatro.	*The cinema is less expensive than the theatre.*
Este hotel es tan grande como el otro.	*This hotel is as big as the other one.*

Note: There is no need to repeat **más, menos** or **tan** before more than one adjective:

El coche de Juan es más rápido y cómodo que el mío.
Juan's car is faster and more comfortable than mine.

2.2 Irregular comparative forms

Although there is no equivalent of the English -*er* ending, a small number of adjectives have irregular comparative forms. These are:

bueno	**mejor**	*good*	*better*
malo	**peor**	*bad*	*worse*
grande	**mayor**	*big*	*bigger*
pequeño	**menor**	*small*	*smaller*

2.2.1

They have the same form in masculine and feminine, but change from singular to plural:

¿No tienes mejores pantalones?	*Don't you have any better trousers?*
Estas manzanas son peores que las de ayer.	*These apples are worse than yesterday's.*
Tengo dos hermanos mayores.	*I have two older (bigger) brothers.*
Hay un grupo de islas menores.	*There is a group of smaller islands.*

2.2.2

They are followed by **que** in the comparative:

Este café es mejor que el café de la cafetería.	*This coffee is better than the coffee in the cafe.*
Mi madre es mayor que mi padre.	*My mother is older than my father.*
Esta playa es peor que la otra.	*This beach is worse than the other one.*
Mis problemas son menores que los suyos.	*My problems are smaller than his.*
Las tapas de María son mejores que las de Fernando.	*Maria's snacks are better than Fernando's.*

2.2.3

These irregular comparatives are often replaced by equivalent regular ones such as **más grande** for **mayor** and **más pequeño** for **menor** when referring to size:

Tu casa es más pequeña que la mía.	*Your house is smaller than mine.*
El abrigo verde es más grande que el abrigo azul.	*The green coat is bigger than the blue one.*

Mayor and **menor** are more frequently used when expressing age (*older, younger*):

Mi madre es mayor que mi padre.	*My mother is older than my father.*
Mi padre es menor que mi madre.	*My father is younger than my mother.*

3 Comparatives of adverbs

3.1 Forms

These are formed in a similar way to the comparatives of adjectives:

más . . . que	*more . . . than*
menos . . . que	*less . . . than*
tan . . . como	*as . . . as*

Siempre llegas más tarde que yo.	*You always arrive later than I do.*
El autobús va menos deprisa que el tren.	*The bus goes less quickly than the train.*
Habla tan despacio como siempre.	*He talks as slowly as always.*

3.1.1 *Mejor* (better) *and peor* (worse)

These can also be used as adverbs. They act as the comparatives of **bien** (*well*) and **mal** (*badly*).

Habla inglés mejor que su hermana.	*She speaks English better than her sister.*
Mi tía está peor que ayer.	*My aunt is worse than yesterday.*

4 Comparatives of nouns

4.1 Formation

These are formed in the same way as comparatives of adjectives:

más . . . que	*more . . . than*
menos . . . que	*less / fewer . . . than*
Tengo más problemas que tú.	*I have more problems than you.*
Juan tiene menos juguetes que Pepe.	*Juan has fewer toys than Pepe.*

4.2 *Tanto*

The exception is **tan . . . como** which becomes **tanto** before a noun. **Tanto** changes in gender and number to agree with the noun it accompanies. It may mean *as much . . . as, as many . . . as, so much . . . as* or *so many . . . as*, depending on context.

Ana no tiene tantas vacaciones como yo.	*Ana doesn't have as many holidays as I do.*
Mi hermano tiene tanto tiempo. como yo	*My brother has as much time as I do.*
Juan tiene tanta comida como tú.	*Juan has as much food as you.*
Pedro tiene tantos libros como Ana.	*Pedro has as many books as Ana.*

5 Comparatives of verbs

These are formed in the same way as the comparatives of nouns.
Tanto used with verbs can be translated as *as much as, as little as*:

Mi hermano estudia menos que antes.	*My brother studies less than before.*
Ana cocina más que el año pasado.	*Ana cooks more than last year.*
Juan gana tanto como su primo.	*Juan earns as much as his cousin.*

6 Other comparative expressions

6.1 Igual que

The expression **igual que** (*the same as*) is also used as a comparative. It can also have a plural form: **iguales que**:

Este coche es igual que el mío.	*This car is the same as mine.*
Estos pantalones son iguales que los míos.	*These trousers are the same as mine.*

6.2 Como

Used also to compare, to say who or what you or someone or something are like.

Soy como mi madre.	*I'm like my mother.*
Juan es como su padre.	*Juan is like his father.*
El clima de mi ciudad es como el de Londres.	*The climate of my city is like that of London.*

7 Superlatives

7.1 Superlatives of adjectives

We can add a superlative meaning to an adjective by simply adding the adverb **muy**:

La chica es guapa.	*The girl is good-looking.*
La chica es muy guapa.	*The girl is very good-looking.*

7.2 Formation

The superlative can also be formed by adding the suffix **-ísimo, -ísima** and the plural **-ísimos, -ísimas**.

We use this if we want to emphasise an adjective but not compare it with anything else.

Mi coche es rapidísimo.	*My car is really fast.*
Aquel tren es lentísimo.	*That train is really slow.*
Esa niña es guapísima.	*That little girl is really pretty.*

La camisa es baratísima.	The shirt is really cheap.
Aquellos coches son carísimos.	Those cars are really expensive.
Las casas son viejísimas.	The houses are really old.

7.2.1 More examples (with orthographic changes)

difícil > dificilísimo	difficult	(changes in accent/stress)
fácil > facilísimo	easy	(changes in accent/stress)
rico > riquísimo	rich	(changes in accent/stress and in consonant)
largo > larguísimo	long	(changes in accent/stress and in consonant)
feliz > felicísimo	happy	(changes in accent/stress and in consonant)

7.2.2 Irregulars

joven > jovencísimo	young
antiguo > antiquísimo	ancient
amable > amabilísimo	friendly
nuevo > novísimo	new

7.3 The superlative form

If we want to say something is the best or biggest of a number of items, we use:

el / la / los / las más . . . (de)   *the most + adjective*

or

el / la / los / las menos. . .(de)   *the least + adjective*

El Talgo es el más rápido.	The Talgo is the fastest.
La bicicleta es la más barata.	The bicycle is the cheapest.
Esta mesa es la más cara de todas las de la tienda.	This table is the most expensive of all in the shop.
Esta figura es la menos pesada de todas.	This figure is the lightest (least heavy) of all.
Éste es el (coche) más caro de todos.	This is the most expensive (car) of all.

7.3.1

Note the word order:

el juego más interesante	the most interesting game (lit: the game most interesting)
el juego menos interesante	the least interesting game
el mejor / peor juego	the best / worst game

8 Superlatives of adverbs

Some adverbs can go with other adverbs, e.g.: **muy bien, muy mal**.

Adverbs can also take the endings **-ísimo / -ísima / -ísimos / -ísimas** to form the superlative:

lejísimos	a very long way away
cerquísima	really nearby
tardísimo	really late
prontísimo	very soon
tantísimo	so much

9 Gramática práctica

8.9.1 Write complete sentences with the comparatives.

Example: coche + cómodo / autobús > El coche es más cómodo que el autobús.

1. Coche + rápido / bicicleta
2. Autobús – caro / tren
3. Bicicleta + lenta / moto
4. Tren + cómodo / autobús
5. Autobús – rápido / avión
6. Tren = barato / autobús

8.9.2 Choose the correct form of the irregular comparatives **mayor, menor, mejor, peor** for each sentence.

1. Tu hijo es mal estudiante, pero mi hijo es _____.
2. Tu apartamento es grande, pero el mío es _____.
3. Tu lavadora es buena, pero la mía es _____.
4. Tu hijo tiene 20 años, el mío 18, mi hijo es _____.
5. Las manzanas son malas, pero las peras son _____.
6. Yo tengo 30 años y mi hermana 40, es _____ que yo.
7. Yo nací primero, soy la _____ y tengo dos hermanos _____.
8. Las notas de Alberto son excelentes, son mucho _____ que las mías.

8.9.3 Complete the sentences with **tanto(s)** or **tanta(s)**.

1. Tú tienes _____ problemas como yo.
2. Tenemos _____ maletas como vosotros.
3. No tengo _____ tiempo como ayer.
4. No compres _____ naranjas como ayer.
5. No bebo _____ agua como vosotros.
6. No quiero _____ leche con el café.

8.9.4 Translate the following sentences into Spanish.

1. My brother is older than my sister.
2. Your house is bigger than my house.
3. He always arrives later than you.
4. My paella is as good as my mother's.
5. He has got as much money as you.
6. Fernando works less than Pepe.
7. Ana studies more than me.
8. Luis has as many books as Julia.
9. I speak Spanish better than my sister.

10. Juan is worse than last week.
11. The boy is like his mother.
12. This coat is the same as mine.

8.9.5 Write the superlative form of the adjectives: **-ísimo/a/os/as**.

Example: El tren AVE es muy rápido. El tren AVE es rapidísimo.

1. El pollo está muy bueno.
2. Los pendientes son caros.
3. El coche está muy viejo.
4. El chico es muy alto.
5. Las calles son muy estrechas.
6. La niña es muy guapa.

10 Más allá

10.1 *igual de; igual que* (invariable)*; lo mismo que*

Son igual de listos.	*They are as clever as each other*
Son igual de buenos.	*They're both good / they're as good as each other.*
María habla inglés igual que tú	*Maria speaks English as well as you*
lo mismo que tú.	*the same as you.*

10.2 *tan . . . que*

With adjectives, although **tan** is normally followed by **como**, there are some expressions in which it is followed by **que**. In this case, the expression is used to indicate emphasis and the translation of **tan** is *so* (not *as*):

Es tan caro que no puedo comprarlo. *It's so expensive I can't buy it.*

10.3

It can also be used with nouns, verbs and adverbs:
Nouns: **tanto/a/os/as . . . que**.
Verbs: the invariable adverb **tanto . . . que**.
Adverbs: **tan . . . que**.

Hay tantas personas que no podemos entrar.	*There are so many people we can't get in.*
Habla tanto que me da dolor de cabeza.	*He talks so much he gives me a headache.*
Habla tan deprisa que no le entiendo.	*He speaks so quickly I don't understand him.*

10.4 Comparatives of numerals or quantities

10.4.1 más de / menos de

Cuesta más de dos euros.	*It costs more than two euros.*
Cuesta menos de dos euros.	*It costs less than two euros.*

There is a difference between **más de** and **más que** in a negative sentence.
más de is used when we want to express the maximum number.
más que is used when we mean that we expect more.

No hay más de diez pasajeros en el autobús.	*There are no more than ten passengers on the bus.*
No hay más que diez pasajeros en el autobús.	*There are only ten passengers in the bus.*

10.4.2 no más de / no menos de

No cuesta más de dos euros.	*It doesn't cost more than two euros. (implying this is cheap)*
No cuesta menos de dos euros.	*It doesn't cost less than two euros. (implying this is expensive)*

10.4.3 *To express the exact quantity:*

No cuesta más que 20 euros.	*It costs no more than 20 euros. (said for effect: this is its price)*

10.5

Special constructions with relatives: comparatives.

el que / la que / los que

 See Unit 13 Section 5.

10.5.1 más / menos . . . + que + el (la / los / las) que

Esta casa es más bonita que la que vimos ayer.	*This house is nicer than the one we saw yesterday.*

10.5.2 más / menos . . . + de + el (la / los / las) que

Tienen menos dinero del* que gastan.	*They have less money than they spend.*

*Note: **de + el que = del que**

10.5.3 más / menos . . . + de + lo que

Esto es más interesante de lo que piensas.	*This is more interesting than you think.*
Es más guapo de lo que dicen.	*He is better looking than they say.*

10.5.4 Saying what you like most or least (gustar)

10.5.4.1

We can refer to a specific type of thing (like a TV programme or a film) that we like most or least:

El programa que más me gusta es Música Sí.	The programme I like most is Música Sí.
La película que menos me gusta es La Bestia.	The film I like least is La Bestia.
Los libros que más me gustan son las biografías.	The books I like most are biographies.

10.5.4.2

Note that **gusta** changes in these cases, and if used without the noun, the article also changes:

El que más me gusta es Música Sí.	The one I like most is Música Sí.
La que menos me gusta es La Bestia.	The one I like least is La Bestia.
Los que más me gustan son las biografías.	The ones I like best are biographies.

Note that when we want to say what we like most or least, we use the following structure:

10.5.4.3

Lo que más me gusta es el sol.	What I like most is the sun.
Lo que menos me gusta es el mal tiempo.	What I like least is bad weather.

Note that **lo** and **gusta** don't change.

10.6 Special constructions with relatives: superlatives

el que más corre de todos	the one who runs fastest (masculine)
la que más estudia de todas	the one who studies most (feminine)
el último de todos	the last of all
el mejor de la clase	the best in the class

10.7 Comparative words

There are a number of words that act as comparatives:

superior (a): es superior a = es mejor que

El hotel Goya es superior al hotel Príncipe.	The Goya hotel is better than the Príncipe hotel.

inferior (a): es inferior a = es peor que

El hotel Príncipe es inferior al hotel Goya.	The Príncipe hotel is worse than the Goya hotel.

anterior (a): es anterior a = antes que
posterior (a): es posterior a = después que

10.8 Special superlative forms

There are some special superlative forms, but they tend not be used often in spoken Spanish: **máximo = el más grande; mínimo = el más pequeño; óptimo = el mejor; pésimo = el peor**.

El salario mínimo es bajísimo en este país.	*The minimum wage is very low in this country.*
El precio máximo que puedo pagar es éste.	*The highest price I can pay is this.*
Aquí tenemos las condiciones óptimas para el campeonato.	*Here we have the best conditions for the championship.*
El tiempo es pésimo esta semana.	*The weather is the worst this week.*

10.8.1

The forms for the irregular comparatives and superlatives are:

más grande	mayor	máximo
más pequeño	menor	mínimo
más bueno	mejor	óptimo
más malo	peor	pésimo

10.9 Superlatives with prefixes

These are words with prefixes like: **super-, extra-, re-, archi-** and **ultra-**.

es superfácil	*it's really easy*
es extrafino	*it's top quality*

10.10 Making superlatives through repetition

Esto es barato barato.	*This is really cheap.*
Pedro es guapo guapísimo.	*Pedro is good looking, really good looking.*

11 Más práctica

8.11.1 Use the words in the box to complete the sentences. You will need to use some of them more than once.

mejor   más   tantas   menos   tantos   tan

1. El piso es _____ caro que no puedo pagarlo.
2. Hay _____niños gritando que no podemos oír nada.
3. Isabel es la _____ de la clase.
4. Ana habla _____ despacio que me aburre.
5. El billete no cuesta _____de 100 euros.
6. Este coche es _____bonito que el que he comprado yo.
7. Los pantalones cuestan _____de 40 euros.
8. El libro es _____interesante de lo que dicen.
9. Me gusta mucho cantar, pero lo que _____me gusta es bailar.
10. Vinieron _____personas a la fiesta que no hubo suficiente comida.

8.11.2 Complete the sentences with the words in the box, making any necessary changes.

posterior óptimo máxima pésima superior mínimo inferior anterior

1. Este abrigo es más barato porque la calidad es_____.
2. Las condiciones de las carreteras son excelentes hoy, son _____.
3. La velocidad _____es de 20 kms por hora.
4. Estos vinos son exquisitos, son _____a aquéllos.
5. La iglesia de San Miguel se construyó cien años antes, es _____a la catedral.
6. Goya pintó aquel cuadro mucho después que éste, aquél es_____.
7. Esta fruta es muy mala, es _____.
8. El número _____de estudiantes para abrir el grupo es de doce.

9 Personal pronouns *Pronombres personales*

1 ¿Qué es?

Personal pronouns are used to replace nouns (the names of people, objects and ideas or concepts) in the sentence.

There are two kind of personal pronouns: subject pronouns and object pronouns.
Subject pronouns are words like: *I, you, he, she, it, we, they.*
Object pronouns are words like: *me, him, her, us, them.*

2 Form of subject pronouns

2.1 Gender

Subject pronouns vary in gender except the first and second person singular which are the same in the masculine and the feminine: **yo, tú** (informal), **usted** (formal) and the formal second person plural **ustedes**.

2.2 Number

Subject pronouns all change according to number.

| Person | singular | | plural | |
	masculine	feminine	masculine	feminine
Ist	yo (*I*)		nosotros (*we*)	nosotras (*we*)
2nd (informal)	tú (*you*)		vosotros (*you*)	vosotras (*you*)
2nd (formal)	usted (*you*)		ustedes (*you*)	
3rd	él (*he*)	ella (*she*)	ellos (*they*)	ellas (*they*)
3rd person neuter	ello (*it*)*			

*él, ella, ellos and ellas always refer to people. There is a neuter form in the third person singular which means *it*: **ello**, but it is not used much.

 See point 5.7 below.

2.3 Accents

Note that **tú** and **él** have an accent to distinguish them from the possessive adjective **tu** and the article **el**, which don't have accents.

¿Tú eres estudiante?	*Are you a student?*
¿Es tu libro?	*Is it your book?*
¿Él viene aquí mucho?	*Does he come here often?*
Viene el chico.	*The boy is coming.*

2.4 Abbreviations

The written form of **usted** and **ustedes** is often abbreviated:

ud. or **vd.**; **uds.** or **vds.**

2.5 Two subjects

When there are two subjects, one female and one male, the masculine plural form is used to refer to both: **ellos** (*they*) = **él** (*he*) + **ella** (*she*).

Ellos (Ana y David) tienen una casa muy grande.	*They have a very big house.*

Él, ella and **usted** all use the third person singular of the verb.
Ellos, ellas and **ustedes** go with the third person plural.

3 Position of subject pronouns

3.1 Before the verb

These usually (but not always) go before the verb and at the beginning of the sentence.

Ellos vendrán más tarde.	*They'll come later.*

3.2 Questions

In questions the subject pronoun normally goes after the verb:

¿Vienen ellos a la fiesta?	*Are they coming to the party?*
¿Cocino yo hoy?	*Am I cooking today?*
¿Vienes tú conmigo?	*Are you coming with me?*

3.3

But it also can go at the beginning, especially in informal speech:

¿Ellos vienen a la fiesta?

3.4 Emphasis

It can add emphasis to who does the action:

¿Yo cocino?	*Am I cooking?*
¿Tú vienes conmigo?	*Are you coming with me?*

3.5 Imperatives

With imperatives they go after the verb:

Abre tú la puerta.	*You open the door.*
Prepara tú la mesa.	*You set the table.*

3.6 Reported speech

The same occurs with reported speech:

Vamos todos juntos, dijo ella.	*We'll all go together, she said.*

4 Combinations of subject pronouns with other words

4.1 With mismo/a/os/as and solo/a/os/as to add emphasis

Yo mismo preparo la cena.	*I'll prepare dinner myself.*
Vosotros solos no podéis viajar.	*You can't travel on your own.*

4.2 With numerals

e.g.: **nosotros tres, ellos dos**:

Nosotros dos viajaremos en tren y vosotros tres en coche.	*We two will travel by train and you three by car.*

4.3 With indefinite pronouns

todos ellos	*all of them*
alguno de vosotros	*one of you*

5 Use of subject pronouns

5.1

Subject pronouns are not often used in Spanish as the verb ending is enough to indicate the person speaking or doing the action:

Como en el restaurante, cenamos en casa.	*I have lunch in the restaurant, we have dinner at home.*

5.2

The personal subject pronoun is used for emphasis, contrast, or clarity.

5.2.1 Emphasis

Used to identify and point out the person who is talking:

Esto lo pago yo.	*I'll pay this one.*
¿Tú trabajas aquí?	*You work here?*

5.2.2 Opposition or contrast

Between the people who take part in the conversation.

Compare:

Quiero un café, por favor.	*I'd like a coffee, please.*
Ana quiere un café y yo quiero un agua mineral.	*Ana wants a coffee and I want water.*

Other examples:

Tú vas al cine y yo al teatro.	*You go to the cinema and I'll go to the theatre.*
Yo no quiero postre, pero él sí quiere.	*I don't want dessert, but he does.*

5.2.3 Clarity

The pronoun is also used when the verb forms coincide (e.g. first and third person singular in the imperfect) and it's not clear from the context who or what we refer to:

Iba al cine todos los fines de semana. (Who? It could be: **yo, él, ella, usted**)

so

Yo iba al cine todos los fines de semana.

5.3

The pronoun can stand alone as an answer to a question:

¿Quién es?	*Who is it?*
Yo.	*Me.*
¿Quién ha sido?	*Who was it?*
Nosotros.	*(It was) us.*

5.4

It can also be used in sentences such as:

Yo soy Isabel, ¿y tú?	*I'm Isabel. And you?*
Soy yo.	*It's me.*
Es él, es ella, somos nosotros, son ellos.	*It's him, it's her, it's us, it's them.*
Yo también / yo tampoco.	*Me too / me neither.*

5.5

Subject pronouns are used in comparative sentences:

Pedro es más fuerte que tú.	*Pedro is stronger than you.*

5.6 ¡Es diferente! Uses of tú and usted

The form **tú** is used with family, children or youngsters, friends or people you know well. You might also use it if the person you are speaking to invites you to do so.

Young people amongst themselves use **tú**, older people use **tú** when addressing people younger then them.

Usted is used in formal situations, in business, when talking to employees (shop assistants, waiters) or when addressing someone you don't know, unless it is a child or a young person.

Usted and the corresponding plural form **ustedes** are often included in the sentence to avoid confusion with the third person **él, ella, ellos, ellas**, as they all use the same form of the verb. It's also used to stress the polite tone.

¿Es usted el conductor?	*Are you the driver?*
¿Pueden acompañarme ustedes?	*Could you all accompany me?*

If you are not sure whether to use the **tú** or **usted** form, use the latter until or unless the other person invites you to use **tú**. They might say:

Puede / puedes tutearme.

or

Puede(s) hablarme / llamarme de tú.

5.7 The neuter form ello (*it*)

This is not commonly used in spoken Spanish, and not so frequently even in written texts. It refers more to ideas and sentences rather than to concrete objects and nouns.

It's often replaced by the demonstrative **eso**:

Eso es muy probable.	*That's very probable.*
(not: **ello es muy probable.**)	
No hablamos más	*We won't speak any more*
de ello.	*about that.*

This is more formal than: **No hablamos más de eso.**

5.8

In most cases Spanish doesn't use a pronoun at all when in English the pronoun is used.

In sentences where *it* is a subject and refers to things, Spanish doesn't use a personal pronoun equivalent to *it*:

es un animal	*it's an animal*

The same applies to the plural, where *they* refers to objects:

Son botas de esquí.	*They are ski boots.*

In English, *it* is used in sentences such as: *There is a house, it's big*. In Spanish the demonstrative **ésta** is used instead of the personal pronoun **ella** (*it*):

Hay una casa, ésta (casa) es grande.   *There's a house; it's big.*

With impersonal weather expressions, *it* is used in English, but there is no equivalent in Spanish:

llueve	*it rains / it's raining*
nieva	*it snows / it's snowing*
hace frío	*it's cold*

6 Object pronouns *Pronombres objeto*

6.1 ¿Qué es?

There are two kinds of object pronouns: **átonos** (*unstressed*) and **tónicos** (*stressed*).

In this section we will study the unstressed pronouns (**átonos**). These are never stressed and always appear with a verb.

 See also Section 6.5.6 below for stressed object pronouns.

6.1.1

There are two kinds of unstressed object pronouns: direct object pronouns and indirect object pronouns. They are words like **me, te, le, lo**.

6.1.2 The direct object

This is the recipient of a direct action of the verb:

A: ¿Ves a María?	*Do you see Maria?*
B: Sí, la veo.	*Yes, I see her.*

In this exchange, **a María** and **la** are direct objects.

¿Compras el libro?	*Are you buying the book?*
Sí, lo compro.	*Yes, I'm buying it.*

In this exchange, **el libro** and **lo** are direct objects.

6.1.3 The indirect object

This is indirectly affected by the action of the verb:

Le compré un regalo.	*I bought him a gift.*
	(I bought a gift <u>for</u> him)

In this sentence the direct object is **un regalo** and the indirect object is **le**.

6.2 Forms of the object pronouns

6.2.1

	Direct object pronouns		Indirect object pronouns	
	Singular	**Plural**	**Singular**	**Plural**
1st person	me (*me*)	nos (*us*)	me (*me*)	nos (*us*)
2nd person	te (*you*)	os (*you*)	te (*you*)	os (*you*)
3rd person	lo / le (*him*)	los / les (*them*)	le / se* (*him / her / you / it*)	les / se* (*them*)
	la (*her*)	las (*them*)		
	lo / la (*it*)			

*__se__ is used instead of **le** when combined with other pronouns such as **lo, la, los, las**.

 See point 6.3.3 below.

6.2.1.1

1st and 2nd person singular, **me, te**, and plural, **nos, os**, are the same for masculine and feminine. These are also the same for the direct and indirect object pronouns:

Te espero en la cafetería.   *I'll wait for you in the cafe.*

(**te** = direct object pronoun, 2nd person singular masculine or feminine)

Te doy un regalo.   *I'll give you a present.*

(**te** = indirect object pronoun, 2nd person singular masculine or feminine)

6.2.1.2 The 3rd person forms

These are different for the direct and indirect object. Their use is therefore more complicated.

They are also different in gender and in number, except the invariable **se**, which is used instead of **le** when combined with other pronouns such as **lo, la, los, las**.

La espero en la cafetería   *I'll wait for her in the cafe.*

(**la** = direct object pronoun singular 3rd person feminine)

Lo llamo ahora.   *I'll call him now*

(**lo** = direct object pronoun singular 3rd person masculine)

Le doy un regalo.   *I'll give him/her a present.*

(**le** = indirect object pronoun singular 3rd person masculine or feminine)

6.2.2

Object pronouns referring to objects: **lo, la, los, las** = *it, them*

They agree with the gender and number of the objects they describe:

El pañuelo: <u>lo</u> quiero.	*The handkerchief: I want it / I'd like it.*
La pulsera: <u>la</u> quiero.	*The bracelet: I want it / I'd like it.*
Los pendientes: <u>los</u> quiero.	*The earrings: I want them / I'd like them.*
Las gafas de sol: <u>las</u> quiero.	*The sunglasses: I want them / I'd like them.*

The neuter pronoun **lo** is used as a direct object when it refers to part of a sentence or to a concept:

No lo sé. (el tema)	*I don't know (about it).*
No lo comprendo. (el problema)	*I don't understand it. (the problem)*
Lo pasamos bien.*	*We had a good time.*

*Note: in Latin America: **La** pasamos bien.

 For structures with indirect objects such as **me gusta, te interesa, nos encanta**, see Unit 26.

6.3 Use of object pronouns

6.3.1 First and second person pronouns

These always refer to people.

Mi madre me compró una guitarra.	*My mother bought me a guitar.*
	My mother bought a guitar for me.
¿Nos lleváis al aeropuerto?	*Will you take us to the airport?*

6.3.2 Uses of *lo, le, la* and their plural forms

6.3.2.1 Direct object pronouns

Lo and **los** are always used as a direct object pronoun for objects which are masculine:

A: **¿Preparas el pastel?**	*Will you prepare the cake?*
B: **Sí, lo preparo.**	*Yes, I'll prepare it.*
A: **¿Lees estos libros?**	*Do you read these books?*
B: **Sí, los leo.**	*Yes, I read them.*

6.3.2.2 Direct objects

Lo and **los** are also used for males as direct objects.

A: **¿Viste a Pedro?**	*Did you see Pedro?*
B: **Sí, lo vi.**	*Yes, I saw him.*
A: **¿Llamaste a Francisco y José?**	*Did you call Francisco and José?*
B: **Sí, los llamé.**	*Yes, I called them.*

Remember that the preposition **a** is used before people (male and female, see point 6.3.2.4 below) when they are the direct object of a sentence, but not with objects, ideas or concepts. This can sometimes cause confusion as the indirect object can also take **a**; observe the difference:

Llamo a Juan.	*I call Juan.*
(direct object)	
Escribió una carta a Juan.	*He wrote a letter to Juan.*
(indirect object)	

6.3.2.3 Lo *and* los *replaced by* le *and* les *in the case of males*

This is called **leísmo** and is accepted as correct. The use of one or the other is a matter of choice and may differ in different geographical areas. They are often even interchanged by the same person, especially in spoken language.

Llamo a Juan > lo llamo / le llamo.	*I'll call Juan > I'll call him.*
Invito a Pedro a la fiesta > lo invito / le invito.	*I'll invite Pedro to the party > I'll invite him.*

6.3.2.4 La, las

These are always used as the direct object pronoun for a feminine object:

A: **¿Verás la película esta tarde?**	*Are you going to see the film this afternoon?*
B: **No, no la veré.**	*No, I'm not going to see it.*
A: **¿Comprarás las revistas?**	*Will you buy the magazines?*
B: **Sí, las compraré.**	*Yes, I'll buy them.*

And also for females:

A: **¿Conoces a Isabel?**	*Do you know Isabel?*
B: **Sí, la conozco.**	*Yes, I know her.*
A: **¿Conoces a Isabel y a María?**	*Do you know Isabel and María?*
B: **Sí, las conozco.**	*Yes, I know them.*

 See point 6.3.2.2 above about the use of the preposition **a** before people when they are the direct object.

6.3.2.5

Le and **les** are indirect object pronouns which are only used for people, both male and female, never for objects.

Di un regalo a Juan. > Le di un regalo.	*I gave a present to Juan. > I gave him a present.*
Di un regalo a María. > Le di un regalo.	*I gave a present to María. > I gave her a present.*
Envié el documento a mis hermanos. > Les envié el documento.	*I sent the document to my brothers. > I sent them the document.*
Envié el documento a mis hermanas. > Les envié el documento.	*I sent the document to my sisters. > I sent them the document.*

6.3.2.6

For clarification or emphasis, the name of the person preceded by the preposition **a** (*a Juan, a María*) or the corresponding stressed pronoun (*a él / ella / ellos / ellas*) is often included in addition to the object pronoun.

 See point 6.5.8 below.

Le di un regalo a Juan.	*I gave him, Juan, a present.*
or	
Le di un regalo a él.	*I gave him a present (to him).*
Le di un regalo a María.	*I gave her, María, a present.*
or	
Le di un regalo a ella.	*I gave her a present (to her).*
Les envié el documento a mis hermanos.	*I sent them, my brothers, the document.*
or	
Les envié el documento a ellos.	*I sent them the documents (to them).*

Note that sometimes you might hear **la** or **las** instead of **le** or **les** for the feminine form of the indirect object pronoun. This use of **la** and **las**, although widespread in certain areas, is not considered grammatically correct.

6.3.3 *se (3rd person indirect object pronoun)*

Sometimes we need to use two object pronouns, for example in sentences like:

Di el libro a Juan.	*I gave the book to Juan.*
Se lo di.	*I gave it to him.*
(not: le lo di)	

If **le** or **les** (3rd person indirect pron.) is used together with **lo, la, los** or **las** (3rd person direct pron.), **le** or **les**, the indirect object, becomes **se** and appears first. **Se** doesn't change in gender nor in number: it means *(to, for) him / her / them*.

Le, les + lo, la, los, las > se + lo, la, los, las.

Se lo doy.	*I give it to him / her / them.*
Se la preparo.	*I'll prepare it for him / her / them.*
Se los envío.	*I send them to him / her / them.*
Se las vendo.	*I sell them to him / her / them.*

This is the way the language has evolved in order to avoid two pronouns beginning with 'l' occurring next to each other; **se lo** is easier to say than **le lo**.

 See Unit 10 for the reflexive pronoun se. For other uses of se see Unit 40.

6.4 Position

In most statements or questions personal pronouns appear before the verb:

A: Quiero un bolso, lo quiero negro.	*I want a bag; I'd like it black.*
B: ¿Lo quiere grande?	*Do you want a big one?*

This also happens when there is a compound verb:

A: ¿Lo has visto?	*Have you seen him / it?*
B: Sí, lo he visto.	*Yes, I've seen him / it.*

Other examples:

Los pantalones me van muy bien.	*The trousers fit (me) well.*
¿Me da un recibo?	*Could you give me a receipt?*
¿Cuánto le debo?	*How much do I owe you?*
¿Qué me recomienda?	*What do you recommend (to me)?*
Nos cobra, por favor.	*Can you take (payment) for this (from us) please.*

6.5 ¡Es diferente!

6.5.1 *With an infinitive*

With verbs in the infinitive the rule is that the pronoun goes at the end of the infinitive.

Notice also how it agrees with the noun.

El espejo está roto; ¿puede cambiarlo?	*The mirror is broken; can you change it?*
La cama está estropeada; ¿puede arreglarla?	*The bed is damaged; can you repair it?*
Los grifos no funcionan; ¿puede arreglarlos?	*The taps don't work; can you fix them?*
Las cortinas no cierran; ¿puede mirarlas?	*The curtains don't close; can you look at them?*

BUT Note that this rule is often not followed, especially in the spoken language, or when the infinitive depends on another verb.

This happens with the direct object pronouns:

Quiero comprarlo. > Lo quiero comprar.	*I want to buy it.*
Voy a buscarlos. > Los voy a buscar.	*I'm going to pick them up.*
Vienen a vernos. > Nos vienen a ver.	*They're coming to see us.*

And also with the indirect object pronouns:

Voy a mandarte un paquete. > Te voy a mandar un paquete.	*I'm going to send you a packet.*
Voy a darle un regalo. > Le voy a dar un regalo.	*I'm going to give him a present.*
Quiero escribirles hoy. > Les quiero escribir hoy.	*I want to write to them today.*

This happens most frequently when the infinitive appears after a modal verb such as **poder** or **soler**:

¿Puedes llamarla? > ¿La puedes llamar?	*Can you call her?*
¿Podría darme otros? > ¿Me podría dar otros?	*Could you give me some others?*
Suele leerlo. > Lo suele leer.	*He usually reads it.*

You will see either being used. For your own use and if in doubt follow the rule of placing the pronoun at the end of the infinitive; this should be easier to remember for English speakers as it is the same as English:

Quiero comprar<u>lo</u>.	*I want to buy <u>it</u>.*

6.5.2 With the gerund

When the gerund follows a main verb the pronoun usually appears after the gerund.

A: ¿Ha pagado la cuenta?	*Has he paid the bill?*
B: No, está pagándola ahora.	*No, he's paying it now.*

A: ¿Estás limpiando la casa?	*Are you cleaning the house?*
B: Sí, estoy limpiándola.	*Yes, I'm cleaning it.*

But as happens with the infinitive, the object pronoun is sometimes placed before the main verb:

Estoy comiéndolo. > Lo estoy comiendo.	*I'm eating it.*
Estoy limpiándola. > La estoy limpiando.	*I'm cleaning it.*

6.5.3 With the imperative

When we use object pronouns (**me / te / le** etc.) with imperatives, we join them to the end of the imperative verb:

Deme un pollo.	*(Can you) give me a chicken.*
Póngame un kilo de patatas.	*(Can you) give me a kilo of potatoes.*
Dime la verdad.	*Tell me the truth.*

These expressions are often used in a restaurant, or when we are eating at home:

Informal		Formal	
ponme	*give me / can you give me*	póngame	*could you give me*
tráeme	*bring me / can you bring me*	tráigame	*could you bring me*
pásame la sal	*pass me the salt*	páseme la sal	*could you pass me the salt*

6.5.4 Accents and spelling

6.5.4.1 Stress and accents

When the pronouns are attached to the imperative or the gerund form of the verb, the stress often changes and they need an accent:
ponga > póngame; comprando > comprándola.

This happens with an infinitive only when it is followed by two pronouns:

comprar > comprarlo (no stress change, no accent needed)

but

comprárselo (followed by two pronouns so stress change and accent needed)

 See Unit 2 Section 3 for accents.

6.5.4.2 *Spelling*

If the pronoun **os** follows the 2nd person informal imperative, the verb loses the final **-d**:

¡Callad! > ¡Callaos!	*Shut up!*
Terminad la sopa. > Terminaos la sopa.	*Finish the soup.*

6.5.5 *Two pronouns together*

Subject pronoun + object pronoun (**me, te, lo, nos** etc.)

When the object pronoun (**me, te, lo, nos, os** etc.) is used with a subject pronoun (**yo, tú, él** etc.) in the same sentence, the subject pronoun always goes before the object pronoun:

Yo te quiero.	*I love you.*
Yo te envié el paquete.	*I sent you the package.*
Nosotros los encontramos en la calle.	*We met them in the street.*

 See point 8.1.1 in Más allá below for two object pronouns (one indirect and the other one direct) together.

6.5.6 *Personal pronouns with prepositions*

The forms of the subject personal pronouns studied in Section 2 above can all be used with prepositions and behave as a prepositional object. They are always stressed forms (remember that object pronouns are not stressed). Their form does not change except for the first and second person singular where **yo** becomes **mí** and **tú** becomes **ti**.

1st person singular:	**mí** (para mí)
2nd person singular:	**ti** (para ti)
3rd person singular	**él / ella / usted** (para él, con ella, sin usted)
1st person plural	**nosotros/as** (para nosotras)
2nd person plural	**vosotros/as** (con vosotros)
3rd person plural	**ellos / ellas / ustedes** (sin ustedes)

 There is a third person form **sí** which has a reflexive or reciprocal meaning. For this see Unit 10 Section 5.

El café con leche es para mí y el café solo para ella.	*The white coffee is for me and the black coffee for her.*
He comprado un regalo para ti.	*I've bought a present for you.*
Voy al cine con vosotros.	*I'm going to the cinema with you.*
El regalo es de ellos.	*The gift is theirs.*

Important: **ti** doesn't have an accent. You might see it written sometimes, but it's a common mistake of Spanish speakers as they think it's like **mí**. The reason **mí** has an accent is to avoid confusion with the possessive **mi** as in **mi casa**. This doesn't happen in the second person: **tu / ti**.

 See Unit 2 section 3 for accents.

Éste es mi libro. / Este libro es para mí.	*This is my book. / This book is for me.*
Éste es tu libro. / Este libro es para ti.	*This is your book. / This book is for you.*

6.5.7

If **mí** and **ti** are accompanied by the preposition **con** their forms change:

mí > conmigo (con + mí + go); **ti > contigo** (con + ti + go).

A: **¿Quieres ir a la fiesta conmigo?**	*Do you want to go to the party with me?*
B: **Sí, quiero ir contigo.**	*Yes, I want to go with you.*

If **él** follows the prepositions **a** and **de** there is no contraction as **él** is stressed: **a él; de él**.

 See Unit 4 Section 2.2.2 for the contractions **al, del**.

There are two prepositions with which **yo** and **tú** stay the same:

entre (*between*), **según** (*according to*).

Según tú no hay problemas entre tú y yo.	*According to you there are no problems between you and me.*

6.5.8 Use of pronouns with the preposition a

Prepositional stressed pronouns with the preposition **a** are used to reinforce and clarify the object pronouns:

a mí / a ti / a él / a ella / a usted / a nosotros / a nosotras / a ellos / a ellas / a ustedes

Le traigo un paquete a él.	*I've brought him a package. (to him).*
Te doy la bolsa a ti.	*I'll give you the bag. (to you)*
Me compró un regalo a mí, no a ti.	*He bought me a present (for me) not you.*

This is very common with **gustar** and similar verbs to emphasise the fact that you like or dislike something or to compare your likes with someone else's.

A mí me gusta la música clásica pero a él le gusta el rock.	*I like classical music but he likes rock.*

 See Unit 26 on **gustar** and similar verbs.

7 Gramática práctica

9.7.1 Give the subject pronoun for these verbs.

1. Como pollo con ensalada.
2. Cenas en mi casa.
3. Abren la tienda a las nueve.
4. Encontramos a mis amigos esta tarde.
5. ¿Sois estudiantes?
6. Habla español muy bien.

9.7.2 Choose the correct pronoun to complete the gap.

1. Quiero una falda, por favor.
¿De qué color ＿＿＿quiere?
＿＿＿ quiero verde.

2. Quiero un jersey, por favor.
¿De qué color ＿＿＿quiere?
＿＿ quiero azul.

3. Quiero unos pantalones, por favor.
¿De qué color ＿＿＿ quiere?
＿＿＿ quiero negros.

4. Quiero unas botas, por favor.
¿De qué color ＿＿ quiere?
＿＿＿ quiero marrones.

9.7.3 Replace the nouns with the direct object pronouns.

Example: Ayer vi a María. **>** Ayer la vi.

1. Ayer vi a Juan.
2. El domingo llamé a Alicia.
3. El fin de semana vi a tus padres.
4. Conocí a María en un cine.
5. El domingo saludé a tus amigas.
6. Miré a Carlos con sorpresa.

9.7.4 Rewrite these sentences as in the example.

Example: ¿Compras un libro para tu hermana? > Le compras un libro?

1. ¿Traes un regalo para mí?
2. ¿Regalas el libro a María?
3. ¿Das la comida a los gatos?
4. ¿Sacas las entradas para tus amigas?
5. ¿Compras el reloj a tu padre?
6. ¿Comprará la guitarra a vosotros?
7. ¿Entregarás el paquete a nosotros?
8. ¿Escribirás un email a mí?

9.7.5 Now rewrite the above sentences with two pronouns.

Example: ¿Le compras un libro? > Se lo compras?

9.7.6 Answer the questions using the infinitive or gerund and the appropriate pronoun.

Example: ¿Quieres comprar la chaqueta? Sí, quiero comprarla.

1. ¿Quieres comprar el coche?
2. ¿Estás arreglando la bicicleta?
3. ¿Quieres escribir a los chicos?
4. ¿Estás pintando la casa?
5. ¿Quieres cerrar las ventanas?
6. ¿Vienes a ver a tu madre?
7. ¿Estás comiendo las verduras?
8. ¿Quieres llamar a las niñas?

8 Más allá

8.1 Position

8.1.1 Two object pronouns together

When two object pronouns appear together, the indirect object (**me, te, nos, os, se**) always goes before the direct object, and they both go before the verb.

¿Me lo dices?	*Will you tell me (it)?*
¿Te lo pruebas?	*Do you want to try it?*
Me la compro.	*I'll buy it (for me).*

Me (indirect object) always follows **te** and **se** when they go together.

Se me ha hecho tarde.	*I've made myself late.*
No te me escapes.	*Don't get away from me.*

Note that in any combination of pronouns **se** always goes first:

Se lo dije.	*I told him (it).*
Se me perdió.	*I lost it. (Lit: It got lost from me.)*
Se os cayó.	*You dropped it. (Lit: It fell from you.)*

Se must be used even when we mention the person it refers to (as reinforcement):

Se lo doy a Luis.	*I'll give it to him, to Luis.*

8.1.2 After the infinitive

We saw above that an object pronoun goes after the infinitive but that it can also go before the main verb.

Here are some cases when the pronoun cannot be placed before the verb, and must therefore follow the infinitive.

8.1.2.1 With impersonal structures

Hay que:

Hay que hacer el trabajo. > Hay que hacerlo.	*It's necessary to do the work.* *It's necessary to do it.*

(<u>Not</u>: **Lo hay que hacer.**)

Other examples:

Es importante estudiarlo.   *It's important to study it.*
Conviene comprarlo ahora.   *It's convenient to buy it now.*

8.1.2.2 *With verbs such as* sentir *and* lamentar

Siento llamarte tan tarde.   *I'm sorry to phone you so late.*

8.1.3 *Two pronouns after the infinitive, the gerund and the imperative*

After a verb in the infinitive which depends on a main verb, the two pronouns can go at the end of the verb. They keep the same order.

<u>Se</u> <u>lo</u> quiero dar > Quiero dár<u>selo</u>.   *I want to give it to him.*

This also happens with the gerund:

Se la está comiendo. > Está comiéndosela. *He's eating it.*

In the case of the imperative, they must always follow it:

Cómpraselo.   *Buy it for him / her.*
Dámelos.   *Give them to me.*
Póntelas.   *Put them on.*

8.2 Questions: ¿Y a ti?

The construction with the preposition **a** is used for questions such as:

A mí me gusta ésta. ¿Y a ti?   *I like this one, and you?*
A ella le va mal. ¿Y a él?   *It doesn't suit her. And him?*
Le has traído un regalo a Juan.   *You've brought a gift for Juan.*
  ¿Y a mí?   *And for me?*
¿Y a mí, me has traído un regalo?   *And me, have you brought me a gift?*
Les compraste helados a ellos.   *You bought ice creams for them.*
  ¿Y a nosotros?   *And for us?*
¿Y a nosotros nos compraste helados?   *And did you buy ice cream for us?*
Me gusta la leche. ¿Y a ti?   *I like milk. And you?*
¿Y a ti, te gusta?   *And you, do you like it?*

 See Unit 26 for **gustar**.

9 Order of pronouns

The following is the order that pronouns follow in Spanish.

9.1

Subj Pron	Indirect Obj	Direct Obj	Verb	Prepositional pron
Yo	te	lo	doy	a ti
Tú	me	las	compras	a mí

9.2 With infinitive, gerund and imperative

Subj Pron	Verb		Indirect Obj	Direct Obj	Prepositional pron
Yo	voy a	*<u>dár</u>	<u>te</u>	<u>lo</u>	a ti
Ella	está	*<u>contándo</u>	<u>se</u>	<u>lo</u>	a ellos
Tú		*<u>píde</u>	<u>nos</u>	<u>lo</u>	a nosotros

*Note: all one word:

dártelo   *to give it to you*
contándoselo   *telling it to him*
pídenoslo   *ask us for it*

10 Más práctica

9.10.1 Rewrite the sentences using pronouns.

Example: Trae el libro a Juan. > Tráeselo.

1. Regala el bolso a María.
2. Compra la cartera a Manolo.
3. Da los libros a Ana.
4. Compra las gafas a tu padre.
5. Presta el bolígrafo a tu amiga.
6. Regala los pantalones a Luis.
7. Compra la camiseta a tu hermano.

9.10.2 Rewrite these sentences using pronouns.

Example: Llevo la bebida a ti. > Te la llevo.

1. Recomiendo el pescado a usted.
2. Traigo la comida a ustedes.
3. Digo la noticia a vosotros.
4. ¿Compras el libro para ti?
5. Compro la bicicleta para mí.
6. ¿Pruebas el vestido tú?
7. ¿Pides la cuenta al camarero?
8. ¿Compramos un coche para nosotros?

10 Reflexive pronouns
Pronombres reflexivos

1 ¿Qué es?

Reflexive pronouns form part of a reflexive verb. These are verbs where the subject and the object are the same. The reflexive pronoun is the equivalent of *oneself* in English:

Me levanto a las ocho, me ducho y me visto.

I get (myself) up, I shower (myself) and I dress (myself).
or *I get up, have a shower and get dressed.*

2 Form

Reflexive pronoun	Refers to / accompanies subject pronoun
me (myself)	yo
te (yourself)	tú
se (himself / herself / itself / yourself)	él / ella / usted
nos (ourselves)	nosotros/as
os (yourselves)	vosotros/as
se (themselves / yourselves)	ellos / ellas / ustedes

All the forms are the same as for personal object pronouns except in the third person **se**.

Note:

Remember the 3rd person object pronouns are **le / les**, which change to **se** when combined with **lo, la, los, las**.

 See Unit 9 section 6.3.3.

It is important not to confuse the reflexive **se** with the object pronoun **se** or with the impersonal and passive **se.**

 See Units 40 and 44.

3 Position

The same rules apply as for the personal pronouns.

 See Unit 9 section 6.4.

Reflexive pronouns always go before the verb, except with the infinitive, gerund or imperative when they appear after the verb:

Me levanto a las siete.	*I get up at seven.*
¿Te acuestas muy tarde?	*Do you go to bed late?*
Luis se baña en el mar.	*Luis bathes in the sea.*
Nos vestimos para la fiesta.	*We are getting dressed for the party.*
¿Os despertáis pronto?	*Do you wake up early?*
El niño se ha lavado las manos.	*The boy has washed his hands.*

Infinitive:

No quiere levantarse temprano.   *He doesn't want to get up early.*

Gerund:

Estoy duchándome.   *I'm having a shower.*

Imperative:

Despiértame a las siete.   *Wake me up at seven.*

4 Use

They are used with reflexive verbs. They can also accompany other verbs that are called pronominal verbs.

 See Unit 41 for pronominal verbs.

5 Más allá

sí, consigo

There is also a third person form that is rarely used in spoken Spanish.

We can use the pronoun **sí** in the third person if we want to refer to him or her as *himself* or *herself*. It is always preceded by a preposition and is often accompanied by **mismo/a/os/as** for added emphasis.

Sí = *himself / herself / yourself*

Habla para sí.   *He speaks to himself.*
Habla para sí mismo.

If **sí** is preceded by the preposition **con** it becomes **consigo** (*with him/her (self)*).

This follows the same rule as **conmigo, contigo**.

 See Unit 9 point 6.5.7.

Está contento consigo mismo.	*He's pleased with himself.*
Están satisfechos de sí mismos	*They're satisfied with themselves.*

There is a tendency to replace **sí** with the equivalent subject forms, often accompanied by **mismo/a/os/as**, in order to emphasise that we are talking about himself / herself / themselves:

Habla para él mismo.	*He speaks for himself.*
Están satisfechos de ellos mismos.	*They are satisfied with themselves.*

Note that these forms do not always have a reflexive meaning. The meaning is different if the preposition **entre** (*between, among*) is added. **Entre sí** means *among themselves* in sentences like these:

Sus hijos hablan español entre sí.	*Her children speak Spanish among themselves.*

But more commonly:

Sus hijos hablan español entre ellos.	*Her children speak Spanish among themselves.*

6 Gramática práctica

10.6.1 Give the correct forms of the infinitives.

1. Yo (levantarse) a las ocho.
2. Mis hermanos (acostarse) muy tarde.
3. Elena (bañarse) en la piscina.
4. Ellos (vestirse) para la fiesta.
5. Nosotros (despertarse) siempre tarde.
6. Tú (ducharse) por las noches.
7. Yo (arreglarse) para ir a bailar.
8. Nosotros (acostarse) pronto.

10.6.2 Give the correct forms of the infinitives.

Example: Yo estoy (ducharse). > Yo estoy duchándome.

1. Yo estoy (bañarse) en la playa.
2. Los niños no quieren (levantarse) temprano.
3. Nosotros estamos (arreglarse) para la fiesta.
4. Vosotros (vestirse) para salir.
5. A mí no me gusta (ducharse) por la noche.
6. Javier está (lavarse) los dientes.
7. A nosotros nos encanta (bañarse) en el mar.

❚❚ Demonstrative adjectives and pronouns
Adjetivos y pronombres demostrativos

1 ¿Qué es?

1.1 Demonstrative adjectives and pronouns

These determine or specify what nouns or phrases we refer to. They tell us whether the noun is near or far from the speaker in terms of time and space.

1.2 Use

Demonstrative adjectives accompany nouns. In English, there are four: *this (car)*, *that (car)*, *these (cars)*, *those (cars)*. Demonstrative pronouns substitute for or replace the noun: *this (one)*, *that (one)*, *these*, *those*.

1.3 Forms

Adjective and pronoun forms are exactly the same except for accents on the pronouns:

este chico	*this boy*	**Mi amigo es éste.**	*My friend is this one.*
aquel piso	*that flat*	**Mi piso es aquél.**	*My flat is that one.*

1.4 ¡Es diferente!

Spanish has a masculine and feminine form for the demonstrative adjectives meaning *this* and *these*: **este / esta** and **estos / estas**.

1.5 ¡Es diferente!

Spanish has two forms of adjectives that mean *that*, each with a masculine and feminine form: **ese / esa, aquel / aquella**.

The difference is in the distance in space and time between the speaker and the object referred to:

ese coche	*that car (quite near you)*
aquel coche	*that car (further from you)*

2 Form and position of demonstrative adjectives

2.1 Demonstrative adjectives

These change in gender and number depending on the noun they accompany:

	Masculine	Feminine	
singular	este	esta	*this*
	ese	esa	*that (near)*
	aquel	aquella	*that (far)*
plural	estos	estas	*these*
	esos	esas	*those (near)*
	aquellos	aquellas	*those (far)*

2.2 Adjectives usually appear before the noun

Este libro es muy interesante.   *This book is very interesting.*
Aquella niña es muy inteligente.   *That little girl is very intelligent.*

But they can go after the noun if it's preceded by an article, to express enphasis.

El chico ese que viene todas las tardes.   *That boy who comes every afternoon.*
La historia aquella que te conté.   *That story I told you.*

3 Use

3.1 este, esta, estos, estas

The noun is near to the speaker and the listener in space or time.

Space = near. Time = present or recent past.

Este libro me gusta mucho.   *I like this book a lot.*
Estas fotos son muy buenas.   *These photos are very good.*

3.2 ese, esa, esos, esas

The noun is far from the speaker but nearer to the listener.

Space = far from the speaker and nearer to the listener. Time = past.

Quiero esa camisa, por favor.   *I'd like that shirt, please.*
¿Cuánto cuestan esos pantalones?   *How much are those trousers?*
Tuve los exámenes en junio,   *I took the exams in June, I had a bad*
    esos días lo pasé muy mal.   *time during those days.*

3.3 aquel, aquella, aquellos, aquellas

The noun is far from both the speaker and the listener.

Space = far from the speaker and from the listener. Time = past.

¿Puedes traer aquella silla?	*Can you bring that chair?*
Quiero aquellos zapatos de arriba.	*I'd like those shoes from up there.*

Aquellas vacaciones de la infancia
   eran muy divertidas.
	*Those childhood holidays were
	   great fun.*

3.4 ese and aquel

The difference between **ese** and **aquel** is often subjective; it depends on what the speaker wants to express:

A: Quiero un kilo de esas manzanas.	*I'd like a kilo of those apples.*
B: ¿Estas manzanas grandes?	*These big apples?*
A: No, quiero esas pequeñas.	*No, I want those small ones.*

Y un kilo de aquellas
     naranjas.
	*And a kilo of those oranges
	     (over there).*

In this example the apples (**esas**) are nearer to the client than the oranges (**aquellas**). The shop assistant has the apples next to him or her and therefore uses **estas**.

A: ¿Es tuyo ese coche azul?	*Is that blue car yours?*
B: No, ese coche no es mío.	*No, that car isn't mine.*
El mío es aquel coche verde, al final de la calle.	*Mine is that green car (over there) at the end of the street.*
Esta casa es de mi madre y aquella casa es de mi abuela.	*This house is my mother's and that house is my grandmother's.*
Esta tarde voy al cine.	*This afternoon I'm going to the cinema.*

Esa tarde fui al cine con
   mi hermano.
	*That afternoon I went to the cinema
	   with my brother. (not too long ago)*

Aquel año fue malo
   para mi familia.
	*That year was bad for my family.
	   (a long time ago)*

4 Forms and use of demonstrative pronouns

4.1 Forms

The forms of the pronouns are the same as for the adjectives except for the accents which distinguish them (with the exception of the neuter forms: see point 5.1 below).

	Masculine	**Feminine**	
singular	éste	ésta	*this (one)*
	ése	ésa	*that (one) (near)*
	aquél	aquélla	*that (one) (far)*
plural	éstos	éstas	*these (ones)*
	ésos	ésas	*those (ones) (near)*
	aquéllos	aquéllas	*those (ones) (far)*

4.2 Use

They substitute for or replace nouns previously referred to. Each form agrees with the noun it replaces. They can be the subject of a sentence (usually before the verb):

Éste es muy bonito.   *This one is very nice.*

or the object of a sentence (usually after the verb):

Quiero ése.   *I'd like that one.*

More examples:

A: ¿Quieres este libro?   *Would you like this book?*
B: No, no quiero éste,   *No, I don't want this one,*
   prefiero ése.   *I prefer that one.*

A: ¿Te gusta ese vestido?   *Do you like that dress?*
B: Sí, me gusta ése, pero me   *Yes, I like it, but I like that*
   gusta más aquél.   *one more.*

4.3

They also present or introduce things or people:

éste / ésta es   *this is*
éstos / éstas son   *these are*
Éste es mi padre.   *This is my father.*
Éstas son mis hermanas.   *These are my sisters.*

5 Neuter demonstrative pronouns

5.1 Forms

esto *this*; **eso** *that*; **aquello** *that* (= that one over there)

They do not carry accents as they cannot be confused with adjectives. They have no gender, and they are never used to refer to people.

5.2 Use

5.2.1 When we don't know or remember the name of an object

¿Qué es esto?	*What's this?*
¿Cómo se llama esto?	*What's the name of this?*

5.2.2 Neuter forms when talking about objects, actions or ideas without saying what they are

Esto no me gusta.	*I don't like this.*

5.2.3

Note the difference:

Dame ése.	*Give me that one. (not the other one)*
Dame eso.	*Give me that. (generic)*

5.2.4 To ask, describe, explain or clarify what something is

A: ¿Qué es eso?	*What's that?*
B: Eso es un teléfono móvil.	*That's a mobile phone.*

5.3 Difference in meaning

The difference between **esto** (*this*), **eso** (*that*) and **aquello** (*that, further or distant*) reflects the different meanings of **este, ese, aquel** (see points 3.1 to 3.3 above).

No me gusta esto.	*I don't like this.*
Dame eso.	*Give me that.*
Quiero aquello.	*I want that one. (over there)*

6 Gramática práctica

11.6.1 Answer the questions as in the example:

¿Quiere este vestido? > No, no quiero éste, prefiero aquél.

1. ¿Quiere esta chaqueta?
2. ¿Quiere estos calcetines?
3. ¿Quiere este abrigo?
4. ¿Quiere estas gafas?
5. ¿Quiere esto?

11.6.2 Translate into Spanish.

1. I would like those oranges over there.
2. I prefer these apples.
3. He prefers those bananas, not those ones over there.
4. What's this? This is a watch.
5. We would like that cake over there.
6. Can I have these apples, not those.
7. I don't want those peaches, I prefer these ones.
8. What's that called?
9. How do you say this?

7 Más allá

7.1

We can use the demonstrative pronoun to refer to someone or something we have mentioned in the previous phrase or sentence:

Llamé al profesor, pero éste no me contestó.	*I called the teacher but he didn't answer.*

7.2

The pronoun can be used with other words: **otro** and **mismo**:

este otro / esta otra	*this other one*
estos mismos / estas mismas	*these same ones*
No quiero este abrigo, quiero este otro.	*I don't want this coat, I want this other one.*
A: ¿Quieres éste?	*Do you want this one?*
B: Sí, éste mismo.	*Yes, (exactly) this one. (or Yes, that's the one.)*

7.3

We use the neuter form **esto, eso, aquello** when we refer to an idea or situation:

Escucha esto.	*Listen to this.*
Esto es ridículo.	*This is ridiculous.*
Eso no me interesa.	*That doesn't interest me.*
No pienso eso.	*I don't think that.*

7.4

The following are some common expressions in which neuter demonstrative pronouns are used:

¡Eso es!	*Exactly!*
Por eso.	*That's why.*
A eso de las ocho.	*About eight o'clock.*
Eso está bien / mal.	*That's fine / bad.*

8 Más práctica

11.8.1 Complete the dialogue with the correct adjective or pronoun.

Example: Quiero (that) falda. > Quiero <u>esa</u> falda

1. A: Quiero (that) falda.
2. B: ¿Cuál, (this) falda azul?
3. A: No, quiero (that one), la verde. También quiero (that – over there) jersey.
4. B: ¿Cuál, (that) jersey blanco?
5. A: No, (that one over there), el jersey gris. ¿Cuánto cuestan (these) pantalones?
6. B: (These) pantalones cuestan cien euros.
7. A: Pues no quiero (these), son muy caros. ¿Cuánto cuestan (those ones), de color negro?
8. B: (Those ones) cuestan treinta euros.
9. A: Pues quiero (those ones). Oiga, ¿qué es (this)? ¿Es una camiseta?
10. B: No, (this) no es una camiseta, es un vestido muy corto.
11. A: Pues quiero (this) vestido, pero de color blanco.
12. B: Mire, (this one) es muy bonito.
13. A: Sí, pero (this one) no es mi talla. Yo uso la talla cuarenta.
14. B: Pues no tengo (this) vestido en la talla cuarenta. ¿Le gusta (that one – over there)? (That – over there) vestido es muy parecido a (this one).
15. A: Bueno, ¿puedo probarme (that one over there)?
16. B: Sí, claro.

12 Possessive adjectives and pronouns
Adjetivos y pronombres posesivos

1 ¿Qué es?

Possessive adjectives and pronouns indicate possession of the noun, i.e. when we say something is *mine, yours, his, theirs* etc.

1.1 Possessive adjectives used with the noun

mi coche	*my car*
su casa	*his / her / their house*

1.2 Possessive pronouns replacing the noun

El coche es mío.	*The car is mine.*
¿Es tuyo?	*Is it yours?*

1.3 **de** to express possession or family relation

el coche de mi amigo	*my friend's car (the car of my friend).*
el padre de Isabel	*Isabel's father*
	(lit: the father of Isabel)

 See also point 2.1.4 below.

2 Possessive adjectives

Possessive adjectives indicate who the noun belongs to. They usually appear before the noun but in some cases can appear after.

2.1 Form and position of possessive adjectives

Possessive adjectives have two forms:

a short form:	**mi** (*my*), **tu** (*your*), **su** (*his, her, your* formal) etc.
a full form:	**mío** (*mine*), **tuyo** (*your*), **suyo** (*his, hers, yours* formal) etc.

Their forms change in gender and number, depending on the noun they accompany.

¡Es diferente! Important! Possessive adjectives and pronouns agree with the possessed object or item and <u>not</u> with the person it belongs to, the owner, as we see in these examples:

su coche   *his / her / your (formal) / their car*
sus coches   *his / her / your (formal) / their cars*

2.1.1 Short forms

This is how the short forms of the possessive adjectives appear when accompanied by masculine and feminine nouns:

m sing	mi	tu	su	nuestro	vuestro	su	coche
	my	*your*	*his, her, your*	*our*	*your*	*their*	*car*
f sing	mi	tu	su	nuestra	vuestra	su	casa
	my	*your*	*his, her, your*	*our*	*your*	*their*	*house*
m pl	mis	tus	sus	nuestros	vuestros	sus	coches
	my	*your*	*his, her, your*	*our*	*your*	*their*	*cars*
f pl	mis	tus	sus	nuestras	vuestras	sus	casas
	my	*your*	*his, her, your*	*our*	*your*	*their*	*houses*

2.1.2 Before the noun and changing only in number, from singular to plural: mi / tu / su / mis / tus / sus:

mi padre   *my father*   **mis padres**   *my parents.*
tu hermana   *your sister*   **tus hermanas**   *your sisters*
su tío   *his / her uncle* **sus tíos**   *his / her aunts and uncles*

2.1.3 First and second person plural possessive adjectives

These have a masculine and a feminine form as well as a singular and plural form. They are the same for the short and full forms.

nuestro tío   nuestra tía   nuestros tíos   nuestras tías
vuestro tío   vuestra tía   vuestros tíos   vuestras tías

2.1.4 Third person forms

The third person forms can be ambiguous. **Su** can mean **his, her, their** or **your** (polite form = **usted**). If the context doesn't make it clear who the possessor is, we have to clarify the meaning with **de** followed by the personal pronoun.

su coche (el coche de él)	*his car*
su coche (el coche de ella)	*her car*
su coche (el coche de usted)	*your car (polite form)*
su coche (el coche de ellos)	*their car*
su coche (el coche de ellas)	*their car*
su coche (el coche de ustedes)	*your car (plural polite form)*

This also happens with the plural **sus**:
sus coches (de él, de ella, de usted, de ellos, de ellas, de ustedes).

2.1.5 With todos and otros

The possessive adjective can be combined with **todos** and with **otros**:

Todos mis amigos van a venir a la fiesta.	*All my friends are coming to the party.*
Mis otros compañeros también vienen.	*My other friends are also coming.*

2.1.6 Full forms:

	Singular	**Plural**	
Masculine	mío	míos	*mine*
	tuyo	tuyos	*yours*
	suyo	suyos	*his / hers / yours*
	nuestro	nuestros	*ours*
	vuestro	vuestros	*yours*
	suyo	suyos	*his / hers / yours*
Feminine	mía	mías	*mine*
	tuya	tuyas	*yours*
	suya	suyas	*his / hers / yours*
	nuestra	nuestras	*ours*
	vuestra	vuestras	*yours*
	suya	suyas	*his / hers / yours*

Remember: First and second person plural of the full forms are the same as the short form (see 2.1.3 above).

2.1.7 With de

As with the short forms, in the case of the third person (**suyo / suya / suyos / suyas**) it may not be obvious who the possessor is. So unless it's clear from the context we clarify this by using **de**.

la casa suya, de ella	*her house, hers*
la casa suya, de él	*his house, his*
el coche suyo, de María	*her car, María's*

2.1.8

The full forms change in gender and number. The meaning is the same as the short form.

el bolso mío	*my bag*	la maleta mía	*my suitcase*
los bolsos míos	*my bags*	las maletas mías	*my suitcases*

2.1.9 Position

They follow the noun, with the noun usually preceded by the article:

la casa suya	las casas suyas
el libro nuestro	los libros nuestros

El bolso suyo es el verde.	*His / her / your bag is the green one.*
No tengo noticias suyas.	*I don't have any news (about him / her).*

2.1.10

These full forms often appear on their own after the verb **ser** (**to be**).

El bolígrafo es mío.	*The pen is mine.*
La cartera es suya.	*The wallet is his / hers / yours.*

3 Possessive pronouns

Possessive pronouns substitute for or replace the noun. They are the equivalent of *mine, yours, his, hers, ours, theirs*. They are preceded by the article. They change in gender and number to match the noun they replace.

Este libro es el mío.	*This book is mine.*
¿Es esta bolsa la tuya?	*Is this bag yours?*
La maleta verde es la nuestra.	*The green case is ours.*

Notice the difference between the adjective and pronoun:

Ésta es <u>nuestra</u> habitación.	*This is our room. (adjective)*
Esta habitación es <u>la nuestra</u>.	*This room is ours. (pronoun)*
A: ¿Son éstos <u>nuestros</u> cuadernos?	*Are these our notebooks?*
B: <u>El mío</u> es el azul, <u>el tuyo</u> es el rojo.	*Mine is the blue one, yours is the red one*

3.1 Form and position of possessive pronouns

	Singular	**Plural**	
Masculine	el mío	los míos	*mine*
	el tuyo	los tuyos	*yours*
	el suyo	los suyos	*his / hers / yours*
	el nuestro	los nuestros	*ours*
	el vuestro	los vuestros	*yours*
	el suyo	los suyos	*his / hers / yours*
Feminine	la mía	las mías	*mine*
	la tuya	las tuyas	*yours*
	la suya	las suyas	*his / hers / yours*
	la nuestra	las nuestras	*ours*
	la vuestra	las vuestras	*yours*
	la suya	las suyas	*his / hers / yours*

A: ¿Es tu casa?　　　　　　*Is it your house?*
B: Sí, es la mía.　　　　　　*Yes, it's mine.*

A: ¿Éstos son los libros de Juan?　*Are these John's books?*
B: Sí, son los suyos.　　　　　　*Yes, they're his.*

3.1.1 With de

As with the adjectives (see 2.1.4 above) the third person forms **el suyo / la suya / los suyos / las suyas** can be ambiguous, and we sometimes have to clarify the meaning using **de**.

La casa es la suya, de ella.　　*The house is hers.*
La casa es la suya, de él.　　　*The house is his.*

3.1.2 Position

Possessive pronouns always appear after the verb. Sometimes the article **el, la, los, las** is left out after the verb **ser** (*to be*) (see 2.1.10 above). In some cases, though, the use of the article places emphasis on who owns the object:

Estos bolígrafos son míos.　　*These pens are mine.*
　　　　　　　　　　　　　　(or: these are my pens)

Estos bolígrafos son　　　　*These pens are mine.*
　los míos.　　　　　　　　*(not yours or his/hers)*

3.1.3

The article (**el / la / los / las**) is always used before the possessive after all verbs except **ser** (*to be*):

Juan encontró su pasaporte, pero　*Juan found his passport, but I*
　yo no encontré el mío.*　　　　*didn't find mine.*
*It is not possible to say: **yo no encontré mío.**

Voy a comprar mi billete, tú compra el tuyo.*	*I'm going to buy my ticket, you buy yours.*

*It is not possible to say: **tú compra tuyo.**

3.1.4

The article is always included when the possessive pronoun appears after a preposition:

Mi coche está detrás del tuyo.	*My car is behind yours.*
Mi padre conoce al tuyo.	*My father knows yours.*

4

En breve

Compare the ways of writing about ownership (masculine forms):

es mi libro	**es tu libro**	**es su libro**
it's my / your / his / her book		
es mío	**es tuyo**	**es suyo**
it's mine / yours / his / hers		
este libro es el mío	**este libro es el tuyo**	**este libro es el suyo**
this book is mine / yours / his / hers		
es nuestro libro	**es vuestro libro**	**es su libro**
it's our / your / their book		
es nuestro	**es vuestro**	**es suyo**
it's ours / yours / theirs		
este libro es el nuestro	**este libro es el vuestro**	**este libro es el suyo**
this book is ours / yours / theirs		

Feminine singular: **(la) mía / (la) tuya / (la) suya / (la) nuestra / (la) vuestra / (la) suya**

Masculine plural: **los (míos) / (los) tuyos / (los) suyos / (los) nuestros / (los) vuestros / (los) suyos**

Feminine plural: **las (mías) / (las) tuyas / (las) suyas / (las) nuestras / (las) vuestras / (las) suyas**

Note that the article (**el / la / los / las**) is added if we want to emphasise the ownership (it's mine, not yours!):
el libro es el suyo (*it's _his_ book*) but **es suyo** (*it's his*).

---

5 Uses of the possessive pronouns

5.1 To replace the noun or to represent the noun when we don't need it or don't wish to repeat it

¿Es éste vuestro coche?	*Is this your car?*
Sí, es el nuestro.	*Yes, it's ours.*

5.2 When preceded by an article

In this case, the pronoun can act as a noun and can be the subject or object of the verb, as in the example above and in the following:

Mi padre conoce al tuyo. (= a tu padre)	*My father knows yours.*
A: Mis gafas están rotas.	*My glasses are broken.*
B: Las mías están rotas también.	*Mine are broken as well.*

5.3 Without an article

The possessive pronoun can appear on its own (without the article) just as an answer to a question:

¿De quién es esta cartera?	*Whose is this wallet?*
Mía. (es mía)	*Mine. (it's mine)*

6 ¡Es diferente!

6.1 de

There is no equivalent to the English apostrophe followed by 's' (*Maria's book* or *the secretary's office*). Nor is there an equivalent of two nouns together (*the company car*). This is expressed in Spanish by the use of **de**:

el libro de María	*Maria's book*
la oficina de la secretaria	*the secretary's office*
el coche de la compañía	*the company car*

Note that the order of the nouns is the opposite of that in English:

la casa de Antonio	*Antonio's house*
estudiante de universidad	*university student*

6.2

The possessive is not used with parts of the body, articles of clothing and with reflexive verbs: the articles are used instead. In these cases it's clear who the owner is, so the possessive is not necessary.

¿Te pones el abrigo?	*Are you putting your coat on?*
Le duele la cabeza.	*His head aches.*
	(lit: It hurts him the head.)
No me pinto nunca los labios.	*I never paint my lips.*

 See point 8.4 below for expressions with personal pronouns instead of possessives, such as **me han robado el bolso** (*they've stolen my bag*).

---

7 Gramática práctica

12.7.1 Transform the following sentences using possessive adjectives.

Example: Yo tengo un coche. > Es mi coche.

1. Yo tengo un apartamento.
2. Ana tiene una casa.
3. Luisa tiene dos maletas.
4. Pedro y María tienen cinco hijos.
5. Juan y yo tenemos dos coches.
6. Susana y Pepe tienen una hija.
7. Ustedes tienen dos casas.
8. Tu hermana y tú tenéis un coche.

12.7.2 Rewrite the sentences from Exercise 12.7.1 using possessive pronouns.

Example: Yo tengo un coche. > Es el mío.

12.7.3 Answer the questions in Spanish.

Example: ¿Es tu casa? > Sí, la casa es mía.

1. ¿Es tu apartamento?
2. ¿Son tus bolsas?
3. ¿Son vuestros coches?
4. ¿Es nuestra maleta?
5. ¿Es mi libro?
6. ¿Es su casa?
7. ¿Es vuestro coche?
8. ¿Son vuestras fotos?

8 Más allá

8.1 To express contrast:

Tu chaqueta es bonita, pero la mía es mucho más bonita.	*Your jacket is nice, but mine is much nicer.*
Este coche no está mal, pero prefiero el mío.	*This car isn't bad, but I prefer mine.*

8.2 To express emphasis (not yours, mine!)

¡Ese bolso es el mío!	*That bag is mine!*
Esta cuenta no es la mía.	*This bill isn't mine.*
No, esa maleta no es la vuestra, ¡es la nuestra!	*No, that case isn't yours, it's ours!*

8.3

Note the differences in the following cases:

mi amigo	*my friend*
un amigo mío	*a friend of mine*
Es su sobrino.	*He's his nephew.*
Es sobrino suyo.	*He's a nephew of his.*

8.4

The possessive is replaced by the personal pronouns in the following examples:

¿Te preparo la cena?	*Shall I get your dinner ready?*
(Not: ¿Preparo <u>tu</u> cena?)	
Me cortan bien el pelo en	*They cut my hair well in*
esa peluquería.	* that hairdresser's.*
(Not: Cortan bien <u>mi</u> pelo . . .)	
Me han robado el coche.	*They have stolen my car.*
Te he planchado la camisa.	*I've ironed your shirt.*
No me han pagado el sueldo.	*They haven't paid me my salary.*

8.5 Fixed expressions, exclamations

¡Madre mía!	*Oh my goodness! (Lit: My mother!)*
¡Cariño mío!	*My darling!*

8.6 Forms of address

¡Hijo mío!	*Lit: My son!*
Ven aquí, hija mía.*	*Come here, my girl.*

* In this case the preferred usage in Latin America is **mi hija**: **Ven aquí, mi hija**.

8.7 Fixed expressions to begin a formal letter

Muy señor mío / muy señora mía / muy señores míos / muy señoras mías

8.8 Used before numerals

Vienen sus tres hijos y	*His three sons and five grandchildren*
sus cinco nietos.	* are coming.*
Nuestros tres gatos son	*Our three cats are*
muy traviesos.	* very naughty.*

8.9 Use of the possessive after the neuter form of the article lo

Esto es lo mío y aquello	*This is my stuff (these are my things),*
lo tuyo.	* that is your stuff.*

9 Más práctica

12.9.1 Reply as in the example.

Example: Mis gafas están rotas. > Las mías también.

1. Mi coche está sucio.
2. Nuestra casa está lejos.
3. Nuestros hijos son mayores.
4. Tu apartamento es grande.
5. Su maleta pesa mucho.
6. Nuestras profesoras son excelentes.
7. Tu hijo es muy inteligente.
8. Vuestros padres son muy simpáticos.

12.9.2 Translate into Spanish.

1. This pen is mine.
2. Is this wallet yours (your one, formal)?
3. Is this umbrella his (one)?
4. Are these earrings hers?
5. This car isn't ours (our one).
6. These suitcases are yours (informal).
7. Antonio's house is very nice.
8. I found your (informal) bag but I can't find mine (my one).
9. I have got mine (fpl), but I haven't got theirs (fpl).
10. Isabel's father is a friend of mine.

12.9.3 Read the dialogue then write similar dialogues.

A: Es mi libro.   **B:** No es tu libro.
A: Sí, el libro es mío.   **B:** No, el libro no es tuyo.
A: Sí, es el mío.   **B:** No, no es el tuyo.

Use these sentences to start your dialogues.
A: Es nuestra cartera.
A: Son sus cuadernos.
A: Es su teléfono.
A: Son sus bolsas.

13 Relative pronouns and adverbs
Pronombres y adverbios relativos

1 ¿Qué es?

They refer to a noun or an action from earlier in the sentence. They are used to avoid repeating the noun or the action we are referring to.

They have no accents, which distinguishes them from interrogatives.

2 Form

2.1 Relative pronouns

Their form is the same as that of the interrogative pronouns except that the interrogative pronouns have accents.

The most commonly used is **que**, which cannot change.

The others are not used as much, especially in spoken language.

Masculine		Feminine	
Singular	**plural**	**Singular**	**Plural**
que		que	
quien	quienes	quien	quienes
cual	cuales	cual	cuales
cuanto	cuantos	cuanta	cuantas
cuyo	cuyos	cuya	cuyas

2.1.1
Note the following:

que (*that, who*) doesn't change.
quien, quienes (*who*) changes in number.
cual, cuales (*which*) changes in number. These are always accompanied by an article:
el cual, la cual, los cuales, las cuales.
cuanto, cuanta, cuantos, cuantas (*how much / how many*). These change in number and gender.
cuyo, cuyos, cuya, cuyas (*whose*). These change in number and gender.

2.2 Relative adverbs

These never change in form.

They are: **donde, adonde, como, cuando.**

They are the same words as the interrogatives but without accents.

La plaza donde vivo es muy bonita.	*The square where I live is very pretty.*
El perro siempre va adonde va él.	*The dog always goes where he goes.*
Mi hijo hace todo como yo le digo.	*My son does everything I tell him.*
Sólo estudia cuando tiene exámenes.	*He only studies when he has exams.*

3 Uses

3.1 Use of que

The most important relative pronoun to know is **que**. It is the most frequently used, especially in spoken Spanish. The others are mostly used in written and formal language and will be studied in the **Más allá** section below.

Que can refer to both things and people. It means *who, whom, which* and *that*.

La profesora que tengo es muy buena.	*The teacher (who) I have is very good.*
Los chicos que vienen a esta clase son muy inteligentes.	*The boys who come to this class are very intelligent.*
La mujer que vimos ayer es mi tía.	*The woman (whom) we saw yesterday is my aunt.*
El libro que lees es excelente.	*The book (that) you're reading is excellent.*
Las manzanas que has comprado son muy malas.	*The apples (that) you bought are very bad.*
Tengo una amiga que trabaja contigo.	*I have a friend who works with you.*
Éste es el bolso que he comprado para mi madre.	*This is the bag (that) I bought for my mother.*
Éstas son las sandalias que compré ayer.	*These are the sandals (that) I bought yesterday.*

4 Gramática práctica

13.4.1 Write sentences in Spanish.

Example: María / red dress > María es la chica que lleva el vestido rojo.

1. Juan / yellow T-shirt
2. Isabel / green sweater
3. Carlos / white shirt
4. Elena / black jeans

13.4.2 Put the words in the correct order and translate the sentences.

1. excelente profesor tiene el Isabel es que
2. sale chico con el Ana amigo es quien mío
3. mercado las compré buenísimas uvas el en que son
4. te amigos quienes hoy hablé de los llegan
5. chica la es esta la limpia oficina que
6. es vive ésta la Juan casa donde

5 Más allá

5.1 que with an article

Que can be preceded by an article:

el que, la que, los que, las que	*the one who / which / those who / which*

Notice that the article varies in gender and number.

Este amigo es el que yo te recomendé.	*This friend is the one who I recommended to you.*
Esta casa es la que quiero comprar.	*This house is the one I want to buy.*

5.1.1

In some cases it can go at the beginning of the sentence as a subject, or it can act as an object after the verb **ser** (*to be*):

El (chico) que entra ahora es mi hermano.	*The one (the boy) coming in now is my brother.*

or:

Mi hermano es el (chico) que entra ahora.	*My brother is the one (the boy) who is coming in now.*
La (tienda) que te recomendé.	*The one (the shop) I recommended to you.*

or:

Ésta es la (tienda) que te recomendé.	*This is the one (the shop) I recommended to you.*

5.2 que after a preposition

If **que** is preceded by a preposition, it is often accompanied by the article: **el que, la que, los que, las que**.

El bolígrafo con el que escribo es muy caro.	*The pen with which I write is very expensive.* (*The pen I write with*)
La casa en la que nací está en esta calle.	*The house in which I was born is in this street.* (*The house I was born in*)
Los equipos contra los que jugamos son difíciles.	*The teams against which we play are difficult.* (*The teams we play against*)
Las películas en las que actúa no son muy buenas.	*The films in which he acts aren't very good.* (*The films he acts in*)

5.2.1

If **que** refers to people it can be replaced by **quien** or **quienes**. This is more formal but still fairly common.

Los amigos de los que hablamos ayer.	*The friends we spoke about yesterday.*
Los amigos de quienes hablamos ayer.	*The friends about whom we spoke yesterday.*
La secretaria con la que trabajo.	*The secretary (whom) I work with.*
La secretaria con quien trabajo.	

5.2.2

After the prepositions **a** and **de** there is a contraction: **al que, del que**:

El profesor del que te hablé da una conferencia.	*The teacher I spoke to you about is giving a conference.*
El hombre al que saludaste es amigo mío.	*The man you greeted is my friend.*

5.2.3

Que accompanied by a preposition can also be used without the article in some cases, except when the preposition has two or more syllables:

El tren en que viajamos es muy rápido.	*The train we are travelling is very fast.*
El tren contra el que chocó el coche iba muy rápido.	*The train the car crashed into was going very fast.*

5.3 lo que

Que accompanied by the neuter article **lo** means *what* or *which* and is a neuter form. It refers to ideas and concepts or to a whole sentence:

No sé lo que quieres.	*I don't know what you want.*
Lo que más me gusta de mi ciudad es el clima.	*What I like most about my city is the climate.*

Lo que can sometimes be replaced by the interrogative **qué**:

No sé lo que dice.	*I don't know what he's saying.*
No sé qué dice.	
Dime lo que te pasa.	*Tell me what's the matter with you.*
Dime qué te pasa.	

5.4 quien

The plural form is **quienes**. Both remain unchanged in the masculine and feminine.

It is only used when referring to people. It means *who* or *whom* and is normally only found in formal speech or literary texts.

It can be used on its own at the beginning of the sentence:

Quien canta ahora es mi hermana.	*The one who is singing now is my sister.*

Also possible:

La que canta ahora
es mi hermana.

The one who is singing now
is my sister.

But it is used more often with a preposition:

La mujer a quien vimos ayer
es mi profesora.

The woman (whom) we saw
yesterday is my teacher.

Compare with:

La mujer a la que vimos ayer
es mi profesora.

The woman (whom) we saw
yesterday is my teacher.

or more commonly

La mujer que vimos ayer es mi profesora.

Each means the same but can be formed in a slightly different way.

Note that in the following examples the preposition **con** must be included:

Los hombres con los que hablamos viven en Madrid.
Los hombres con quienes hablamos
viven en Madrid.

The men with whom we spoke
live in Madrid.

5.5 cual

This can refer to a person or an object. It is the same when referring to masculine or feminine and only changes from singular to plural: **cuales**.

It is the equivalent of **que** and is used as an alternative, but mainly in very formal and literary language. It is only used when preceded by an article: **el cual, la cual, los cuales, las cuales**.

It is used more often when accompanied by a preposition.

La mujer de la cual me hablas
es amiga mía.

The woman of whom you speak
is a friend of mine.

5.6 cuyo

This relative pronoun changes in gender and number and it means *whose*. It is only used to express ownership. It is the equivalent of **de quien, del que** and **del cual**.

It is rarely used in modern Spanish, but you might find it in literary texts.

Un actor cuyo nombre no
recuerdo ganó el premio.

An actor whose name I don't
remember won the prize.

6 Más práctica

13.6.1 Rewrite these sentences.

Example: Este bolso / he comprado para mi madre > Este bolso es el que he comprado para mi madre.

1. Este libro / leí la semana pasada
2. Esta película / vi ayer
3. Aquellos chicos / vinieron a mi casa
4. Estas amigas / conocí en la playa
5. Este chico / sale con mi hermana
6. Aquellas profesora / me da clase
7. Esas chicas / siempre llegan tarde
8. Aquellas gafas / compré en el mercado
9. Este chico / trabaja con mi padre
10. Estos chicos / compraron las chaquetas

13.6.2 Rewrite the sentences with **el / la / los / las que** instead of **quien** or **quienes**.

Example: Ése es el chico de quien te hablé. > Ése es el chico del que te hablé.

1. Ésas son las chicas con quienes salimos la semana pasada.
2. El hombre a quien encontré es mi profesor.
3. Éstos son los estudiantes a quienes doy clase de español.
4. Ésta es la chica de quien hablamos ayer.
5. Éste es el hombre para quien trabajo.
6. Los chicos a quienes viste ayer son amigos míos.

13.6.3 Rewrite the sentences from 13.6.2 with **el / la / los / las cual / cuales** instead of **quien** or **quienes**.

Example: Ése es el chico de quien te hablé. > Ése es el chico del cual te hablé.

14 Interrogative pronouns and adverbs
Pronombres y adverbios interrogativos

1 ¿Qué es?

Question words in Spanish can be of two categories: interrogative pronouns and interrogative adverbs.

Interrogative pronouns replace a noun. Some can also act as adjectives, followed by a noun. They can change in number or gender or both:

¿Quién es? / ¿Quiénes son?   *Who is it? / Who are they?*

Interrogative adverbs don't change:

¿Cómo estás?   *How are you?*

They have accents to distinguish them from the same words used in statements:

¿Cómo es María?   *What's María like?*
Es como tú.   *She's like you.*

 To form questions: see Unit 22 Section 1.2.

2 Interrogative pronouns

2.1 Form and position

2.1.1

Their form is the same as that of relative pronouns, except that interrogative pronouns have accents.

 See Unit 13 point 2.1.

Masculine		Feminine		Neuter
Singular	**Plural**	**Singular**	**Plural**	
qué		qué		qué
quién	quiénes	quién	quiénes	
cuál	cuáles	cuál	cuáles	
cuánto	cuántos	cuánta	cuántas	cuánto

The most commonly used is **qué**, which is invariable.

2.1.2

En breve
Qué (*what, which*) doesn't change.
Quién, Quiénes (*who*) changes in number.
Cuál, Cuáles (*what, which*) changes in number.
Cuánto, Cuánta, Cuántos, Cuántas (*how much / how many*) changes in
number and gender.

2.2 Uses of the interrogative pronouns

2.2.1 *qué* (what, which)

It goes at the beginning of the sentence. It is used to ask about objects or
actions:

¿Qué es eso?	*What's that?*
¿Qué haces?	*What do you do? /*
	What are you doing?

It can be used as a pronoun:

¿Qué tienes en la	*What do you have in your*
cartera?	*wallet / briefcase?*

And as an adjective:

¿Qué abrigo prefieres?	*Which coat do you prefer?*

Or it can be used on its own, as *Pardon?* to ask for repetition or clarification:

¿Qué?	*What? Pardon?*
¿Qué dices?	*What did you say?*

¿Qué? is more informal.

Note: You might use **¿Cómo?** if you wish to be formal.

More examples:

¿Qué pasa?	*What's the matter?*
¿Qué bebes?	*What are you drinking?*
¿Qué es María?	*What is María?*

2.2.2 *quién* (who, whom)

The plural form is **quiénes**. Both forms are the same for masculine and
feminine. It acts only as a pronoun

These are only used when asking about people.

¿Quién es esa chica?	*Who is that girl?*
¿Quién viene a comer?	*Who is coming to have lunch?*
¿Quiénes son esos hombres?	*Who are those men?*

If used with **de** it means *whose?*

¿De quién es este bolso?	*Whose is this bag?*

2.2.3 *cuál* (which, which one)

The plural form is **cuáles** (*which ones?*). Both forms are the same for masculine and feminine. It is used in cases of choice. **Cuál** and **cuáles** don't act as adjectives, and they are followed by a verb and not by a noun.

 See point 5.1.3 below for differences between **cuál** and **qué**.

¿Cuál te gusta más, el rojo o el azul?	*Which one do you like more, the red one or the blue one?*
¿Cuál quieres, el grande o el pequeño?	*Which one do you want, the big one or the small one?*
¿Cuáles son tus libros?	*Which ones are your books?*

2.2.4 *cuánto* (how much)

2.2.4.1

This can function as a pronoun or as an adjective. It changes to *cuánta* (feminine singular), and *cuántos* (masculine plural) or *cuántas* (feminine plural) to mean *how many?*

¿Cuántos años tienes?   *How old are you?*
         (lit: how many years do you have?)

(cuánt**os** agrees with añ**os**, masculine plural)
¿Cuántas hermanas tienes?   *How many sisters do you have?*
(cuánt**as** agrees with herman**as** (feminine plural)

More examples:

¿Cuánta leche compro?	*How much milk shall I buy?*
¿Cuántos plátanos quiere?	*How many bananas would you like?*
¿Cuántas naranjas le pongo?	*How many oranges shall I give you?*

2.2.4.2

Cuánto can also be an adverb (see point 3.1 below) and in this case it means *how much?*

¿Cuánto es?   *How much is it?*

3 Interrogative adverbs

3.1 ¿Cuánto? *How much?*

As an adverb, it is invariable, which means it doesn't change.

¿Cuánto es?	*How much is it?*
¿Cuánto cuesta?	*How much does it cost?*
¿Cuánto pesa la maleta?	*How much does the case weigh?*

3.2 ¿Cómo? *How?*

¿Cómo estás?	*How are you?*
¿Cómo vas al trabajo?	*How do you get to work?*

It is also used to ask for repetition or clarification in a more formal way than ¿qué?

¿Cómo? / ¿Cómo dice?	*What? What did you say?*

3.3 ¿Dónde? *Where?*

Used to ask about a location. It can be accompanied by different prepositions:

¿Dónde vives?	*Where do you live?*
¿De dónde eres?	*Where are you from?*
¿Por dónde se va a la calle Flor?	*How does one get to Flower Street? (lit: through where)*

3.4 ¿Cuándo? *When?*

Used to ask about time:

¿Cuándo llega el tren?	*When does the train arrive?*
¿Cuándo es tu cumpleaños?	*When is your birthday?*

3.5 ¿Por qué? *Why?*

¿Por qué estudias español?	*Why do you study Spanish?*
¿Por qué no vamos al cine?	*Why don't we go to the cinema?*

Be careful not to confuse **¿por qué?** (*why?*) with **porque**, which means *because*. Notice that **por qué**, the question, is two words and includes an accent, while **porque** is one word with no accent. There is also a difference in intonation: **por qué** rises at the end and **porque** falls at the end.

4 Gramática práctica

14.4.1 Make questions for these answers.

1. Soy el Sr. González.
2. Mi nombre es Pedro.
3. Estoy muy bien.
4. Soy de Málaga.
5. Vivo en Madrid.
6. Avenida América, 102.
7. Tengo 40 años.
8. Trabajo en esta empresa porque me gusta.
9. Gano treinta mil euros al mes.
10. Llego a la oficina a las ocho.
11. Yo quiero una cerveza.

14.4.2 Fill in the gaps with the correct interrogative pronoun.

1. ¿_____ se llama tu hermana?
2. ¿_____ viene a comer hoy?
3. ¿De _____ es tu padre?
4. ¿_____ vive Juan?
5. ¿_____ quieres para beber?
6. ¿_____ dice?

7. ¿_____ te gusta más, el grande o el pequeño?
8. ¿ _____ es Ana?
9. ¿_____ está Juan?
10. ¿_____ hermanos tiene Juan?

14.4.3 Put the sentences in the plural.

Example: ¿Quién es tu amigo? > ¿Quiénes son tus amigos?

1. ¿Qué libro compras?
2. ¿Quién estudia español?
3. ¿Cuánto pastel quiere?
4. ¿Cuál es más bonito?
5. ¿Cuánta pizza compras?
6. ¿Qué abrigo quieres?
7. ¿Quién vive en Madrid?
8. ¿Cuánto cuesta la chaqueta?
9. ¿De quién hablas?

5 Más allá

5.1 Interrogative pronouns

5.1.1 *Qué and Quién*

These can be preceded by a preposition:

¿Con qué limpias esto?	*What are you cleaning that with?*
¿A qué juegas?	*What are you playing (at)?*
¿De quién es este coche?	*Whose is this car? (lit: of whom)*
¿Con quién trabajas?	*Who do you work with?*
¿A quién viste ayer?	*Who did you see yesterday?*

Note the difference:

¿Qué buscas?	*What are you looking for?*

but

¿A quién buscas?	*Who are you looking for?*

In this case the preposition **a** is added because the question refers to a person.

5.1.2 *Quién and cuánto/a/os/as*

These can be followed by a phrase starting with **de** which indicates 'partial value':

¿Quién de tus amigas es Elena?	*Which (Who) of your friends is Elena?*
¿Cuántos de tus amigos vienen a la fiesta?	*How many of your friends are coming to the party?*

5.1.3 *The difference between qué and cuál*

¿Qué . . . ? and **¿Cuál . . . ?** both mean *What . . .?* or *Which . . .?*.

Notice the difference: **qué** can be followed by a noun or a verb but **cuál** can only be followed by a verb (usually expressing preference), or by the preposition **de** followed by a pronoun or a noun:

¿Qué profesor te da clase?	*Which teacher gives you the class?*
¿Qué vas a hacer?	*What are you going to do?*
¿Cuál es tu bebida favorita?	*What is your favourite drink?*
¿Cuál de los dos pisos te gusta más?	*Which of the two flats do you like more?*
¿Cuál de ellos es el mejor?	*Which of them is better?*

Both **qué** and **cuál** can be followed by a verb. In this case **qué** is used to ask for general information (e.g. the type, the nature of something):

A: ¿Qué quieres comprar?	*What do you want to buy?*
B: Un anillo.	*A ring.*

Cuál is used to ask for more specific information, where there is a choice:

A: Los dos anillos son bonitos, ¿cuál quieres comprar?	*Both rings are nice, which do you want to buy?*
B: El de oro blanco.	*The white gold one.*

5.2 Interrogative adverbs

¿Adónde? means *where (to)?* with verbs that need the preposition **a** in Spanish: **ir (a)**:

¿Adónde vas de vacaciones?	*(To) where are you going on holiday?*

It can also be written as two separate words: **¿A dónde?**

Compare:

¿Dónde estás?	*Where are you?*
¿Adónde vas?	*Where are you going?*

You might also hear **¿Dónde vas?** in informal and colloquial situations.

5.3 Other interrogatives

¿Para qué?	What for?
¿Para qué estudias español?	*(For what) Why are you studying Spanish?*
Para ir a España de vacaciones.	*(In order) To go to Spain on holiday.*
¿Por qué estudias español?	*Why are you studying Spanish?*
Porque me gusta y porque quiero ir a España de vacaciones.	*Because I like it and because I want to go to Spain on holiday.*

5.4 Indirect questions

5.4.1 Interrogative pronouns and adverbs

These can also be used in indirect questions. They keep their accent. Indirect questions do not need question marks:

No sé qué hacer.	*I don't know what to do.*
No sé dónde está mi cartera.	*I don't know where my wallet is.*

5.4.2 lo que

This means *what* and can replace **qué** in indirect questions. Note that there is no accent in **lo que**:

No sé lo que quiero tomar.   *I don't know what I want to have.*
Dime lo que prefieres.   *Tell me what you prefer.*

6 Más práctica

14.6.1 You want to use the tour bus in a Spanish town. Put the words in each question in order.

1. ¿ el horario Bus tiene turístico qué?
2. ¿ mañana sale a hora por qué el Bus la?
3. ¿ el por termina tarde cuándo Bus la?
4. ¿ a horas el Bus cuántas mediodía para?
5. ¿ ciudad dura la el por itinerario cuánto?
6. ¿ bus de el sale turístico dónde?
7. ¿ los se pueden billetes dónde comprar?
8. ¿cuánto billete el cuesta?
9. ¿ en cuántas hay paradas centro el?

14.6.2 Ask your friend about her day out yesterday. Use the words in the box.

Cuándo Con quién Cuál Adónde A qué Qué Por qué Cuántas Qué Cuánto

1. ¿_____ hiciste?
2. ¿_____fuiste?
3. ¿_____tuviste el día libre?
4. ¿_____ hora te levantaste?
5. ¿_____tiempo estudiaste?
6. ¿_____fuiste de compras?
7. ¿_____cosas compraste?
8. ¿_____fuiste al cine?
9. ¿_____tal lo pasaste?
10. ¿_____prefieres, el grande o el pequeño?

15 Exclamatory pronouns and adverbs
Pronombres y adverbios exclamativos

1 ¿Qué es?

Exclamation words in Spanish are the same as the question words, but used for a different purpose: to express surprise or emphasis.

They can be of two categories: exclamatory pronouns and exclamatory adverbs.

Exclamatory pronouns replace a noun. Some can also act as adjectives, followed by a noun. They can change in number or gender or both:

¡Cuántos hay!   *There are so many!*

Exclamatory adverbs don't change:

¡Cómo corre!   *He runs so fast!*

2 Form and position

Their form is the same as that of interrogative pronouns:

Masculine		Feminine		Neuter
Singular	**Plural**	**Singular**	**Plural**	
qué		qué		qué
quién	quiénes	quién	quiénes	
cuánto	cuántos	cuánta	cuántas	cuánto

The most commonly used is **qué**, which is invariable.

2.1

> **En breve**
> **Qué** (*what, which*) doesn't change.
> **Quién, Quiénes** (*who*) changes in number.
> **Cuál, Cuáles** (*what, which*) changes in number.
> **Cuánto, Cuánta, Cuántos, Cuántas** (*how much / how many*) changes in number and gender.

3 Uses of exclamation words

3.1 ¡Qué! (*what, how*)

It goes at the beginning of the sentence and it's used in many idiomatic expressions. It can be a pronoun and an adjective.

¡Qué dices!	*What are you talking about?*	**¡Qué bueno está!**	*It's so good!*
¡Qué bonito!	*It's so pretty!*	**¡Qué calor!**	*It's so hot!*

3.2 ¡Quién! (*who*)

The plural form is **quiénes**. Both forms are the same for masculine and feminine.

Quién is used in many idiomatic expressions:

¡Mira quién viene!	*Look who's coming!*
¡Quién lo diría!	*Who'd have thought it?*
¡Quién sabe!	*Who knows!*

3.3 ¡Cuánto/a/os/as! (*how much / how many*)

This changes in number and gender:

¡Cuánto (dinero) tienes!	*You have so much (money)!*
¡Cuánta (comida) hay!	*There's so much (food)!*
¡Cuántos amigos tiene!	*He has so many friends!*

(**cuántos** agrees with **amigos**, masculine plural)
¡Cuántas chicas vienen!
(**cuántas** agrees with **chicas** (feminine plural)

3.4

¡Cuánto! can also be an adverb, and in this case it means **how much!**, **so much!** As an adverb, it is invariable:

¡Cuánto come!	*He eats so much!*
¡Cuánto pesa la maleta!	*The case weighs so much!*

3.5 ¡Cómo! (*how*)

This adverb is also invariable:

¡Cómo trabajas!	*You work so much!*
¡Cómo te atreves!	*How dare you!*

It is also used in expressions such as **¡Cómo no!**

4 Gramática práctica

15.4.1 Write an appropriate exclamation.

Example: La paella está muy buena. > ¡Qué buena está la paella!

1. Tiene mucho trabajo.
2. El bolso es muy caro.
3. El equipo juega muy bien.
4. Tienes muchos libros.
5. Luis estudia mucho.
6. El exámen es muy difícil.
7. Tienes muchas cosas.
8. La casa es muy grande.

15.4.2 Translate the answers from 15.4.1 into English.

16 Indefinite adjectives and pronouns
Adjetivos y pronombres indefinidos

1 ¿Qué es?

Indefinite adjectives and pronouns are used to talk about people or things without identifying who or what they are. They are words such as **algo** (*something*), **nada** (*nothing*), **otro** (*other*) or **alguien** (*someone*).

Many of them also refer to quantity:

poco, mucho, bastante, demasiado   *a little, a lot, enough, too much*

For this reason they are also called **cuantitativos** (*quantitatives*), or **de cantidad** (*quantity*). They can refer to one person or object or a group or part of a group without specifying who or what they are and how many of them there are.

2 Form and use

The forms of the majority of indefinite adjectives and pronouns are the same, but some can only be pronouns, a few can only be adjectives and some can also be adverbs.

 See the sections below for translations, use and examples.

2.1 Only pronouns

algo, nada, alguien, nadie

Note: **algo** and **nada** can also act as adverbs.

 See point 5.6 below.

2.2 Adjectives and pronouns

alguno (algún)* / alguna / algunos / algunas
ninguno (ningún*) / ninguna / ningunos / ningunas
uno (un)* / una / unos / unas
otro / otra / otros / otras

*The short form of the adjective appears only in the singular before a masculine noun. Remember, this is the same as the rule for the **adjetivo calificativo** (*qualifying adjective*) where some lose their last vowel in the masculine singular form:

buen, mal, primer, tercer.

 See Unit 6, points 3.2, 6.1.

2.3 Adjectives and pronouns   &   adverbs

todo / toda / todos / todas	todo
mucho / mucha / muchos / muchas	mucho
poco / poca / pocos / pocas	poco
demasiado / demasiada / demasiados / demasiadas	demasiado
tanto (tan) / tanta / tantos / tantas	tanto (tan)
bastante / bastantes	bastante

2.4

Note: adverbs use the masculine form and don't change, but note that **tanto** becomes **tan** even as an adverb.

¡Me gusta tanto!	*I like it so much!*
¡Es tan lejos!	*It's so far!*

3 Use

3.1 Only pronouns

The following can only be pronouns. They are very frequently used and they don't vary in gender and number:

Referring to objects or concepts:	algo	*something anything* (in questions)
	nada	*nothing / anything*
Referring to people:	alguien	*someone / somebody / anyone / anybody*
	nadie	*no-one / nobody*

Tenemos algo para comer.	*We have something to eat.*
¿Quiere algo más?	*Do you want anything else?*
No quiero nada más.	*I don't want anything else.*
Nada me interesa.	*Nothing interests me.*
Alguien ha llamado.	*Sonmeone has called.*
No hay nadie en la fiesta.	*There isn't anybody at the party.*
¿Ha venido alguien?	*Has anyone come?*
No ha venido nadie.	*Nobody has come.*

3.2 Adjectives and pronouns

These can refer to people, objects and ideas or concepts.

In affirmative sentences:

alguno (algún) / alguna / algunos / algunas   *some*

In negative sentences:

ninguno (ningún) / ninguna/ ningunos / ningunas   *none*

Tengo algunas amigas colombianas. (adjective)	*I have some Colombian friends.*
Tengo muchos amigos, algunos son colombianos. (pronoun)	*I have many friends, some are Colombians.*

Tengo muchos amigos aquí, pero
   ninguno es colombiano.
(pronoun)

I have many friends here, but
   none are Colombian.

No tiene ninguna preocupación.
(adjective)

He has no worries.

3.2.1 algún / ningún

If used as adjectives with masculine singular nouns, **alguno** becomes **algún** and **ninguno** becomes **ningún**. The other forms stay the same.

A: ¿Tiene algún amigo allí? (adj)

Does he have any friends there?

B: Tiene amigos, pero no sale
   con ninguno. (pron)

He has friends, but he doesn't go
   out with any of them.

A: ¿Ha venido algún estudiante a
   clase? (adj)

Have any students come
   to class?

B: No, no ha venido ningún
   estudiante. (adj)

No, no students have
   come.

or No, no ha venido ninguno. (pron)

No, none have come.

A: ¿Tienes algún mensaje para mí? (adj)

Do you have any messages for me?

B: No, no tengo ningún mensaje (adj)

No, I don't have any message.

or: No, no tengo ninguno. (pron)

No, I don't have any.

A: ¿Hay algún parque en esta zona? (adj)

Are there any parks in this area?

B: No, en esta zona no hay ningún
   parque. (adj)

No, there are no parks in
   this area.

or: En esta zona no hay ninguno. (pron)

There aren't any in this area.

 See points 5.1 and 5.2 below for comparison of **algo / alguien / alguno; nada / nadie / ninguno.**

3.2.2 uno / una / unos / unas (a, one, some, a few)

Uno becomes **un** as a masculine singular adjective. This form coincides with the numeral **un** and is like the indefinite article **un**.

Their meaning is often the same or very similar.

 See Unit 17 for numerals and Unit 5 for the indefinite article.

It is sometimes used instead of **alguno/a/os/as**, with the same meaning.

A: ¿Quieres un bocadillo?

Would you like a sandwich?

B: Sí, quiero uno.

Yes, I'd like one.

¿Quieres unas tapas?

Do you want some tapas?

Estoy comiendo unos calamares.

I'm eating some squid.

Note that it is also possible to make these sentences without using the adjective:

¿Quieres tapas?

Do you want tapas?

Estoy comiendo calamares.

I'm eating squid.

The use of **unos** limits the general concept of **calamares** (*squid*) to give the meaning of *some* or *a few calamares*:

Quiero calamares.	*I want squid.*
Quiero unos calamares.	*I want some squid*

It can also transform general concepts into countable individual items:

Quiero vino.	*I'd like wine.*
	(as opposed to water or
	beer for example)
Quiero unos vinos.	*I'd like a few (glasses of) wine(s).*
Quiere agua con gas.	*He'd like sparkling water.*
Quieren un agua con gas.	*They'd like a sparkling water.*

3.2.3 *otro / otra / otros / otras* (another / other / others)

¿Quieres otro café? (adj)	*Would you like another coffee?*
¿Tienes otros pantalones? (adj)	*Do you have any other trousers?*
No me gusta esta tienda, vamos	*I don't like this shop, let's*
a otra. (pron)	*go to another one.*

They can also be accompanied by the article:

Las otras cajas están allí. (adj)	*The other boxes are there.*
No quiero éstas, prefiero las otras. (pron)	*I don't want these, I prefer the others.*

3.3 Adjectives, pronouns and adverbs

3.3.1 *todo / toda / todos / todas* (everything, all)

A: ¿Compras toda la ropa en	*Do you buy all your clothes*
esta tienda? (adj)	*in this shop?*
B: Sí, la compro toda aquí. (pron)	*Yes, I buy them all here.*
A: ¿Quieres todo el pastel? (adj)	*Do you want all of the cake?*
B: Sí, lo quiero todo. (pron)	*Yes, I'd like it all.*
A: ¿Quieres todos los caramelos? (adj)	*Do you want all the sweets?*
B: Sí, los quiero todos. (pron)	*Yes, I'd like all of them.*

Todos and **todas** can be the subject of the sentence, meaning *everybody, we all*:

Todos somos iguales.	*We are all equal.*
Todas hablan el mismo idioma.	*They all speak the same language.*

3.3.1.1 *Adverb:* todo (everything)

A: ¿Qué prefieres para comer?	*What do you prefer to eat?*
B: No sé, me gusta todo. (adverb)	*I don't know, I like everything.*

Todo is used in the expressions:

todo recto	*straight on*
todo seguido	*all at once*

It can also be used on its own:

A: ¿Qué te gusta de México?	*What do you like about Mexico?*
B: Todo.	*Everything.*

3.3.2 *mucho / mucha / muchos / muchas* (a lot, much, many)

A: ¿Tienes mucho dinero? (adj)
B: No, no tengo mucho. (pron)

Do you have much money?
No, I don't have much.

A: ¿Tienes muchas amigas? (adj)
B: Sí, tengo muchas. (pron) / No, no tengo muchas. (pron)

Do you have many girlfriends?
Yes, I have a lot. / No, I don't have many.

3.3.2.1 *Adverb:* mucho

Te quiero mucho.

I love you a lot.

3.3.3 *poco / poca / pocos / pocas* (a little, not much, a few, not many)

A: ¿Tienes poco dinero? (adj)
B: Sí, tengo poco. (pron)

Do you have little money? (Don't you have much money?)
Yes, I have little. (No, I don't have much.)

A: ¿Tienes pocas amigas aquí? (adj)
B: Sí, tengo pocas. (pron)

Do you (only) have a few friends here?
Yes I (only) have a few.

3.3.3.1 *Adverb:* poco

Este libro me gusta poco.

I don't like this book much.

3.3.3.2 poco / un poco

Note the difference: **Estudio poco**. (negative meaning: *I study very little.*); **Estudio un poco**. (positive meaning: *I study a bit.*)

3.3.4 *demasiado / demasiada / demasiados / demasiadas* (too much, too many)

A: Tienes demasiado trabajo. (adj)
B: Sí, tengo demasiado. (pron)

You have too much work.
Yes, I have too much.

A: Tienes demasiadas cosas. (adj)
B: Sí, tengo demasiadas. (pron)

You have too many things.
Yes, I have too many.

3.3.4.1 *Adverb:* demasiado

Comes demasiado.

You eat too much.

3.3.5 *tanto (tan) / tanta / tantos / tantas* (so much, so many)

This is often used in exclamatory sentences:

¡Es tan bueno! (adj)
¡Lo quiero tanto! (adv)

It's so good!
I love it so much!

No quiero tanto vino. (adj)

I don't want so much wine.

A: ¿Quieres tanta comida? (adj)
B: No, no quiero tanta. (pron)

Do you want so much food?
No, I don't want so much.

A: ¡Tienes tantas cosas! (adj)   You have so many things!
B: No, no tengo tantas. (pron)   No, I don't have so many.

3.3.5.1 Adverb: tanto (tan) = so (much)

No puedo comer tanto.   I can't eat so much.
¡Me duele tanto!   It hurts me so much!
¡Se acuesta tan tarde!   He goes to bed so late!

 For the use of **tan** and **tanto** as comparatives see Unit 8.

3.3.6 bastante / bastantes (a lot, enough)

Tengo bastante leche, pero no   I have enough milk but I don't
   tengo bastante azúcar.   have enough sugar.
Tiene bastantes problemas.   He has enough problems.

3.3.6.1 Adverb

Note how the meaning can change slightly when it is used as an adverb:

Esta ciudad me gusta   I quite like this city. / I like this
   bastante.   city quite a lot.
Ha bebido bastante.   He's drunk enough.

4 Gramática práctica

16.4.1 Read the dialogues and underline the indefinite.

1.
A: ¿Tienes muchos amigos en el pueblo?
B: No, tengo pocos amigos. ¿Y tú? Tienes algún amigo en la ciudad?
A: No tengo ningún amigo. Este pueblo es demasiado pequeño y bastante aburrido.

2.
A: ¿Te gusta algún vestido?
B: No me gusta ninguno.
A: ¿Te gusta alguna chaqueta?
B: No, no me gusta ninguna. Además esta tienda es demasiado cara.
A: Pues vamos a otra. Hay una tienda bastante barata muy cerca.

3.
A: Tengo demasiado trabajo y demasiados problemas.
B: Pues yo no tengo tanto trabajo esta semana. Si quieres te ayudo con algo.
A: Muchas gracias, pero tengo que hacerlo todo yo solo.

16.4.2 Complete the questions with the words from the box.

bastante   algo   ninguna   mucha   alguna   otro   algún   algunas

1. A: ¿Quieres _____? B: No, no quiero nada.
2. A: ¿Tienes _____libro de Lorca? B: No, no tengo ninguno.

3. A: ¿Quieres _____ sopa o poca? B: Quiero poca.
4. A: ¿Han venido _____ amigas suyas? B: No, no ha venido ninguna.
5. A: ¿Ha comprado _____bebida para la fiesta? B: No, no ha comprado ninguna bebida.
6. A: ¿No has tomado_____ pastilla para el dolor? B: Sí, he tomado muchas pastillas.
7. A: ¿Has traído _____dinero? B: No, he traído muy poco.
8. A: ¿Prefieres este abrigo o el _____? B: Prefiero éste.

5 Más allá

Comparison of **algo, nada; alguien, nadie; alguno, ninguno**

5.1 algo / alguien / alguno

5.1.1 Form

Algo and **alguien** are invariable; they do not change.
Alguno changes in gender and number: **alguno (algún) / alguna / algunos / algunas**.

Algo and **alguien** can only be pronouns.
Alguno (algún) can be an adjective and a pronoun.

5.1.2 Meaning

	Affirmative	**In questions**
algo	something	anything
alguien	someone / somebody	anyone / anybody
alguno	some	any

5.1.3 Use

Algo refers only to objects, things and ideas or concepts.
Alguien always refers to people.
Alguno refers to both objects and people.

A: ¿Quieres algo para comer?　　　*Do you want something to eat?*
B: Sí, quiero algo para comer.　　　*Yes, I'd like something to eat.*

A: ¿Viene alguien a comer?　　　*Is someone / anyone coming to eat?*
B: Sí, viene alguien a comer.　　　*Yes, someone is coming to eat.*

A: ¿Vienen algunos amigos a comer? (adj) *Are some friends coming to eat?*
B: Sí, vienen algunos. (pron)　　　*Yes, some of them are coming.*

5.2 nada / nadie / ninguno

5.2.1 Form

Nada and **nadie** are invariable: they do not change.

Ninguno changes in gender and number: **ninguno (ningún) / ninguna / ningunos / ningunas**.

Nada and **nadie** can only be pronouns.
Ninguno (ningún) can be an adjective and a pronoun.

5.2.2 Meaning

	Affirmative	**In questions**
nada	nothing	anything
nadie	nobody / no-one	anyone / anybody
ninguno	any / none	any / none

5.2.3 Use

Nada refers only to objects, things and ideas or concepts.
Nadie always refers to people.
Ninguno can refer to both objects and people.

A: ¿No quieres nada para comer?   *Don't you want anything to eat?*
B: No quiero nada.   *I don't want anything.*

A: ¿No viene nadie a   *Is no-one / Isn't anyone*
    comer?   *coming to eat?*
B: No, no viene nadie.   *No, no-one is coming.*

A: ¿No viene ningún amigo a   *Aren't any of your friends*
    comer? (adj)   *coming to eat?*
B: No, no viene ninguno. (pron)   *No, none of them are coming.*

 For the position of the negative pronouns in the sentence, and for
    double negatives, see Unit 19.

5.3

Alguno and **ninguno** are similar to **alguien** and **nadie**. The first two are more specific, and they are used to specify someone in a group:

alguno (de ellos) / ninguno (de ellos)   *one of them / none of them*

Alguno and **ninguno** can refer to people and also to objects or ideas or concepts.

The meaning of **alguien** and **nadie** is more general and vague. They are only used for people, not for objects.

¿Viene alguien a la fiesta?   *Is anybody coming to the party?*
¿Viene alguno (de ellos) a la fiesta?   *Is any of them coming to the party?*
Tengo algunos libros para ti.   *I have some books for you.*

All these can be combined with **más**:

A: ¿Quiere algo más?   *Do you want anything else?*
B: No quiero nada más.   *I don't want anything else.*

A: ¿No ha llegado nadie más?   *Hasn't anyone else arrived?*

A: ¿Puede entrar alguno más?　　　*Can anyone else come in?*
B: No puede entrar ninguno más.　　*No-one else can come in.*

5.4　More indefinites

5.4.1　Only adjectives: *cada / cierto*

These can only be used as adjectives.

Cada (*each* or *every*) does not change in number or gender.

Cada mañana se levanta a las siete.　*Every morning he gets up at seven.*
Cada niño debe tener un libro.　　　*Each child should have a book.*

5.4.2　*cada + uno*

Cada uno vendrá a una hora　　*Each one will come at a*
　diferente.　　　　　　　　　*different time.*

5.4.3

Cierto (*certain*) is variable in both gender and number: **cierto / cierta / ciertos / ciertas**.

Ciertos científicos confirman　　*Certain scientists confirm*
　estas teorías.　　　　　　　　*these theories.*

5.4.4

If **cierto** is placed after a noun it becomes a qualifying adjective, meaning *true* or *accurate*:

La noticia es cierta.　　　　*The news is accurate.*
Los rumores son ciertos.　　*The rumours are true.*

Compare:
una historia cierta (*a true story*)

and

una cierta historia (*a certain story*).

5.4.5

Cierto can also be an adverb, meaning *true*, and in this case it's invariable:

Es cierto.　　　　　　　*It's true.*

5.5　Adjectives and pronouns

5.5.1　*varios / varias* (several, various)

They only exist in the plural.

Tengo varias cosas que decirte.　*I have a few things to tell you.*
Tengo muchos libros de historia,　*I have lots of history books,*
　hay varios en este armario.　　　*there are several in this cupboard.*
La exposición incluye varios　　*The exhibition includes various*
　estilos de pintura.　　　　　　*painting styles.*

Note that **varios / varias** can also mean many:

Había varias personas. *There were many people.*

5.5.2 cualquiera (cualquier)

As an adjective: *any*: as a pronoun: *anybody, anyone, anything.*

5.5.2.1 Form

This word does not change in gender or number. The form **cualquiera** can never occur before a noun. As an adjective before a noun the final **-a** is dropped: **cualquiera > cualquier**. Note that this happens with both the masculine and the feminine, contrary to the general rule for adjectives such as **ningún, algún, primer, buen** and **mal** that lose the last vowel **-o** only in the masculine.

Puedes usar cualquier taza. (adj) *You can use any cup.*
Se pone cualquier cosa para ir *He puts on anything to go*
  al trabajo. (adj)   *to work.*
No habla con cualquiera. (pron) *She doesn't speak to just anybody.*
No sé qué libro leer, voy a comprar *I don't know which book to read,*
  cualquiera. (pron)   *I'm going to buy any one.*

5.5.2.2 With otro/a

It is possible to combine **cualquier** with **otro/a**:

No tengo ese libro, pero *I don't have that book, but take*
  toma cualquier otro.   *any other one.*

A: No tengo esa marca. *I don't have that make.*
B: Es igual, dame cualquiera. *It doesn't matter, give me any one.*

or

Dame cualquier otra. *Give me any other one.*

5.5.2.3 With de

Also with the preposition **de**:

Elige cualquiera de estos. *Choose any one of these.*

5.5.2.4 Position

Cualquiera usually goes before the noun when it is an adjective, but it can also be placed after the noun to indicate its random quality.

Dame una camisa cualquiera. *Give me any (old) shirt.*
Dame unos pantalones cualquiera. *Give me any (old) trousers.*

5.6 algo / nada as adverbs

As adverbs these are invariable: **algo** (*rather / a bit*); **nada** (*not at all*).

Este libro es algo largo. *This book is rather long*
No es nada importante. *It's not at all important /*
    it's nothing important

6 Más práctica

16.6.1 Complete the sentences with **alguien, nadie, algo, nada, algún, alguno/a/os/as, ningún** or **ninguno/a/os/as**.

1. ¿Conociste a _____ en la fiesta? No, no conocí a _____ en la fiesta.
2. ¿Tienes _____ zapatillas para mí? No, no tengo _____ zapatillas.
3. ¿Tienes _____ para desayunar? No, no tengo _____ para desayunar.
4. ¿Oyes _____ ? No, no oigo _____.
5. ¿Vienen _____ de tus amigos para comer? Sí, vienen _____.
6. ¿Quieres _____ libro para leer? Sí, ¿tienes _____ de misterio?
7. ¿Hay _____ en casa? No, no hay _____ en casa.
8. ¿Quieres ir a _____ cafetería? No quiero ir a _____ cafetería, prefiero tomar el café en casa.

16.6.2 Complete the sentences with **alguien, nadie, algo** or **nada**.

1. Ana, ¿no comes _____? No, no quiero comer _____.
2. La clase está completamente vacía, ¿no hay _____? No, no hay _____.
3. ¿No quieres _____ más? No gracias, no quiero _____ más.
4. ¿No quieres ir de vacaciones con _____? No, prefiero ir solo, no me gusta ir de vacaciones con _____.
5. ¿No ves a _____? Sí, veo a _____.
6. ¿No conoces a _____ en esta ciudad? No, no conozco a _____.
7. ¿No viene _____ al cine? Sí, creo que viene _____.
8. ¿No has traído _____ para comer? No, no he traído _____.

16.6.3 Fill the gaps with the correct word from the box. Some will be used more than once.

cualquier	cierta	varias	cualquiera	cada	varios

1. Pedro sale de casa _____mañana a las diez.
2. Tiene _____ amigos en la universidad.
3. ¿Sabes si la noticia es _____?
4. Compraremos _____ camisetas porque son baratas.
5. Puedes leer _____libro, todos son buenos.
6. Este hombre es muy simpático, habla con _____
7. _____ estudiante tiene un cuaderno.
8. _____ vino de esta región es bueno.

17 Numbers, times and dates
Los números, la hora y la fecha

1 ¿Qué es?

Numerals are cardinal or normal numbers such as:

cuatro, cinco, quince   *four, five, fifteen*

or ordinal numbers, used to express the order of things in a sequence:

primero, segundo, tercero . . .   *first, second, third . . .*

2 Forms: cardinal numbers

0 cero		
1 uno	11 once	21 veintiuno
2 dos	12 doce	22 veintidós
3 tres	13 trece	23 veintitrés
4 cuatro	14 catorce	24 veinticuatro
5 cinco	15 quince	25 veinticinco
6 seis	16 dieciséis	26 veintiséis
7 siete	17 diecisiete	27 veintisiete
8 ocho	18 dieciocho	28 veintiocho
9 nueve	19 diecinueve	29 veintinueve
10 diez	20 veinte	30 treinta

2.1 cero (*zero*)

The plural of **cero** is **ceros**:

un cero, tres ceros   *one zero, three zeros*

2.2 uno, una, un

Uno is masculine and **una** is feminine.

The short version **un** goes before masculine nouns:

A: ¿Cuántos hermanos   *How many brothers and sisters*
   tienes?   *do you have?*
B: Tengo uno, ¿y tú?   *I have one, and you?*
A: Tengo dos, un hermano   *I have two, a brother and*
   y una hermana.   *a sister.*

2.3 Numbers ending in uno

Other numbers ending in **uno** also change to **un** before a masculine noun:

veintiuno > veintiún

hay veintiún chicos — *there are twenty-one boys*
hay veintiuna chicas — *there are twenty-one girls*

treinta y uno

vienen treinta y un estudiantes — *thirty-one students are coming*
vienen treinta y una alumnas — *thirty-one female pupils are coming*

2.4 Numbers from 11 to 15

These all finish in **-ce**:

once, trece, quince — *eleven, thirteen, fifteen*

2.5 Numbers from 16 to 30

From 16 to 30 the numbers are contracted into one word. It's best to learn them by heart, but the following explanations will help you understand them better.

diez y ocho (18) > dieciocho

Note: 'y' becomes 'i' and 'z' changes to 'c' because of orthographic rules ('z' cannot go before 'i').

 See Unit 2 point 2.2.2.

The same happens with **dieciséis**, but an accent is added according to the rule when **seis** becomes part of one word.

 See Unit 2 point 3.3.1.

The same happens with the 20s:

veinte y uno (21) > veintiuno ('e' + 'y' = 'i')

veintidós (22), **veintitrés** (23) and **veintiséis** (26) also carry an accent at the end of the word.

 See Unit 2 point 3.3.1.

2.6

30, 40, 50, 60, 70, 80, 90 all end in **-enta**, except **treinta**, which ends in **-inta**. Also, from number 30 the tens and units are separated by **y** (*and*), e.g.: **cincuenta y cinco** (55).

30 tre**inta**	40 cuar**enta**	50 cincu**enta**	60 ses**enta**
31 treinta y uno	43 cuarenta y tres	55 cincuenta y cinco	66 sesenta y seis
32 treinta y dos	44 cuarenta y cuatro		
70 set**enta**	80 och**enta**	90 nov**enta**	
77 setenta y siete	88 ochenta y ocho	99 noventa y nueve	

2.7 cien (100)

Cien is used on its own and before **mil** and **millón**:

cien	*a hundred*
cien mil	*a hundred thousand*
cien millones	*a hundred million*

Cien becomes **ciento** when followed by any other numbers:

101	**ciento uno**	111	**ciento once**
102	**ciento dos**	116	**ciento dieciséis**
105	**ciento cinco**	127	**ciento veintisiete**
110	**ciento diez**	135	**ciento treinta y cinco**

Note: numbers after 100 do not require **y**.

2.8 Ciento used to express percentages

Note that the article **el** or **un** is used with percentages:

El cincuenta por ciento de los estudiantes es bilingüe.	*Fifty per cent of the students are bilingual.*
El abrigo tiene un diez por ciento de descuento.	*There's a ten per cent discount on the coat.*

2.9 Masculine and feminine

2.9.1

Numbers up to 200 are masculine except for **uno / una**. If we identify a number as an entity we use the article **el**:

A: ¿Qué número es?	*What number is it?*
B: Es el cinco.	*The five.*
Vivo en el ciento dos.	*I live at (number) 102.*
Vivo en el número ciento dos.	*I live at number 102.*

2.9.2

But from 200 up to 900 numbers can be masculine or feminine depending on the noun they accompany or refer to:

doscientos euros	*two hundred euros*
trescientas libras	*three hundred pounds*

Notice also that these numbers appear in the plural and they form one word:

dos + ciento + s   >   doscientos

200 **doscientos / doscientas**	500 **quinientos/as**	800 **ochocientos/as**
300 **trescientos/as**	600 **seiscientos/as**	900 **novecientos/as**
400 **cuatrocientos/as**	700 **setecientos/as**	

Note the irregular formations: **quin**ientos, **sete**cientos, **nove**cientos.

2.10

From **mil** (*one thousand*) the numbers do not change.

Note that a full stop is used to separate the thousands and that *one* or *a* in *one thousand* or *a thousand* does not appear in Spanish.

1.000 **mil** 2.000 **dos mil** 3.000 **tres mil** 4.000 **cuatro mil** 5.000 **cinco mil**

6.000 **seis mil** 7.000 **siete mil** 8.000 **ocho mil** 9.000 **nueve mil** 10.000 **diez mil**

For decimal numbers, a comma is used:
7,50 **siete (con) cincuenta** or **siete coma cincuenta**.

2.11 Higher numbers

These are formed as follows:

1.117 **mil ciento diecisiete**
1.954 **mil novecientos cincuenta y cuatro**
2.746 **dos mil setecientos cuarenta y seis**

1.000.000 **un millón** (*one million*)

Note that this doesn't change to the feminine but does change to the plural from 2 million on: **dos millones** (2.000.000).

After the amount in millions and before the noun the preposition **de** is used:

un millón de dólares	*a million dollars*
dos millones de libras	*two million pounds*

 Note the loss of the accent: see Unit 2 point 3.3.1.

The same rules apply to billions:

un billón de euros	*a billion euros*
dos billones de dólares	*two billion dollars*

But **de** does not appear between the parts of the numbers:
un millón quinientos mil = 1.500.000.

2.12

> **En breve**
>
> | | | |
> |---|---|---|
> | uno | > | un niño / una niña |
> | veintiuno | > | veintiún (but feminine: **veintiuna**) |
> | one word (from 16 to 30): | | diéciséis / veintinueve |
> | cien | > | ciento + another number (ciento diez) |
>
> From 200 to 999, **ciento** changes to feminine and plural: **doscientos / doscientas**
>
> **ciento** and **mil** don't change; **millón** changes only to plural: **millones**
>
> After the tens **y** is added: either becoming 'i' when in one word > **dieciséis, veinticinco**
>
> or after 30: **treinta y uno, cuarenta y cinco**
>
> After the hundreds and the thousands there is no **y**: **doscientos veinte, mil quinientos**

3 Forms: ordinal numbers

primero	*first*
segundo	*second*
tercero	*third*
cuarto	*fourth*
quinto	*fifth*
sexto	*sixth*
séptimo	*seventh*
octavo	*eighth*
noveno	*ninth*
décimo	*tenth*

3.1

Primero and **tercero** lose the final **-o** before a masculine singular noun and become **primer** and **tercer**:

Su primer hijo se llama José.	*His first son is called José.*
Vamos al tercer piso.	*We're going to the third floor.*

3.2 cuatro and cuarto

These appear similar and may be confused:

Son las cuatro y cuarto.	*It's a quarter past four.*
Vivo en el número cuatro, cuarto piso.	*I live in number four, fourth floor.*

3.3

Ordinal numbers change to feminine:
primera, segunda, quinta, décima

and to plural:
terceros, cuartas, sextos, octavas

Estos estudiantes siempre son los primeros en llegar.	*These students are always the first to arrive.*
Ahora vienen los segundos platos.	*The main courses are coming now. (second dishes)*

3.4 Symbols

Note the consistent symbol for ordinals in Spanish, unlike English:

1º	1st
2º	2nd
3º	3rd
4º	4th

If they refer to the feminine the º changes to ª: 1ª, 2ª. etc.

Note that ordinal forms after **décimo** (*tenth*) are rarely used and even then only in formal and written language. Instead, ordinal numbers are used:

el piso once	*the eleventh floor*

4 Time *La hora*

To ask the time we say:

¿Qué hora es?	*What time is it?*
Es la una.	*It's one o'clock.*
Son las dos.	*It's two o'clock.*

Note:
We say **es la una** because **una** is singular. The other times are all in the plural and so we use **son**.

4.1

The equivalent to the English expression *o'clock* is **en punto**, although it is not necessary in Spanish, and it is only used for emphasis.

You can either say:

Son las diez en punto.	*It's exactly ten o'clock.*

or

Son las diez.	*It's ten o'clock.*

4.2

The Spanish equivalent of a.m. and p.m. is:

de la mañana	*in the morning*
de la tarde	*in the afternoon / evening*
de la noche	*at night*
Son las cinco de la mañana.	*It's 5 a.m.*
Son las ocho de la noche.	*It's 8 p.m.*

4.3

To express 'past' the hour in Spanish, say the hour first followed by **y** (*and*) and then the minutes:

Es la una y veinte.	*It's twenty past one. (lit: it's one (hour) and twenty (minutes))*

To express 'to', i.e. minutes to the hour, we use **menos** (*less / minus*):

Son las tres menos diez.	*It's ten to three. (lit: They are three (hours) minus ten (minutes))*

Look at the following times:

Es la una y cinco	1.05	**Son las dos y diez**	2.10
Son las tres y cuarto	3.15	**Son las cuatro y veinte**	4.20
Son las cinco y veinticinco	5.25	**Son las seis y media**	6.30
Son las siete menos veinticinco	6.35	**Son las ocho menos veinte**	7.40
Son las nueve menos cuarto	8.45	**Son las diez menos diez**	9.50
Son las once menos cinco	10.55		

Note: a.m.: **Es la una y cinco de la mañana** (1.05 a.m.)
         p.m.: **Es la una y cinco de la tarde** (13.05 p.m.)

4.4 The 24-hour clock

The 24-hour clock is used in timetables and on official and formal occasions, but not normally in speech.

Note that **y** is not used when saying the time with the 24-hour clock..

14.30 **Son las catorce treinta.** or: **Son las catorce horas, treinta minutos.**
16.45 **Son las dieciséis cuarenta y cinco.**

4.5 a las tres

When we want to say at what time something happens, has happened or will happen, we use **a** (*at*) followed by the article and the time. The preposition must also be used in the question:

A: **¿A qué hora sale el tren?**   *(At) what time does the train leave?*
B: **El tren sale a las cuatro.**   *The train leaves at four.*

A: **¿A qué hora cenaste**   *(At) what time did you have*
   ayer?   *dinner yesterday?*
B: **Cené a las nueve de la noche.**   *I had dinner at nine o'clock at night.*

A: **¿A qué hora llegará Juan?**   *(At) what time will Juan arrive?*
B: **Juan llegará a las once y**   *Juan will arrive at 11.15*
   cuarto de la mañana.   *in the morning.*

4.6 de la mañana or por la mañana?

When we say the exact time we use the preposition **de**:

A las cuatro de la mañana.   *At four in the morning.*
A las cinco de la tarde.   *At five in the afternoon.*

When we don't specify the time we use **por**:

Llegará por la mañana.   *He'll arrive in the morning.*
Trabajaré por la tarde.   *I'll work in the afternoon.*
Saldré por la noche.   *I'll go out at night.*

Trabajo por la mañana / por las mañanas. *I work in the morning(s).*
Siempre salgo por la noche   *I always go out at*
   / por las noches.   *night(s)*

4.7 el mediodía / la medianoche

We use **es mediodía** or **es medianoche** (note the absence of the article) to talk generally about the middle of the day or the middle of the night. They do not mean the exact hour of 12 o'clock (a.m. or p.m.). Nor can they be used as answers to the question **¿Qué hora es?**.

We can say:
son las doce del mediodía

but

son las doce de la noche (not **de la medianoche**).

Mediodía refers generally to lunchtime, a period of two hours or more.

We can say:

A mediodía como.   *I have lunch around midday.*

We can use the article with **mediodía**: **a mediodía / al mediodía**

Comemos en casa a mediodía   *We have lunch at home*
  / al mediodía.   *at midday.*

5 The calendar *El calendario*

5.1 Days of the week *Los días de la semana*

lunes	*Monday*
martes	*Tuesday*
miércoles	*Wednesday*
jueves	*Thursday*
viernes	*Friday*
sábado	*Saturday*
domingo	*Sunday*

5.1.2

Days of the week in Spanish are masculine and are not wiritten with a capital:
el martes, el jueves, el sábado, etc.

El lunes próximo voy de vacaciones.   *Next Monday I'm going on holiday.*

Lunes, martes, miércoles, jueves, viernes don't change in the plural: **el jueves,
los jueves**.

But these do: **el sábado > los sábados** and **el domingo > los domingos**.

5.1.3

The word **on** is not necessary in Spanish:

Trabajo los domingos.   *I work (on) Sundays.*
Llegará el lunes.   *He'll arrive (on) Monday.*

5.2 The months of the year *Los meses del año*

They are:

**enero, febrero, marzo, abril, mayo, junio, julio, agosto, septiembre, octubre,
noviembre, diciembre**

The months in Spanish are masculine (**el mes**) and, like the days of the week,
are not written with a capital. They are <u>not</u> used with an article.

En España agosto es el mes más caluroso. *In Spain August is the hottest month.*
El mes más corto del año es   *The shortest month of the year is*
  febrero.   *February.*

5.3 Dates *Las fechas*

Unlike in English, dates are expressed in cardinal numbers:

el catorce de abril, el veinte de junio. 14th *April, 20th June.*

Only with the 1st is it possible to use the ordinal number **primero**.

el uno de mayo 1st *May*
or
el primero de mayo

5.3.1

To say the dates we put the preposition **de** before the month and the year:

Hoy es el quince de agosto de 2010. *Today is the fifteenth of August*

5.3.2

It's possible to say:

Hoy es quince de agosto (without the article).

5.3.3

To say **on** plus a date, Spanish simply uses the article:

Mi padre llegará el veinte *My father will arrive on the*
de diciembre. *20th of December.*

5.3.4

We cannot group the numbers to say the year in Spanish as we can in English (19, followed by 92 for 1992). We must say the full number:

1992 **mil novecientos noventa y dos**.

5.3.5

Although normally we put a full stop after a thousand, this doesn't happen with the years. Compare:

1.992 estudiantes
el año 1992

5.4 The seasons *Las estaciones del año*

la primavera	*spring*	**el verano**	*summer*
el otoño	*autumn*	**el invierno**	*winter*

Study the following examples:

Es primavera.	*It's spring.*
Estamos en primavera.	*We are in springtime.*
En verano tengo vacaciones.	*In the summer I have holidays.*

5.5 More time expressions

hoy	*today*
mañana	*tomorrow*

ayer	*yesterday*
pasado mañana	*the day after tomorrow*
antes de ayer / anteayer	*the day before yesterday*
mañana por la mañana / por la tarde / por la noche	*tomorrow morning / afternoon-evening / night*
ayer por la tarde	*yesterday afternoon*
anoche	*last night*
el domingo por la noche	*Sunday night*
la semana que viene	*next week*
el mes próximo	*next month*
una hora	*an hour*
un minuto	*a minute*
un segundo	*a second*
un momento	*a moment*
un cuarto de hora	*a quarter of an hour*
tres cuartos de hora	*three quarters of an hour*
media hora	*half an hour*
de las dos a las siete	*from two to seven*
desde las tres a las cinco	*from three to five*
una vez / dos veces (al día, a la semana, al mes, al año)	*once, twice (a day, a week, a month, a year)*
todos los días	*every day*
cada día / semana / mes / año	*each day / week / month / year*

6 Gramática práctica

17.6.1 Write the numbers.

1. Ciento veintiocho
2. Doscientos cuarenta y nueve
3. Quinientos quince
4. Setenta y ocho
5. Cuatrocientos dos
6. Dos mil diez

17.6.2 Write the numbers in words.

Example: 85 > ochenta y cinco

a 723   b 45   c 28   d 259   e 178   f 17   g 349   h 586   i 215   j 176

17.6.3 Write the times in words.

Example: 18.10 > Son las seis y diez de la tarde.

a 11.45   b 14.30   c 22.05   d 16.50   e 19.30   f 6.20   g 15.35

h 7.30   i 4.15   j 12.45

17.6.4 Answer the questions. Put the times in words.

Example: 2.10 p.m. > El tren sale a las dos y diez de la tarde.
1. ¿A qué hora sale el tren? 3.30 p.m.
2. ¿A qué hora abre la tienda? 10.05 a.m.
3. ¿A qué hora empieza la película? 7.15 p.m.

4. ¿A qué hora llega el autobús? 4.25 p.m.
5. ¿A qué hora comes? 12.15 p.m.

17.6.5 Put the words in brackets into Spanish to complete the sentences.

1. Mis amigos llegarán (tomorrow morning).
2. Salí con mi hermana (last night).
3. El tren sale dentro de (an hour and a half).
4. Voy de vacaciones (the day after tomorrow).
5. Empiezo a trabajar (next week).
6. He esperado el autobús (three quarters of an hour).
7. Hace (half an hour) que espero.
8. Tengo clase (from three to five).
9. Voy a clase de español (twice a week).
10. Se levanta a las siete (each day).

7 Más allá

7.1 Numbers

Ciento and **mil** change to **cientos** and **miles** in these expressions:

**Cientos de personas vienen
  a esta playa en verano.**
*Hundreds of people come to this
  beach in the summer.*
**Gastaron miles de euros
  en el viaje.**
*They spent thousands of euros on
  the journey.*

Millón changes to **millones** and can also be used in this way:

**Millones de personas pasan hambre
  en el mundo.**
*Millions of people go hungry
  in the world.*

7.1.1 More high numbers

1.765.498 **un millón setecientos sesenta y cinco mil cuatrocientos noventa y ocho**
2.341.386 **dos millones trescientos cuarenta y un mil trescientos ochenta y seis**
4.702.105 **cuatro millones setecientos dos mil ciento cinco**

7.1.2 Cardinal numbers to refer to centuries

el siglo veintiuno   *the twentieth century*
el siglo catorce   *the fourteenth century*

7.1.3 Ordinals used when talking about kings and queens

Juan Carlos primero   *Juan Carlos I*
Isabel segunda   *Isabel II*

But for numbers above ten, cardinal numbers are more usual:

Alfonso trece   *Alfonso XIII*

7.2 Other quantities

7.2.1

Ambos means *both* and is equivalent to the much more common **los dos**.
It is used mostly in written texts. Its feminine form is **ambas**:

Me interesan ambos documentos.	*I'm interested in both documents.*
Ambas profesoras son excelentes.	*Both teachers are excellent.*

7.2.2 More numerals: quantitatives

la mitad, un tercio, un cuarto, etc.

La mitad de los niños.	*Half of the children.*
Un tercio del pastel.	*A third of the cake.*
Un cuarto de kilo.	*A quarter of a kilo.*
El doble de dinero.	*Double the money.*
Los precios han subido el triple.	*Prices have tripled.*
Una vez / dos veces / diez veces más.	*Once, twice, ten times more.*
una docena	*a dozen*
la mayoría / la minoría	*the majority / the minority*

7.3 More time expressions

a eso de las seis	*about six*
a las ocho más o menos	*at more or less eight*
a las once y pico	*at just after eleven*
dentro de / en una hora	*in an hour*
dentro de unos minutos	*in a few minutes*
dentro de unos momentos	*in a few moments*
una vez / dos veces (al día, a la semana, al mes, al año)	*once, twice (a day, a week, a month, a year)*
cada día	*every day*
cada (dos) años	*every (two) years*
es de día	*it's daylight*
es de noche	*it's dark*
el amanecer	*dawn*
la madrugada	*early morning*
el atardecer	*twilight*
el anochecer	*dusk*
hace tres días / una semana / dos meses / tres años	*three days / a week / two months / three years ago*
los años ochenta / en los años noventa	*the eighties / in the nineties*
el siglo veintiuno (XXI)	*the 21st century*
en el siglo veinte	*in the 20th century*
el siglo pasado	*last century*

8 Más práctica

17.8.1 Write the numbers in words.

a 1.843.576   **b** 5.345.707   **c** 3.830.748   **d** 87.570   **e** 92.000
f 8.789.507   **g** 7.000   **h** 65.135.946

18 Adverbs *Adverbios*

1 ¿Qué es?

Adverbs are words that modify and determine the verb:

Tu hermana habla bien el español.   *Your sister speaks Spanish well.*

They are varied in form and function. They can also modify and determine adjectives:

muy feo   *very ugly*

other adverbs:

muy bien   *very well*

and whole sentences:

Afortunadamente tuve suerte   *Fortunately I was lucky with*
   con el examen.   *the exam.*

They can also accompany prepositions and conjunctions:

antes de ayer   *the day before yesterday*

2 Form

Adverbs are invariable; that means they do not change in number or gender.

There are two forms of adverbs:

2.1

Those that have their own form and appear as one word:

bien	*well*
mal	*badly*
cerca	*near*
hoy	*today*
antes	*before*
etc.	

2.2

Those that are formed from adjectives by adding the ending **-mente** (equivalent to the English **-ly**): these are called adverbs of manner:

tranquilamente	*calmly*
lentamente	*slowly*

especialmente   *especially*
etc.

Most adverbs in **-mente** are formed from the feminine singular form of the adjective:

tranquila > tranquilamente   *calmly*
exacta > exactamente   *exactly*
inmediata > inmediatamente   *immediately*
perfecta > perfectamente   *perfectly*
afortunada > afortunadamente   *fortunately*

But other adjectives that don't change in the feminine (those ending in a consonant or **-e** for example) can also add **-mente** to become an adverb:

fácil > fácilmente   *easily*
especial > especialmente   *especially*
natural > naturalmente   *naturally*
normal > normalmente   *normally*
simple > simplemente   *simply*

2.2.1

Some adjectives cannot take **-mente** to make them into adverbs, such as:

- adjectives of colour: **amarillo**
- nationalities and origin: **español**
- and ordinal numbers: **tercero**

(with the exception of **primero > primeramente** and **último > últimamente**).

2.2.2

When a sentence contains two or more adverbs that finish in **-mente**, only the final one takes the ending **-mente**:

Hizo el trabajo fácil y rápidamente.   *He did the work easily and quickly.*

2.2.3

Adverbs that finish in **-mente** keep their normal stress / accent. As **-mente** is stressed itself, some adverbs consequently have two stressed vowels: **completamente, fácilmente**.

2.3

Although the general rule is that adverbs do not change, a few take special endings (**diminutivos**) in familiar language:

cerca > cerquita   *near*
lejos > lejitos   *far away*
pronto > prontito   *soon*

 See Unit 7.

They can be used in comparative as well as superlative sentences:

más lejos que	*further away than*
más tarde que	*later than*

Note that superlatives can also add a form of these endings:

lejos > lejísimos	*very far away*
cerca > cerquísima	*really near*
pronto > prontísimo	*very soon*
tarde > tardísimo	*really late*

There are also some adverbs called **adverbios cortos**, or short adverbs, that have the same form as the adjective and don't change. These affect the verb, not the noun:

Canta fuerte.	*He sings strongly.*
Habla alto.	*He speaks very loudly.*
Habla bajo.	*He speaks quietly.*

Other examples: **claro, despacio, rápido, demasiado, mucho, poco, tanto**.

3 Position

3.1

Adverbs usually go before adjectives and other adverbs:

muy bueno	*very good*
casi siempre	*almost always*

3.2

Most adverbs usually follow the verb:

Habla bien el español.	*He speaks Spanish well.*
Anda lentamente.	*She walks slowly.*

Exceptions are the following adverbs, which go before the verb:
sí, no, casi, sólo.

Yo sí sé hablar francés.	*I do know how to speak French. (for emphasis)*
Él no trabaja aquí.	*He doesn't work here.*
Casi he terminado los deberes.	*I have almost finished my homework.*
Sólo tengo cinco euros.	*I only have five euros.*

3.3

Adverbs can go before the verb for emphasis, but they can never go between the subject and the verb as they do in English:

Casi terminé mi trabajo ayer.	*I almost finished my work yesterday.*

Nor can they go between the auxiliary and the main verb in compound verbs:

He vivido aquí siempre.	*I have always lived here.*

4 Types of adverbs

There are many types of adverbs:

adverbios de tiempo	*adverbs of time*
lugar	*place*
cantidad	*quantity*
modo	*manner*
afirmación	*affirmation*
negación	*negation*
duda	*doubt*

4.1 Adverbs of time

Common examples of adverbs of time are as follows:

ahora	*now*
hoy	*today*
mañana	*tomorrow*
ayer	*yesterday*
nunca	*never*
jamás	*never*
entonces	*then*
siempre	*always*
luego	*then, next, later, soon, afterwards*
pronto	*soon*
tarde	*late*
temprano	*early*

4.1.1 Common examples

Nunca he estado en México /	*I've never been in*
No he estado en México nunca.	* Mexico.*
Entonces la vida era muy difícil.	*Life was difficult then.*
¿No vienes, entonces?	*You're not coming, then?*
Te veo luego.	*I'll see you soon.*
Luego iremos al cine.	*Later/Then we'll go to the cinema.*
El tren ya ha llegado.	*The train has already arrived.*
Haz los deberes ya.	*Do your homework now.*

4.1.2 Ya, *meaning* already, now, at once

This also has many idiomatic uses:

• Affirmation:	**ya, claro**	*of course*
• Impatience (time):	**Ya voy.**	*I'm coming right now.*
• Certainty:	**Ya habrá terminado.**	*It'll have finished by now.*
• Certainty about the future	**Ya verás.**	*You'll see.*

Also:

Ya lo sé.	*Yes, I know.*
¡Basta ya!	*That's enough!*
Ya que has venido . . .	*Since you're here . . .*

4.1.3 *aún / todavía* (yet or still)

These two words mean the same and are interchangeable:

El avión aún no ha llegado.   *The plane has not arrived yet.*
El avión todavía no ha llegado.
¿Aún duerme?   *Is he still asleep?*
¿Todavía duerme?

4.1.4

Aun without the accent means **even**:

El viaje fue bueno aun con   *The journey was good even with*
   esos problemas.   *those problems.*

4.1.5

There is a difference between **ya no** and **aún no**:

Ya no means that something that formerly took place no longer does so:

Ya no trabaja en ese hospital.   *He no longer works in that hospital.*

Or something you were expecting to happen will not now happen:

Es tarde y ya no puedo salir.   *It's late and now I can't go out.*

Aún no means that something has not happened yet:

Aún no he terminado el trabajo.   *I've not finished my work yet.*

4.1.6

Adverbs showing sequence, order, etc.: **primero / luego / después**:

Vamos a comer primero y después   *We'll go and eat first and afterwards*
   vamos al cine.   *we'll go to the cinema.*

4.1.7

Prepositional adverbs combine with the preposition **de**. Common examples are **antes** and **después**. These translate as **before doing** and **after doing**:

Siempre se ducha antes   *She always showers before leaving*
   de salir de casa.   *the house.*
Después de terminar el   *After finishing work he went*
   trabajo fue al cine.   *to the cinema.*

4.1.8

Adverbs formed by a combination of two or more words:

anteayer   *the day before yesterday*
anoche   *last night*
anteanoche   *the night before last*
pasado mañana   *the day after tomorrow*

(not to be confused with **la semana pasada**, which means *last week*)

4.1.9 Expressions of frequency

a menudo
Voy al cine a menudo.   *I often go to the cinema.*

a veces	
Voy al teatro a veces.	*Sometimes I go to the theatre.*
de vez en cuando	
Juego al tenis de vez en cuando.	*I play tennis from time to time.*
(no) muchas veces	
No voy al centro muchas veces.	*I don't go to the centre much.*
(muy) poco	
Voy a la piscina muy poco.	*I rarely go to the swimming pool.*
normalmente / generalmente	
Normalmente hago las compras el sábado.	*Normally I do the shopping on Saturday.*
siempre que puedo	
Veo la televisión siempre que puedo.	*I watch television whenever I can.*

We can use some of these expressions either at the beginning or at the end of a sentence:

a veces voy al teatro
de vez en cuando juego al tenis
siempre que puedo veo la televisión

But **a menudo** and **muy poco** usually appear at the end of the sentence.

4.1.10 *Adverbs and expressions of the past*

ayer	
Ayer fui al mercado.	*Yesterday I went to the market.*
el fin de semana	
El fin de semana me quedé en casa.	*At the weekend I stayed at home.*
la semana pasada	
La semana pasada fui al pueblo.	*Last week I went to the village.*
el mes pasado	
El mes pasado fui a la montaña.	*Last month I went to the mountains.*

4.1.11 *hace / desde hace*

We use **hace** and **desde hace** when we talk about how long we have been doing something. In the question with **hace** we also use **que**:

¿Cuánto (tiempo) hace que patinas?	*How long have you been skating?*

Notice that the verb is in the present simple form: **patinas**.

The answer can be in two forms:

Patino desde hace ocho años.	*I've been skating for eight years.*
Hace ocho años que patino.	*(lit.) It's eight years that I've been skating.*

4.2 Adverbs of place

4.2.1 *aquí, ahí, allí*

Note: in Latin America, the more usual forms are **acá, allá**.

The use of these adverbs depends on the distance of the person or object mentioned in relation to the speaker. They are related to **este, ese, aquel**:

Este chico está aquí.	*This boy is here.*
Esa chica está ahí.	*That girl is there.*
Aquel hombre está allí.	*That man is over there.*

 See Unit 11.

4.2.2 Intensification

Lejos and **cerca** can be intensified in two ways: **muy lejos, muy cerca, lejísimos, cerquísima**.

But other adverbs, such as **encima**, cannot:

muy encima (but not **encimísima**).

4.2.3 Adverbs that require a preposition

abajo
Vivimos abajo de la montaña.	*We live below the mountain.*

cerca
Su oficina está muy cerca de casa.	*His office is very near home.*

debajo
La maleta esté debajo de la cama.	*The case is under the bed.*

delante
Su coche está delante del mío.	*Her car is in front of mine.*

dentro
Está dentro de casa.	*She's in / inside the house.*

detrás
El enchufe está detrás de la televisión.	*The plug is behind the television.*

encima
Tu cartera está encima de la mesa.	*Your wallet is on the table.*

enfrente
Vivimos enfrente de una panadería.	*We live opposite a baker's.*

fuera
Juan trabaja fuera de la ciudad.	*Juan works out of town.*

lejos
Ahora trabaja lejos de aquí.	*He now works a long way from here.*

Some can be combined: **allí encima, allá lejos**.

4.2.4 Adverbs of quantity

4.2.4.1

The following adverbs all follow the verb:

bastante
En su nuevo trabajo gana bastante.　　　*In his new job he earns quite a lot.*

demasiado
Llegó demasiado tarde.　　　*He arrived too late.*

mucho
Le quiere mucho.　　　*She loves him a lot.*

Estos días llueve mucho.　　　*These days it rains a lot.*
poco

Quiero sólo un poco.　　　*I only want a little.*
Duermo poco.　　　*I sleep little. (I don't sleep much.)*

4.2.4.2 nada

nada can go before or after the verb, but changes its meaning according to its position:

No me gusta nada.　　　*I don't like it at all.*

but

Nada le importa.　　　*Nothing matters to him.*

Compare with:

Algo me preocupa.　　　*Something is worrying me.*

4.2.4.3 mucho *and* muy

Both these words have similar meanings.

Muy is used before adjectives (or adverbs):

La ópera es muy buena.　　　*The opera is very good.*
El banco está muy cerca.　　　*The bank is very near.*

Mucho goes after the verb, but can vary its position in a sentence:

Has trabajado mucho hoy.　　　*You've worked a lot today.*
Has trabajado hoy mucho.

4.2.5 Adverbs of manner

These express the way something is done:

así
Se hace así.　　　*It's done like this.*

bien
Lo has hecho bien.　　　*You did it well.*

deprisa
Va muy deprisa en ese coche.　　　*He goes very fast in that car.*

despacio
Tiene que conducir más despacio. *He should drive more slowly.*

difícilmente
Lo consiguió difícilmente. *He managed it with difficulty.*

dolorosamente
Se levantó dolorosamente *He got up painfully.*

fácilmente
Lo hizo fácilmente. *He did it easily.*

mal
Me encuentro mal. *I feel bad.*

Other adverbs of manner: **afortunadamente, desgraciadamente, estupendamente, lamentablemente, perfectamente, totalmente.**

4.2.6 Affirmative and negative adverbs

Affirmative: **sí, seguramente, claro**
Negative: **no, ni, jamás, tampoco**

 See Unit 19 for more about negation and negatives.

No tengo hermanos. *I don't have any brothers or sisters.*
No quiero sopa. *I don't want soup.*

también, tampoco

A: Me gusta el fútbol. *I like football.*
B: A mí también. *So do I. / Me too.*
A: Pero no me gusta el atletismo. *But I don't like athletics.*
B: A mí tampoco. *Nor do I. / Me neither.*

4.2.7 Interrogative and relative adverbs

 See Unit 13 for relative pronouns and adverbs, and Unit 14 for interrogatives.

Interrogatives: **dónde (adónde), cómo, cuándo**

¿Dónde vive Juan? *Where does Juan live?*
¿Adónde vas? *Where are you going (to)?*
¿Cómo te encuentras hoy? *How do you feel today?*
¿Cuándo vamos a Argentina? *When are we going to Argentina?*

Relatives: **donde, como, cuando**

Note that these are the same as the interrogative adverbs but do not have an accent.

Lo hice como María lo hizo. *I did it the way Maria did it.*
Salí cuando Ana llegó. *I left when Ana arrived.*
Allí es donde vivo. *There is where I live.*
La casa donde vive Luis. *The house where Luis lives.*
Vamos adonde tú quieras. *We'll go wherever you want.*

4.2.8 Other types of adverbs

4.2.8.1 *Adverbs of doubt:* acaso, difícilmente, posiblemente, probablemente, quizás, seguramente, tal vez.

4.2.8.2 *Intensifying adverbs:* realmente, totalmente, verdaderamente.

Quantitative intensifiers: **absolutamente, ligeramente**.

5 Gramática práctica

18.5.1 Add **-mente** to these adjectives to form adverbs.

fácil, difícil, tranquilo, lento, exacto, próximo, especial, normal, simple, inmediato, último, frecuente, anterior, descuidado

18.5.2 Find the adverbs and say what kind they are.

Example: cerca: place

 1. Vivo cerca de la universidad, pero antes vivía muy lejos.
 2. El niño siempre hace los deberes muy bien.
 3. Mi hermano está mal, le duele mucho la cabeza.
 4. Mis padres vienen a comer hoy.
 5. Juan se levanta muy temprano y sale rápidamente de casa.
 6. Todos los días pasean despacio por el parque.
 7. Juan dice que siempre llega tarde a clase porque vive lejos.
 8. Mi hermana vendrá mañana a visitarme.
 9. Sal pronto de casa porque vas a llegar tarde a la oficina.
10. Llámame luego porque ahora estoy ocupada.

18.5.3 Translate the sentences from 18.5.2 into English.

18.5.4 Fill the gaps with **nunca** or **alguna vez**.

1. ¿Has comido paella _____?
2. No, _____ he comido paella.
3. ¿Has probado la sangría _____?
4. No, no he probado la sangría _____.
5. ¿No has tomado café _____?
6. Sí, he tomado café _____.

18.5.5 Complete the sentences with **ya** or **aún**.

1. ¿_____ has hecho los deberes?
2. No, _____ no he hecho los deberes.
3. ¿_____ no has terminado los deberes?
4. Sí, _____ he terminado los deberes
5. _____ has llamado a María?
6. Sí, _____ he llamado a María.

6 Más allá

More adverbs and adverbial expressions

6.1 Adverbs of time

<u>Anteriormente</u> había vivido allí.	*He had lived there previously.*
<u>Últimamente</u> está muy preocupado.	*Lately he is very worried.*
Te veré <u>dentro de dos días</u>.	*I'll see you in two days.*
Fueron <u>la semana anterior</u>.	*They went the week before.*
Terminaron <u>un día antes</u>.	*They finished a day early / before.*
Esto ocurrió <u>dos días después</u>.	*This occurred two days after.*
nunca más / nunca jamás	*never again / not any more.*

Other adverbs of time:
anualmente, continuamente, definitivamente, diariamente, frecuentemente, habitualmente, inmediatamente, instantáneamente.

They can go before or after the verb:
Juan va diariamente a la universidad. / Diariamente Juan va a la universidad.

Some adverbs of time can take other adverbs of quantity:

muy recientemente	*very recently*
poco antes	*a little before*

6.2 Adverbs of quantity

mucho / muy

 See point 4.2.4.3 above.

Note the difference between **poco** and **un poco**:

He aprendido poco.	*I haven't learnt much.*
He aprendido un poco.	*I've learnt a little.*

 See Unit 16 point 3.3.3.

6.3 Adverbs of manner

The following always go after the verb:
correctamente, estupendamente, generosamente, perfectamente, totalmente

The following can go in different positions in the sentence:
afortunadamente, desgraciadamente, dolorosamente, obligatoriamente

Afortunadamente encontró trabajo.	*Luckily, he found a job.*
Trabaja estupendamente.	*He works really well.*

6.4 Comparison of adverbs

Adverbs can be used for comparison and to express the superlative. They work in a similar way to the comparison of adjectives:

Salimos más tarde que vosotros.   *We went out later than you.*
Hago el trabajo tan bien como él.   *I do the work as well as he does.*

The superlative endings **-ísimo/a/os/as** can be added to some adverbs:
cerquísima, muchísimo, prontísimo, tantísimo.

6.5 Alternative expressions

Some adverbs can be replaced by adverbial expressions:

cuidadosamente   **> con cuidado**
rápidamente   **> de prisa**
repentinamente   **> de repente**
tristemente   **> de manera triste**

7 Más práctica

18.7.1 Form adverbs ending in **-mente** from these words.

anterior, último, inmediato, simultáneo, definitivo, continuo, instantáneo,
repetido, repentino, frecuente, mensual, estupendo, total, doloroso,
afortunado, desgraciado, lamentable

19 Negatives *Negativos*

1 ¿Qué es?

A negative statement or sentence can be expressed in different ways in Spanish. An isolated answer of **no** is the same in Spanish and English but when it comes to more elaborate negations there are many differences between the two languages.

Generally the Spanish negative constructions are very simple:

Subject + no + verb

Yo no trabajo.   *I don't work.*

2 Forms

2.1 Negative adverbs

 See also Unit 16, indefinite pronouns and adverbs

no	*no*	**tampoco**	*neither*
ni	*nor*	**nada**	*nothing / at all (in a*
ni . . . ni	*neither . . . nor*		*negative statement)*
nunca	*never*	**nadie**	*nobody*
jamás	*never*	**ninguno**	*none, nobody*

2.2 Other negative expressions (adverbial)

de ningún modo / de ninguna manera	*no way, absolutely not*
claro que no	*of course not*
nada más	*no more / nothing else*

3 Use and position

3.1 no

3.1.1

The absolute answer to a question is normally one word:

affirmative: **Sí** or negative: **No.**

Negation within a sentence places **no** before the verb it negates. If the sentence contains a subject personal pronoun then **no** goes immediately after it:

No tengo dinero.	*I don't have any money.*
No quiero café.	*I don't want any coffee.*
Yo no quiero ir al cine.	*I don't want to go to the cinema.*
María no viene a la fiesta.	*Maria isn't coming to the party.*

3.1.2

If a sentence contains any other personal object pronouns, **no** always goes before them:

No se lo dijo.	*He didn't tell (it to) him.*
Nosotros no se lo enviamos.	*We didn't send it to him.*

3.1.3

With compound verbs, **no** always goes before the auxiliary verb:

No ha venido.	*He hasn't come*

3.1.4

The word **no** is enough in Spanish to form the negative. There is no need for structures such as the English **don't** or **doesn't**. And when in English an answer is **No, I don't** or **He doesn't**, in Spanish the answer is simply **No**.

A: ¿Quieres ensalada?	*Do you want salad?*
B: No.	
or:	
No quiero.	*I don't want any.*
or:	
No quiero ensalada.	*I don't want salad.*
A: ¿Te gusta el fútbol?	*Do you like football?*
B: No.	
or:	
No me gusta.	*I don't like it.*
or:	
No me gusta el fútbol.	*I don't like football.*

3.1.5

To respond with a negative we can use the word **no** followed by a negative sentence starting with another **no**:

A: ¿Quieres patatas fritas?	*Do you want chips?*
B: No, no quiero patatas fritas.	*No, I don't want chips.*
A: ¿Te gustan las películas de terror?	*Do you like horror films?*
B: No, no me gustan.	*No, I don't like them.*

3.2 Double negatives

3.2.1

In Spanish, if there is a negative word after the verb such as **nada, nadie, ninguno, nunca** or **tampoco**, there must be another negative word before the verb; usually this word is **no**:

no . . . nada
No le gusta nada.   *He doesn't like it at all.*

no . . . nadie
No viene nadie a visitarme.   *Nobody comes to visit me.*

no . . . ninguno
No aprobó los exámenes ninguno.   *None of them passed the exams.*

no . . . nunca
No estudia nunca.   *He doesn't ever study.*
           (He never studies.)

no . . . tampoco
No van de vacaciones tampoco.   *They don't go on holiday either.*

3.2.2

Other negatives can also start the sentence and in this case there is no need to use **no**. Compare the above examples with the following:

Nada le gusta.*	*Nothing pleases him.*
Nadie viene a visitarme.	*No-one comes to visit me.*
Ninguno aprobó los exámenes.	*Not one passed the exams.*
Nunca estudia para los exámenes.	*He never studies for the exams.*
Tampoco vamos de vacaciones	*Neither are we going on holiday*
este mes.	*this month.*

*In many cases it is not possible to start a sentence with **nada**:

No quiero nada.   *I don't want anything.*
(<u>not</u> **Nada quiero.**)

But it <u>is</u> possible with verbs similar to **gustar**:

Nada le importa.	*Nothing matters to him.*
Nada te interesa.	*Nothing interests you.*

The use of these structures adds emphasis to the negative meaning.

 For other uses of **nada, nadie** and **ninguno/a/os/as** see Unit 16 Sections 2, 5.

3.3 ni

3.3.1

Ni means **nor / neither**. It is used in a negative sentence that has one subject and two verbs. In this case two negatives must be used: the first one is **no** and goes before the first verb, and **ni** is the second negative and goes before the second verb.

Juan no sale de casa ni ve a   *Juan doesn't leave home nor*
   sus amigos.   *see his friends.*

3.3.2

When there is only one verb and two objects to express the negative we use
ni between the two objects.

Yo no quiero té ni café.	*I don't want tea or coffee.*
or:	
Yo no quiero te, ni quiero café.	*I don't want tea, nor do I want coffee.*

3.4 tampoco

This means *either* (in a negative sentence), *not either, neither*.

The negative **tampoco** is the opposite of the affirmative **también**. It can go
after the verb (see point 3.2.1 above on double negatives) or before the verb.
Compare the following examples:

A: Yo voy al cine.	*I'm going to the cinema.*
B: Yo también.	*So am I.*
A: Yo no voy al teatro.	*I'm not going to the theatre.*
B: Yo tampoco.	*Neither am I.*
A: Yo he hecho los deberes.	*I've done my homework.*
B: También yo.	*Me too.*
A: Yo no he hecho los deberes.	*I haven't done my homework.*
B: Tampoco yo.	*Neither have I.*

3.5 nunca / jamás

Both mean *never* and sometimes *ever* (in a negative sense). The meaning
of **jamás** is stronger (*never ever*). It is used less, and only when we want to
emphasise the negative meaning.

They can be used in double negations (see point 3.2.1 above):

No sale nunca.	*He doesn't ever go out.*
No quiero verlo jamás.	*I don't want to see it, ever.*

Nunca and **jamás** can also go before the verb and in this case **no** is not
used:

Nunca viene a casa.	*He never comes home.*
Jamás viaja en avión.	*Never does he travel by plane.*

4 Gramática práctica

19.4.1 Answer the questions with a negative.

Example: ¿Tomas té con leche? No, no tomo té con leche.

1. ¿Quieres café?
2. ¿Juegas al fútbol?
3. ¿Quieres salir conmigo?
4. ¿Viene Ana a la fiesta?.

5. ¿Tomáis más cerveza?
6. ¿Te gustan las patatas asadas?
7. ¿Vas a comprar el billete esta tarde?
8. ¿Tienes mucho trabajo?

19.4.2 Rewrite these sentences.

Example: Nada le gusta. > No le gusta nada.

1. Nunca sale de casa.
2. Nadie compra en esta tienda.
3. Ninguno aprobará el examen.
4. Tampoco iré a la playa este año.
5. Nada me apetece estos días.
6. Nunca hablamos de trabajo.

19.4.3 Complete the sentences with a suitable negative.

1. No me gusta el té _____el café.
2. Yo no tengo hermanos _____.
3. No quiero _____ más, gracias.
4. Yo _____voy al cine.
5. _____ viajo en tren.
6. _____ viene a visitarnos.

5 Más allá

5.1 Combination of other negatives

It is possible to combine other negatives in the sentence:

Nadie me visita nunca.   *No-one ever visits me.*
or:
Nunca me visita nadie.

Nunca bebe nada*.   *He never drinks anything.*

*But <u>not</u> **Nada bebe nunca.**

5.2 More uses of ni

5.2.1

Sometimes the first negative is also **ni**, and this adds emphasis to the negative meaning:

Ni estudias, ni dejas   *You neither study nor let anyone*
   estudiar.   *else study.*
Juan ni come carne, ni pescado.   *Juan eats neither meat nor fish.*
or:
Juan ni come carne, ni come pescado.

5.2.2

Often, when we want to add even more emphasis, three negatives can be used: **no** before the first verb, **ni** before the first item we want to negate and another **ni**:

No trabaja ni el viernes ni el lunes.	*He doesn't work on either Friday or Monday.*
No me gusta ni la carne ni el pescado.	*I don't like either meat or fish.*

Compare:

No me gusta el té ni el café.	*I don't like tea or coffee.*
No me gusta ni el té ni el café.	*I don't like either tea or coffee.*

5.3 nunca and jamás

5.3.1

Sometimes **nunca** and **jamás** can go together to make a very strong negation:

No quiero verla nunca jamás.	*I don't want to see her, never ever.*

5.3.2

Similarly, **nunca** can be followed by **más**:

No quiero verla nunca más.	*I don't want to see her ever again.*
Nunca más vendré a esta casa.	*Never again will I come to this house.*

5.4 Some expressions with no

5.4.1 ¿No?

This is a question tag, not a negative, and it goes at the end of a sentence. It is the equivalent of, but much more simple than, the English question tags that also go at the end of the sentence: *don't you? doesn't he? didn't you? will you?* etc.:

Estás estudiando ahora, ¿no?	*You're studying now, aren't you?*
Vendrás a mi fiesta, ¿no?	*You'll come to my party, won't you?*
Terminaste el trabajo, ¿no?	*You finished the work, didn't you?*

In such instances, we can use an alternative question tag: **¿verdad?**:

Están trabajando aquí, ¿verdad?	*They're working here, aren't they?*
Terminarás el trabajo, ¿verdad?	*You'll finish the work, won't you?*
Saliste ayer, ¿verdad?	*You went out yesterday, didn't you?*

5.4.2 no más

This expression is used in Latin American Spanish and has different meanings: *only*, *just*, or simply adds emphasis:

Vivo aquí no más.	*I just live here.*
Estuve allí ayer no más.	*I was there only yesterday.*

5.5 Other negative expressions (adverbial)

Some of these translations are only approximate as there is no exact equivalent:

de ningún modo / de ninguna manera *no way, absolutely not.*

claro que no	*of course not*
nada más	*no more / nothing else*
en absoluto	*absolutely not*
casi nada	*almost nothing*
nada de eso	*none of that*
Eso sí que no.	*Not that.*

and the more colloquial:

¡Que no!	*Of course not!*
¡Ni hablar!	*Not at all / Absolutely not!*
¡Qué va!	*Of course not!*

6 Más práctica

19.6.1 Complete the sentences with the negatives from the box.

nunca   no   ninguna   ni   nadie   nada   ninguno   tampoco

1. Susana _____ va a trabajar _____ María _____.
2. _____ viene a verme.
3. _____ se le ocurre _____ idea.
4. _____ he visto a _____ en la calle.
5. _____ Ana _____ yo iremos de vacaciones.
6. _____ me gusta _____ de lo que hay en esta tienda.
7. A ti _____ te gusta _____el café con leche y a mí _____.
8. Ana_____ tiene _____ que hacer esta tarde

19.6.2 Complete these expressions with the words from the box and then translate them into English.

en   qué   manera   nada   eso   modo   no   ni   claro

1. de ningún _____
2. de ninguna _____
3. _____ que no
4. _____ más
5. _____ sí que no
6. _____ absoluto
7. casi _____
8. nada de _____
9. ¡que _____ !
10. _____ hablar
11. _____ mi vida
12. ¡ _____ va!

20 Prepositions and prepositional phrases
Preposiciones y frases preposicionales

Note that this chapter doesn't have a Más allá section, but uses at a higher level are indicated by ** .

1 ¿Qué es?

Prepositions are words that link or relate other words in the same sentence.

Raúl es <u>de</u> Madrid.   *Raúl is <u>from</u> Madrid.*

Prepositional phrases are groups of words that act in the same way as prepositions. We will look at these in Section 5.

**El coche está aparcado
 <u>delante de</u> la casa.**   *The car is parked
 <u>in front of</u> the house.*
El cine está <u>al lado de</u> la tienda.   *The cinema is <u>next to</u> the shop.*

2 Form

2.1

Here is a list of all Spanish prepositions. Some are much more common than others and some have several different meanings in English.

a, ante, bajo, con, contra, de, desde, en, entre, hacia, hasta, para, por, según, sin, sobre, tras

2.2

Prepositions are usually followed by a noun or a pronoun and cannot appear at the end of the sentence as they can in English.

¿<u>Para</u> quién es el libro?   *Who is the book <u>for</u>?*
¿<u>Con</u> quién sales esta noche?   *Who are you going out <u>with</u> tonight?*

3 Use

3.1 a

This is a very common preposition and can be used in a variety of situations. It has several meanings in English, depending on the context. Its English equivalent can be: *to, at, on, down, up, in*.

If followed by the article **el: a + el = al**:

Voy al cine.   *I'm going to the cinema.*

3.1.1 To indicate a destination (to)

Vamos a Madrid.   *We're going to Madrid.*

3.1.2 To express time, meaning at, until or to

El tren sale a las ocho.   *The train leaves at eight.*
Trabajo de las ocho a las tres.   *I work from eight to three.*

3.1.3 With days and dates, in expressions such as

a la mañana siguiente   *(on) the next morning*
al día siguiente   *(on) the next day*

3.1.4 To express purpose

Llevó a Juan a comer.   *He took Juan to eat.*

3.1.5 To indicate direction or place

a la derecha   *to the right*
sentarse a la mesa   *to sit at the table*

3.1.6 To specify price

Las salchichas cuestan a tres   *The sausages cost (at) three*
   euros el kilo.   *euros a kilo.*

3.1.7 To indicate distribution

Tocan a tres helados   *(it works out at) Three ice creams*
   por persona.   *per person.*

3.1.8 To describe ways of doing something

Voy a mi trabajo a pie.   *I go to work on foot.*
Está escrito a mano.   *It's written by hand.*

Note:

ir a pie   *to go on foot*
ir a caballo   *to go on horseback*
ir en bicicleta   *to go by bicycle*
ir en coche   *to go by car*

3.1.9 To indicate distance or speed

La playa está a dos kilómetros   *The beach is (at) two kilometres*
   de la ciudad.   *from the city.*
El coche va a cien   *The car goes at a hundred*
   kilómetros por hora.   *kilometres an hour.*

3.1.10 To describe food and drink

pescado a la plancha
pollo al ajillo

3.1.11 *Before the indirect object*

Escribí una postal a mi hermano para su cumpleaños.	*I wrote a postcard to my brother for his birthday.*

3.1.12 *¡Es diferente!*

Note the very important use of **a** that has no equivalent in English: the personal **a**. This is used when the direct object of a sentence is a person:

Llamé a Juan.	*I called Juan.*

Note that the verb **tener** does not follow this rule:

Tengo dos hermanos.	*I have two brothers.*

** 3.1.13 *In the construction a + el = al in sentences such as*

Al terminar la clase iremos al cine.	*On finishing the class we'll go to the cinema.*

** 3.1.14 *After certain verbs*

aprender a cocinar	*to learn how to cook*
enseñar a leer	*to teach how to read*
empezar a trabajar	*to begin to work*

3.2 de

This usually means *of* or *from*.

If followed by the article **el**: **de + el = del**:

Vengo del cine.	*I've just come from the cinema.*

3.2.1 *To indicate origin*

Soy de Madrid.	*I'm from Madrid.*

Note: In the question form:

¿De qué país eres?	*What country are you from? (lit: From what country are you?)*

3.2.2 *To indicate distance*

Hay trescientos kilómetros de Barcelona a Madrid.	*It's 300 km from Barcelona to Madrid.*

3.2.3 *To indicate time*

Tiene clase de diez a doce.	*He has classes from ten to twelve.*
Trabaja de noche.	*He works at night.*

3.2.4 *To describe material, colour and physical attributes*

¿De qué material es?	*What (material) is it made of?*
Es de oro.	*It's made of gold.*

una pulsera de plata	*a silver bracelet*
La camisa es de algodón.	*The shirt is made of cotton.*
¿De qué color es?	*What colour is it?*
Es de color azul.	*It's (a) blue (colour).*
Un hombre de pelo rubio.	*A man with blond hair.*

3.2.5 ¡Es diferente!

Note in the following that the order of the words is the opposite of English; and also the use of **de** to mean *of*, *for* or *made of*.

3.2.5.1 To indicate possession

el bolso de mi madre	*my mother's bag (lit: the bag of my mother)*
la casa de Ana	*Ana's house (lit: the house of Ana)*
Esta cartera es de mi hermano.	*This is my brother's wallet.*

Note also:

el programa de hoy	*today's programme (lit: the programme for today)*

3.2.5.2 To indicate purpose

Son botas de montaña.	*They are mountain boots. (lit: boots for the mountain)*
gafas de sol	*sunglasses (lit: glasses for the sun)*

Note the difference between Spanish and English in the following:

las zapatillas de deporte	*sports shoes (shoes for sport)*
un helado de chocolate	*a chocolate ice cream (an ice cream made of chocolate)*
un número de teléfono	*a telephone number (a number for the telephone)*
una película de terror	*a horror film (a film of horror)*
un pastel de queso	*a cheese cake (a cake made of cheese)*

**3.2.6 Used in comparatives and superlatives

 See Unit 8.

Es el pueblo más pequeño de la región.	*It's the smallest town in the region.*

** 3.2.7 Used with numbers

To mean *than*:

No tiene más de mil euros.	*He doesn't have more than a thousand euros.*

To refer to price or value:

Compré un bolso de doscientos euros.	*I bought a bag for two hundred euros.*

3.2.8 *To indicate a topic*

hablar de	to talk about
quejarse de	to complain about
tratar de	to be about

Hablo de mis problemas.	*I talk about my problems.*

3.2.9 *Used with some verbs*

acabar de
Acabo de cenar.	*I've just had dinner.*

cambiar(se) de
Voy a cambiar de coche.	*I'm going to change my car.*

hablar de
Hablamos de su vida.	*We talk about his life.*

Notice again the position of **de** at the beginning of a question:

¿De qué habláis?	*What do you talk about?*

3.3 desde

3.3.1 *To describe a place of origin*

El autobús va desde Marbella al aeropuerto en media hora.	*The bus goes from Marbella to the airport in half an hour.*

3.3.2 *To express time, meaning* from

Trabajo desde las nueve hasta las cinco.	*I work from 9 to 5.*

** 3.3.3 *In expressions of time, meaning* since *and* for

Estudio español desde el año pasado.	*I've been studying Spanish since last year.*
Trabaja en la universidad desde hace tres años.	*He's worked in the university for three years. (since three years ago)*

3.4 en

This can mean *in, on, inside, at, into* or *by.*

3.4.1 *To indicate time and place*

Empiezo a trabajar en enero en Barcelona.	*I start working in January in Barcelona.*

3.4.2 *To convey position without being specific*

El bolso está en la mesa.	*The bag is on the table.*
El bolso está en el armario.	*The bag is in the wardrobe.*
Juan está en la oficina.	*Juan is in the office.*

3.4.3 *To state modes of transport*

Voy a mi trabajo en autobús.	*I go to work by bus.*
Siempre vamos a Barcelona en tren.	*We always go to Barcelona by train.*

But note:

Voy a pie.	*I go on foot.*

3.4.4 *To refer to languages spoken*

Siempre hablan en español.	*They always speak in Spanish.*

3.4.5 *Verbs with* **en**

Gasto mi dinero en libros y discos.	*I spend my money on books and records.*

3.5 hacia

3.5.1 *Meaning* towards

El autobús se dirige hacia Barcelona.	*The bus travels towards Barcelona.*

3.5.2 *Meaning* round about, approximately

Llegaremos a casa hacia las dos.	*We'll arrive home at about two.*

3.6 hasta

Meaning *until, as far as*:

Trabajo desde las ocho de la mañana hasta las tres de la tarde.	*I work from eight in the morning till three in the afternoon.*
Iremos en tren desde Barcelona hasta Madrid.	*We'll go by train from Barcelona as far as Madrid.*

3.7 por

3.7.1 *To express the cause of or reason for an action*

Suspendió el examen por estudiar poco.	*He failed the exam because he studied too little.*
La carretera está cortada por obras.	*The road is closed because of road works.*
Gracias por tu ayuda.	*Thanks for your help.*

3.7.2

We use **por** to talk about things that happen in the morning, in the afternoon and at night. It can also mean *during*:

Tengo clases por la mañana.	*I have classes in the morning.*
Hago mis deberes por la noche.	*I do my homework at night.*
Por la tarde descanso.	*During the afternoon I relax.*

3.7.3 *Meaning* through, at *or* by way of

Cruza siempre por el paso de cebra.	*Always cross at the zebra crossing.*
Se pasa por un túnel muy largo para ir a Francia.	*You go through a very long tunnel to get to France.*

3.7.4 *Meaning* along

Vamos a casa por la avenida del Mar.	*We go home along Mar Avenue.*

3.7.5 *Meaning* around *or* nearby

Hay un banco por aquí.	*There's a bank around here.*

3.7.6 *To indicate the means of doing something*

Llámame por teléfono.	*Call me by phone.*
Envía el documento por correo electrónico.	*Send the document by email.*

3.7.7 *To indicate rate and price*

Pagó mucho dinero por la casa, la compró por un millón de euros.	*He paid a lot of money for the house, he bought it for a million euros.*
Pagamos un cinco por ciento de interés.	*We pay five per cent interest.*
El AVE puede ir a más de 300 kilómetros por hora.	*The AVE can go at more than 300 km per hour.*

3.7.8 *To indicate duration*

Estuve en Sevilla por una semana.	*I was in Seville for a week.*

Note:

This is more usual in Latin American Spanish. In Spain you might hear **durante**, or no preposition at all:

Estuve en Sevilla una semana. / Estuve en Sevilla durante una semana.

3.7.9 *Used in expressions of movement*

Pasó por debajo del puente.	*It went under the bridge.*
por encima de	*over*
por delante de	*in front of*
por detrás de	*behind*

**3.7.10 *To express equivalence*

Vale por un viaje a Cuba.	*It's valid for a trip to Cuba.*

**3.7.11 *To indicate distribution*

Pagamos cincuenta euros por persona.	*We paid fifty euros per person.*

**3.7.12 *Meaning* on behalf of

¿Puedo firmar por mi madre?	*Can I sign for my mother?*

****3.7.13** *To indicate changing something for something else*

Quiero cambiar este jersey por uno más grande.	*I'd like to change this sweater for a bigger one.*

****3.7.14** *Meaning* by *when used in passive constructions*

Este libro fue escrito por Cervantes.	*This book was written by Cervantes.*

 See Unit 44 for details of the passive.

3.8 para

This preposition means *for, in order to.*

It expresses intention, purpose or destiny.

Hace todo esto para ayudar a sus hijos.	*She does all this to help her children.*
Estudia mucho para aprobar los exámenes.	*He studies a lot in order to pass his exams.*

3.8.1 *To indicate direction and movement (destination, towards somewhere)*

El tren para Madrid sale a las cinco.	*The train for Madrid leaves at five.*

3.8.2 *To indicate time or duration*

Quiero una habitación para cinco noches.	*I'd like a room for five nights.*
Viajará para la primavera.	*He'll travel in springtime.*

3.8.3 *To indicate what something is used for*

Este jarabe es bueno para el catarro.	*This syrup is good for colds.*
Esto no sirve para nada.	*This is no good for anything.*

3.8.4 *To indicate who or what something is intended for*

Este regalo es para mi madre.	*This gift is for my mother.*
Este libro es para ti.	*This book is for you.*

3.8.5 *To indicate purpose*

Mi hermano estudia para ser arquitecto.	*My brother is studying to be an architect.*

3.8.6 *To accompany* mí *when ordering food or drink*

Para mí un agua con gas, por favor.	*A sparkling water for me, please.*

3.8.7 *To indicate opinion*

Para mí esto está mal.	*As far as I'm concerned this is bad.*

3.8.8 *The proximity or starting of an action*

Juan está para llegar.   *Juan is about to arrive.*

3.8.9 *In expressions of comparison, meaning considering*

Para ser tan joven toca muy   *Considering he's so young he*
   bien el violín.   *plays the violin very well.*

3.9 ¡Es diferente! por and para

3.9.1

Por and **para** may both be translated as *for* in English, but in Spanish they are not normally interchangeable.

In general terms:

- **por** equates with cause and reason. It can be replaced by *because of.*
- **para** equates with finality, intention, and can mean *in order to.*
- **por** also equates with purpose and for this reason can be confused with **para**, which also means *for*. Compare the following:

Trabajo por mis hijos.   *I work because of my children.*
Trabajo para mis hijos.   *I work for my children.*
Hago esto por ti.   *I'm doing this because of / for you.*
Hago esto para ti.   *I'm doing this for you.*
Dejó todo por ella.   *He left everything because of her.*
Dejó todo para ella.   *He left everything for her.*

Note:

por is often followed by a noun: **para** is often followed by a verb:

Trabajo por dinero.   *I work for money.*
Trabajo para ganar dinero   *I work to earn money.*
Fui a vivir a Madrid por   *I went to live in Madrid for reasons*
   motivos de trabajo.   *of work.*
Fui a vivir a Madrid para   *I went to live in Madrid in*
   trabajar.   *order to work.*

3.9.2

Sometimes the distinction is very subtle, so that both **por** and **para** can mean practically the same when stating intention:

Viajó desde muy lejos para venir a verte. *He travelled a long way to see you.*
Viajó desde muy lejos por venir a verte.
Se quedó por estar contigo.   *He stayed (because he wanted)*
                                  to be with you.
Se quedó para estar contigo.   *He stayed in order to be with you.*

The difference is clearer in the question, but not so clear in the answer:

¿Para qué has venido?   *Why have you come?*
                                    (What is the purpose of your visit?)
He venido para hablar contigo.   *I've come (in order) to speak to you.*

¿Por qué has venido?	Why have you come?
He venido por (porque quiero) hablar contigo.	I've come because (I want to) speak to you.
Lo hago para enfadarte.	I do it to annoy you. (with the intention)
Lo hago por enfadarte.	I do it (because I want) to annoy you.

As a useful rule of thumb, if the English meaning could be expressed as *for the sake of*, use **por**; otherwise, use **para**.

3.10 sobre

3.10.1 Meaning on, above *or* over *in expressions of place*

El helicóptero vuela sobre la ciudad.	The helicopter is flying over the city.
El libro está sobre la silla.	The book is on the chair.

Note that in this case it can be replaced by **en**, which has a more general meaning.

3.10.2 Meaning approximately *in expressions of time*

Terminaré el trabajo sobre las cinco.	I'll finish work about five.

3.10.3 Meaning about, *as in the subject of a book or film*

Es un libro sobre un político famoso.	It's a book about a famous politician.

3.11 con (*with*)

3.11.1

Quiero pan con la tortilla.	I'd like bread with the tortilla.
Salgo con mi amigo.	I go out with my friend.

3.11.2 Used in expressions of food and drink

Un agua con gas.	A sparkling water. (lit: a water with gas)
Un café con leche.	A white coffee. (lit: coffee with milk)

3.11.3 Used with instruments or tools

Abre el paquete con las tijeras.	Open the packet with the scissors.

3.11.4 To express manner

Hay que tratar a los clientes con amabilidad.	You have to treat the clients with friendliness.

** 3.11.5 Note the position of con in question forms

¿Con quién sales por la noche?	Who do you go out with at night?
¿Con quién estudias?	Who do you study with?

** *3.11.6 Used with the verb* to dream, *meaning* about:

| Todas las noches sueño con mi hermano. | Every night I dream about my brother. |

3.12 sin (*without*)

| No vayas sin mí. | Don't go without me. |
| Un agua sin gas. | A still water. (lit: water without gas) |

3.13 contra (*against*)

| Mi equipo juega contra los campeones. | My team is playing against the champions. |

3.14 entre (*amongst* or *between*)

3.14.1

| La tienda está entre el cine y la iglesia. | The shop is between the cinema and the church. |

3.14.2

| Paseamos entre los árboles. | We stroll amongst the trees. |

** 3.15 según (*according to*)

| Según mi tía, Pedro no vendrá hoy. | According to my aunt, Pedro won't come today. |
| Según dicen, va a llover. | According to what they say, it's going to rain. |

4 Prepositions that are more often used in the form of prepositional phrases

4.1 ante and delante de (*before, in front of, in the presence of*)

4.1.1

| El coche está aparcado delante de la casa. | The car is parked in front of the house. |

***4.1.2*

| Habló ante mucha gente. | He spoke in front of many people. |

** *4.1.3*

| Sabe actuar ante una dificultad. | He knows how to behave when faced with a difficulty |

**4.1.4 *ante todo* (above all)

Ante todo, no olvides cerrar la puerta.	*Above all, don't forget to lock the door,*

4.2 **bajo** and **debajo, debajo de** (*under, underneath*)

4.2.1

El bolso está debajo de la silla.	*The bag is under the chair.*

**4.2.2*

No podemos trabajar bajo estas condiciones.	*We can't work under these conditions.*

4.3 **tras** and **detrás, detrás de** (*behind, after*)

4.3.1

El bolso está detrás de la puerta.	*The bag is behind the door.*

**4.3.2*

Tras la cena hubo una fiesta.	*After supper there was a party.*

5 Many prepositions combine with other words to form prepositional phrases

We have already seen some above: **ante** > **delante de**; **bajo** > **debajo de**; **tras** > **detrás de**.

5.1 **al lado de** (*next to*)

Carmen está sentada al lado de Ana.	*Carmen is sitting next to Ana.*

5.2 **encima de** (*on, on top of*)

La fruta está encima de la caja.	*The fruit is on top of the box.*

5.3 **enfrente de** (*opposite*)

Mi casa está enfrente del parque.	*My house is opposite the park.*

5.4 **antes de** (*before*)

Antes de cenar fuimos a ver una película.	*Before dinner we went to see a film.*

5.5 **junto a** (*next to*)

Siéntate junto a mí.	*Sit next to me.*

6 Gramática práctica

20.6.1 Add the correct prepositions.

1. Voy ____ la piscina.
2. Hago deporte ____ mi hermano.
3. Estudio ____ la universidad.
4. Voy ____ cine.
5. Bailo ____ la discoteca.
6. Como ____ mi familia.
7. Juego ____ la pelota.
8. Hablo ____ mis amigos ____ el bar.
9. Hago mis deberes ____ casa.
10. Juego ____ fútbol ____ el parque.
11. Estaré aquí ____ las tres ____ las seis de la tarde.

20.6.2 Fill the gaps in the dialogue with **por** or **para**.

1. A: ¿Tiene sitio _____ una tienda pequeña?
2. B: Sí, ¿_____ cuántos días lo quieren?
3. A: _____ una semana. ¿Cuánto cuesta _____ día?
4. B: Cuesta cincuenta euros _____ persona y _____ día.
5. A: ¿Cuánto tenemos que pagar _____ el coche?
6. B: _____ el coche tienen que pagar treinta euros _____ día.
7. A: Queremos cenar a las ocho. ¿Se puede reservar una mesa _____
   cuatro personas en el restaurante _____ esta noche?
8. B: Sí, claro. Una mesa _____ las ocho _____ cuatro personas.

20.6.3 Put prepositions in the correct place.

Example: Queremos vino marca > Queremos vino de marca.

Frases en el restaurante
Pollo asado patatas fritas
Chuleta ternera
Bistec la pimienta
Vino tinto la casa
Cerveza alcohol

Frases en el hotel
Quiero reservar una habitación el día quince
Quiero una habitación vistas la playa
Hay piscina niños
¿Puede despertarme la mañana?
La cena es las nueve la noche

20.6.4 Complete the sentences with **para, sobre, por, con, de, a, sin** or **en**.

1. Este hombre se casó _____ la directora de la empresa.
2. Juan Carlos es el rey _____ España.
3. Goya trabajó _____ el rey de España.
4. Dalí empezó _____ pintar muy joven.
5. No puedes viajar ____ billete.
6. Hay que tener mucha energía _____ bailar flamenco.
7. Goya pintó cuadros _____ las cosas terribles _____ la guerra.

8. El tren está _____ la estación.

9. Los árabes construyeron la Alhambra _____ vivir allí.

10. No podemos leer _____ la noche_____ esta lámpara.

20.6.5 Match the phrases from List A with those from List B to make complete sentences.

List A

I. El libro trata
2. Juan se sentó
3. Yo voy a trabajar
4. Quiero cambiar
5. La película acaba
6. El profesor se queja
7. Juan está aprendiendo
8. Empecé
9. Llegaremos a casa
10. Quiero cambiar este abrigo

List B

a) a trabajar hace dos años
b) a pie
c) de un actor famoso
d) a la mesa con nosotros
e) a cocinar
f) hacia las dos de la tarde
g) de empezar
h) por otro
i) de coche
j) de los estudiantes

20.6.6 Complete the sentences with **por** or **para**.

I. Trabajo _____ una empresa de construcción

2. Compro en este supermercado _____ la calidad de los productos.

3. Trabajo _____ placer no _____ dinero.

4. Yo no compro aquí _____ los precios tan caros.

5. Ve la televisión _____ no aburrirse.

6. Trabajo aquí _____ ganar más dinero.

7. Suspendió el examen _____ estudiar poco.

8. Compré un coche grande _____ toda la familia.

9. Estas pastillas son buenas _____ la garganta.

10. El zumo de naranja es excelente _____ el resfriado.

11. Esta fruta es excelente _____ sus vitaminas.

12. El deporte es excelente _____ la salud.

21 Conjunctions *Las conjunciones*

1 ¿Qué es?

Conjunctions are words that link sentences or parts of sentences. They are words such as **y** (*and*), **o** (*or*) and **pero** (*but*). They can link two separate independent sentences:

Juan estudia y Ana trabaja.   *Juan studies and Ana works.*

or subordinate clauses:

Ana dice que la película es buena.   *Ana says that the film is good.*

2 Forms

Copulatives	Disjunctives	Oppositionals	Causals
y, e (*and*)	o, u (*or*)	pero (*but*)	porque, pues (*because*)
ni (*neither . . . nor*)		sino (*but*)	
que (*that*)			

3 Use and position

3.1 Y and e both mean *and*

Y changes to **e** when the following word starts with 'i' or 'hi':

Tomo un café y leo el periódico.   *I have a coffee and read the newspaper.*

María compró un vestido e Isabel compró una falda.   *María bought a dress and Isabel bought a skirt.*

3.2 Ni is the negative form of y, meaning *nor*

When repeated in a sentence (**ni . . . ni**) it means **neither . . . nor**:

No quiere ir al cine ni a cenar en un restaurante.   *He doesn't want to go to the cinema nor to have dinner in a restaurant.*

Ni quiere estudiar ni quiere trabajar.   *He neither wants to study nor to work.*

3.3 O and u mean *or*

O changes to **u** when the following word starts with 'o' or 'ho':

¿Prefieres zumo de naranja o zumo de piña?	*Do you prefer orange juice or pineapple juice?*
Van a venir siete u ocho amigos a comer.	*Seven or eight friends are coming for lunch.*

It can be repeated in the sentence (**o . . . o**) meaning *either . . . or*:

O estudias más o suspenderás el examen.	*Either you study more or you'll fail the exam.*

3.4 pero, sino

Both mean *but*. **Sino** indicates an opposition between two elements and contradicts the first one, which must always be negative:

Trabaja mucho, pero gana poco dinero.	*He works hard, but he earns little money.*
No está enfermo, sino cansado.	*He's not ill, but tired.*
No es marrón, sino negro.	*It isn't brown, but black.*

3.4.1

Note: be careful not to confuse **sino** with **si no**. **Si no** is two separate words and is used in conditional sentences, meaning **if not**.

Si no vamos al cine, iremos al teatro.	*If we don't go to the cinema we'll go to the theatre.*
No vamos al cine, sino al teatro.	*We aren't going to the cinema, but to the theatre.*

3.5 que

Que means *that*. It may link two sentences or introduce a subordinate sentence. It is often followed by a subjunctive:

Me ha dicho que llega mañana.	*He told me that he is arriving tomorrow.*
Quiero que vengas.	*I'd like you to come.* *(lit: I'd like that you should come)*

3.6 porque

This means *because*, and it links the main sentence with a subordinate causal sentence:

No como la sopa porque está fría.	*I'm not eating the soup because it's cold.*
No voy a salir porque hace frío.	*I'm not going out because it's cold.*

3.6.1 porque and por qué

Remember not to confuse **porque** (*because*) with the question word **por qué** (*why*): the latter is two separate words with an accent on **qué**.

A: ¿Por qué no vienes?	*Why aren't you coming?*
B: Porque no quiero.	*Because I don't want to.*

4 Gramática práctica

21.4.1 Match the phrases from List A with those of List B and add the appropriate conjunctions: **y (e), o (u), ni, pero, sino, que** or **porque**.

List A	List B
1. Vine con Ana	a) es muy caro
2. Trabajo en una tienda	b) está lloviendo
3. Llegaré esta tarde	c) estudio por las noches
4. No quiero tomar primer plato	d) hay clase mañana
5. Me gusta este abrigo	e) Isabel
6. No estoy enfadado	f) mañana por la tarde
7. El profesor dice	g) otro más barato
8. No vamos al parque	h) postre
9. No sé si prefieres éste	i) triste

21.4.2 Put the correct conjunctions in the right place.

Pepe me dijo este pueblo es muy bonito muy tranquilo podemos ir a la playa a la montaña en poco tiempo está muy cerca de las dos. A mí me gusta la playa mi marido prefiere la montaña, mis hijos este año no quieren ir de vacaciones a la playa a la montaña, al extranjero. Dicen quieren visitar Italia Inglaterra. También van a viajar por Alemania Holanda, otros países del norte de Europa.

5 Más allá

5.1 pues

It also means *because*, and it links the main sentence with a subordinate causal sentence:

Voy a comprar un regalo a mi madre pues es su cumpleaños.	*I'm going to buy a gift for my mother because it's her birthday.*
Aprobará los exámenes pues estudia mucho.	*He will pass the exams because he studies a lot.*

Note: **pues** can also mean *so* or *in that case*:

A: Estudio mucho.	*I study a lot.*
B: Pues aprobarás los exámenes.	*So / In that case you will pass the exams.*

5.2 mas

This has the same meaning as **pero**. It is used less frequently, although you might see it in written Spanish. It has no accent and musn't be confused with **más** (more). Compare the following:

Lo busqué, mas no lo encontré.	*I looked for it but I couldn't find it.*
No lo busqué más.	*I didn't look for it any more.*

5.3 Other conjunctive / adverbial expression

Note that the ones more used in spoken language are **sin embargo, aunque** and **menos**.

5.3.1 *por lo tanto* (therefore)

No tiene dinero, por lo tanto no puede
  ir de vacaciones.

He has no money, therefore
* he can't go on holiday.*

5.3.2 *We can also use por eso* (because of that):

No tiene dinero, por eso no puede
  ir de vacaciones.

He has no money, and because
* of that he can't go on holiday.*

5.3.3 *sin embargo* (but, however)

No tiene dinero, sin embargo irá
  de vacaciones.

He has no money, but he'll go
* on holiday.*

5.3.4 *no obstante* (nevertherless)

No tiene dinero, no obstante irá
  de vacaciones.

He has no money, nevertheless he'll
* go on holiday.*

5.3.5 *aunque* (although); *a pesar de que* (despite, in spite of)

Aunque no tiene dinero, irá
  de vacaciones.

Although he has no money,
* he'll go on holiday.*

A pesar de que no tiene dinero, irá
  de vacaciones.

Despite having no money,
* he'll go on holiday.*

5.3.6 *excepto, menos* (with the exception of)

Vendrá toda mi familia, menos mi
  hermana mayor.

All my family will come, except my
* older sister.*

Estaré en casa toda la semana excepto
  el lunes por la tarde.

I'll be at home all week except
* Monday afternoon.*

6 Más práctica

---

sin embargo   aunque   excepto   no obstante   pues   a pesar de menos   por lo tanto

21.6.1 Complete the sentences using the expressions from the box.

1. Voy de vacaciones esta semana _____ no tengo clase hasta el lunes.
2. Todos mis amigos vinieron a la fiesta _____ Luis.
3. Aprobó todos los exámenes, _____ el de matemáticas.
4. No trabaja y _____ no gana dinero.
5. Está enfermo, _____ ha ido a trabajar.
6. _____ que gana mucho dinero, nunca tiene nada.
7. Llegaré tarde, _____ te llamaré al llegar.
8. _____ hace ejercicio todos los días, está bastante gordo.

22 Word order

1 ¿Qué es?

Word order in Spanish is very flexible. The different elements of a sentence can appear in different positions to change the emphasis.

1.1 Statements

In the following sentence, the subject appears before the verb:

Luis estudia mucho. *Luis studies a lot.*

But we can also say:

Estudia mucho Luis.

In the second example the emphasis is on **estudia** (*he studies*).

1.2 Questions

In questions the verb is usually placed before the subject:

¿Tiene Juan el dinero? *Does Juan have the money?*

Notice that the object follows the subject.
The object can also appear before the subject:

¿Tiene el dinero Juan?

1.3 Intonation

Very often, especially in spoken Spanish, the question form is the same as the affirmative form and it is the intonation that differentiates the two.

In the written form we know which is a question because of the inverted question mark at the beginning of the sentence.

Pedro sale contigo. *Pedro is going out with you.*
¿Pedro sale contigo? *Is Pedro going out with you?*

or

Sale Pedro contigo.
¿Sale Pedro contigo?

Remember that in questions the intonation in the sentence usually goes up at the end:

¿Sale Pedro contigo?

2 Other words and expressions

2.1

Any word or expression which is part of the clause can go at the beginning of the sentence, depending on the emphasis we want to give to it.

Juan viene mañana.   *Juan is coming tomorrow.*

or

Mañana viene Juan.   *Tomorrow, Juan is coming.*

In the first sentence the emphasis is on **Juan** and in the second it is on **mañana**.

2.2

Notice the different ways of saying the same thing in the following versions of what is essentially the same sentence:

Juan desayuna todos los días a las siete.	*Juan has breakfast every day at seven.*
Todos los días Juan desayuna a las siete.	*Every day Juan has breakfast at seven.*
A las siete, todos los días, desayuna Juan.	*At seven, every day, Juan has breakfast.*
A las siete desayuna Juan todos los días.	*At seven Juan has breakfast every day.*
A las siete desayuna todos los días Juan.	*At seven he has breakfast every day, does Juan.*

2.3

There are some rules, however.

2.3.1

The negative **no** must always come before the verb:

Juan no viene hoy.   *Juan isn't coming today.*
No viene Juan hoy.
Hoy no viene Juan.

2.3.2

It is not possible for any words to appear between the auxiliary verb and the participle in compound verbs:

Juan no <u>ha venido</u> aún.   *Juan hasn't come yet.*
Aún no <u>ha venido</u> Juan.
Juan aún no <u>ha venido</u>.

2.3.3

Adverbs and adverbial phrases go immediately before or after the word they modify:

María siempre estudia por la noche.   *María always studies at night.*
María estudia siempre por la noche.

2.3.4

 For other word order rules, see Unit 9 on personal pronouns, Unit 19 on negatives and Unit 6 on adjectives.

3 Gramática práctica

22.3.1 Reorder the sentences in these dialogues.

1.
A: ¿quieres al ir hoy conmigo cine?
B: gusta cine me no el
A: ¿cartas las quieres a jugar?
B: cartas las sí me jugar gusta a

2.
A: ¿jugar fútbol quieres al?
B: gusta el me fútbol no
A: ¿música escuchar prefieres?
B: bueno gusta me sí música la

22.3.2 Write questions for these answers.

Example: Yo salgo de la oficina a las tres. > ¿Sales (tú) de la oficina a las tres?

1. Nosotros vamos de compras esta tarde.
2. Ellos vendrán por la mañana.
3. Tú fuiste a la playa.
4. Ella compró mucha ropa en esta tienda.
5. Yo tengo un apartamento en la playa.
6. Mis padres vendrán mañana.

23 Verbs *Los verbos*

1 ¿Qué es?

A verb is a word that describes an action (to speak, to run) or a state (to live, to love).

Here are some examples of Spanish verbs: **hablar** *to speak*; **comer** *to eat*; **vivir** *to live*.

2 Form

2.1 The infinitive

This is the form of the verb we find in the dictionary, without conjugation. It is the basic form of the verb.

English verbs in the infinitive form start with *to*: **to** *speak,* **to** *eat,* **to** *live*.

In Spanish, the basic or infinitive form of the verb comes with one of three different endings:

-ar	**hablar, trabajar**	*to speak, to work*
-er	**comer, beber**	*to eat, to drink*
-ir	**vivir, escribir**	*to live, to write*

These different verb types are all conjugated in a slightly different way.

2.2 Tenses and endings

The tense of a verb indicates the time at which something is done. This may be in the past, in the present or in the future.

Different tenses are formed by changing the endings of the verb. Within each tense the endings change to tell us which person (I, you, he / she etc.) is referred to.

These endings follow a pattern, so we can use them for different verbs.

2.2.1

Tenses are formed by taking away the endings of the infinitive form of the verb, **-ar, -er, -ir**, which leaves what we call the stem of the verb:

habl(~~ar~~), com(~~er~~), viv(~~ir~~):

and by adding to the stem the correct endings for each tense to indicate when the action takes place and who is carrying it out.

Infinitive	Stem	Tenses	
hablar	habl-	Hablo español.	I speak Spanish.
comer	com-	Comió a las dos.	He ate at two.
vivir	viv-	Vivían en Madrid.	They used to live in Madrid.

2.2.2

There are two exceptions to the way we form the tense endings: the future and the conditional. In these cases the endings are added to the complete infinitive form:

hablar

hablar + é / ás / á, etc.	*I / you / he, she, you will speak.*
hablar + ía / ías / ía, etc.	*I / you / he, she, you would speak.*

2.2.3

Spanish has two kinds of tense, simple and compound.

Simple: where the verb consists of one word:

hablaron   *they spoke*

Compound: where the verb consists of two words:

han hablado   *they have spoken*

2.3 Person

The person of the verb indicates who is carrying out the action of the verb:

Person	Singular	Plural
1st	yo (*I*)	nosotros / nosotras (*we*)
2nd	tú (*you*)	vosotros / vosotras (*you*)
3rd	él (*he*), ella (*she*), usted (*you* formal)	ellos / ellas (*they*), ustedes (*you* formal)

Note that in most cases, the verb endings on their own are sufficient to tell us who is the subject of the verb (who is doing the action).

For that reason, **yo, tú** etc. are usually omitted, unless used for emphasis or clarification.

2.4 Mood

This is the word used to describe what we call the 'attitude' of the verb.

Spanish verbs have two moods: indicative and subjunctive.

The indicative is used to state straightforward factual information.

The subjunctive is used to express wishes, doubts, possibilities, etc.

Indicative:

Hago mis deberes.   *I do my homework.*

Subjunctive:

Quiero que hagas los deberes.   *I want you to do your homework.*

24 The present tense *El presente*

1 ¿Qué es?

We use verbs in the present tense to say what we do every day or what we are doing at the moment.

In their infinitive form, all Spanish verbs end in **-ar, -er** or **-ir** (**estudiar**, *to study*; **comer**, *to eat*; **vivir**, *to live*). The Present Tense of regular verbs in Spanish is formed by taking away these infinitive endings, leaving the stem, and adding the present endings to this stem.

2 Forms of the present tense

2.1 Regular verbs

	-ar	**-er**	**-ir**	
	hablar	comer	vivir	
	to speak	*to eat*	*to live*	
(yo)	hablo	como	vivo	*I study / eat / live*
(tú)	hablas	comes	vives	*you . . .*
(él / ella / Vd)	habla	come	vive	*he/she/it/you* (formal)
(nosotros/as)	hablamos	comemos	vivimos	*we . . .*
(vosotros/as)	habláis	coméis	vivís	*you . . .*
(ellos / ellas / Vds)	hablan	comen	viven	*they/you* (formal) *. . .*

Note: the stress is on the stem except in the **nosotros** and **vosotros** forms.

2.2 Irregular verbs

The various irregularities in these verbs have a pattern to them. Generally speaking, the 1st and 2nd persons plural keep the regular pattern and it is the other persons (1st, 2nd and 3rd singular and 3rd plural) that have the changes.

2.2.1 *ser* and *ir*

These are two very common and useful irregular verbs: **ser** and **ir**

	ser *(to be)*	ir *(to go)*
(yo)	soy	voy
(tú)	eres	vas
(él / ella / Vd)	es	va
(nosotros/as)	somos	vamos
(vosotros/as)	sois	vais
(ellos / ellas / Vds)	son	van

Another common irregular verb is **haber: he, has, ha, hemos, habéis, han**

Haber is mostly used as an auxiliary with other verbs, e.g. **he terminado** (I've finished), **has comido** (you've eaten), and in the special impersonal form (formed from the third person): **hay** (*there is, there are*).

2.2.2 *Irregular stem-changing verbs*

Most irregularities in the present tense occur in the stem, while the endings are the same as those of the regular verbs.

Notice that, in all these verbs, the changes to the stem occur in the 1st, 2nd and 3rd person singular and the 3rd person plural.

There are various types of stem-changing verbs.

2.2.3 *Verbs that change the vowel:* e > ie

	empezar *(to start)*	querer *(to want)*	preferir *(to prefer)*
(yo)	empiezo	quiero	prefiero
(tú)	empiezas	quieres	prefieres
(él / ella / Vd)	empieza	quiere	prefiere
(nosotros/as)	empezamos	queremos	preferimos
(vosotros/as)	empezáis	queréis	preferís
(ellos / ellas / Vds)	empiezan	quieren	prefieren

Other verbs that follow the pattern **e > ie** are:

-ar:
pensar (*to think*) **pienso** . . .
cerrar (*to close*) **cierro** . . .;
comenzar (*to begin*) **comienzo** . . .
-er:
entender (*to understand*) **entiendo** . . .
perder (*to lose*) **pierdo** . . .

-ir:
divertir (*to enjoy*) **divierto** . . .
sentir (*to feel / be sorry*) **siento** . . .

The impersonal verbs **nevar** (*to snow*) **nieva**; **helar** (*to freeze*) **hiela**.

2.2.4 Verbs that change the vowel: u > ue and o > ue

	jugar (to play)	**volver (to return)**	**dormir (to sleep)**
(yo)	juego	vuelvo	duermo
(tú)	juegas	vuelves	duermes
(él / ella / Vd)	juega	vuelve	duerme
(nosotros/as)	jugamos	volvemos	dormimos
(vosotros/as)	jugáis	volvéis	dormís
(ellos / ellas / Vds)	juegan	vuelven	duermen

Other verbs that follow the pattern **o, u > ue** are:

-ar:
probar (*to prove, to test, to try on, to taste*) **pruebo** . . .
contar (*to count, to tell a story*) **cuento** . . .
encontrar (*to find*) **encuentro** . . .
recordar (*to remember / to remind*) **recuerdo** . . .
costar (*to cost*) **cuesta (mucho dinero)**
-er:
poder (*to be able*) **puedo** . . .
doler (*to hurt, to ache*) **duele** (*it hurts*)
oler (*to smell*) adds an 'h' to the irregular forms: **huelo, hueles, huele, olemos, oléis, huelen**
-ir:
morir (*to die*) **muero** . . .

The impersonal verb **llover** (*to rain*) **llueve**

2.2.5 Verbs that change the vowel: e > i

pedir (*to ask for, to order*) **pido, pides, pide, pedimos, pedís, piden**

Other verbs that follow the pattern **e > i** are:
repetir (*to repeat*) **repito** . . .
seguir (*to continue*) **sigo** . . .
servir (*to serve*) **sirvo** . . .
vestir (*to dress*) **visto** . . .

2.2.6 Stem-changing verbs: verbs that change the consonant

This happens only in the first person singular (the rest of the forms are regular) in the following verbs:

c > zc
traducir (*to translate*) **traduzco**, **traduces, traduce, traducimos, traducís, traducen**

Other verbs:

conducir (*to drive*) **conduzco, conduces** . . .
parecer (*to appear*) **aparezco, apareces** . . .
ofrecer (*to offer*) **ofrezco, ofreces** . . .
nacer (*to be born*) **nazco, naces** . . .

c > g hacer (*to make / do*) **hago, haces, hace, hacemos, hacéis, hacen**

l > lg salir (*to leave / go out*) **salgo, sales, sale, salimos, salís, salen**

n > ng poner (*to put*) **pongo, pones, pone, ponemos, ponéis, ponen**

2.2.7 Verbs that add -ig to the 1st person singular, while the rest of the persons are regular

traer (*to bring*) **traigo, traes, trae, traemos, traéis, traen**
caer (*to fall*) **caigo, caes, cae, caemos, caéis, caen**
oír (*to hear, to listen*) **oigo, oyes, oye, oímos, oís, oyen** (note the **i > y** change)

2.2.8 Verbs that add -g in the 1st person and also have a vowel change in the rest of the forms (except 1st and 2nd plural)

tener (*to have*) tengo, tienes, tiene, tenemos, tenéis, tienen
venir (*to come*) vengo, vienes, viene, venimos, venís, vienen
decir (*to say, to tell*) digo, dices, dice, decimos, decís, dicen

2.2.9 Verbs that change completely in the first person only

saber (*to know [how to]*) **sé, sabes, sabe, sabemos, sabéis, saben**

2.2.10 Verbs that add -y in the first person; the rest of the forms are regular*

estar (*to be*) **estoy, estás, está, estamos, estáis, están**
dar (*to give*) **doy, das, da, damos, dais, dan**

---

 *See also: **ser: soy** and **ir: voy** (point 2.2.1 above). But these are irregular in all forms.

---

3 Uses of the present tense

3.1

The present tense is used to express an action that is happening at the moment:

A: **¿Qué haces?**   *What are you doing?*
B: **Preparo la cena.**   *I'm preparing dinner.*

A: ¿Adónde vas?   *Where are you going?*
B: Voy al cine.   *I'm going to the cinema.*

3.2

The present tense is used to talk about habitual actions:

Voy al cine todos los domingos.   *I go to the cinema every Sunday.*

3.3

The present tense is used to describe your current status, with no time limit, known as **presente durativo**:

Vivo en Madrid.   *I live in Madrid.*
Trabajo en una tienda.   *I work in a shop.*

3.4

The present tense can refer to the future:

El tren sale a las cinco de la tarde. *The train leaves at five this afternoon.*
Voy a Australia.   *I'm going to Australia.*

3.4.1

When we are arranging to do something in the future we often use the present tense in Spanish. It's often indicated by the context and / or the use of a time adverb. It indicates that what we are discussing is certain to happen.

¿Qué hacemos   *What shall we do (this evening)?*
  (esta tarde)?   *(lit: What do we do?)*
¿Adónde vamos mañana?   *Where shall we go tomorrow?*
¿Dónde quedamos?   *Where shall we meet?*

3.4.2

It also expresses the immediate future:
A ¿Vienes o no?   *Are you coming or not?*
B: Sí, ahora voy / ya voy.   *Yes, I'm coming now.*

4 Gramática práctica

24.4.1 Write the singular form of the verb.

Example: Nosotros jugamos al tenis. > Yo juego al tenis.

1. Nosotros venimos a verte todos los sábados. >
2. Vosotros jugáis al fútbol.
3. Ellos son profesores.
4. Nosotros sabemos tocar el piano.
5. Vosotros conducís muy mal.
6. Nosotros no oímos nada.
7. Ellos van al cine.
8. Nosotros pedimos un café.
9. Nosotros decimos que sí.

24.4.2 Write the correct verb form for the person given.

yo ser – tú poner – vosotros empezar – ellos preferir – yo jugar – nosotros comer – tú salir – vosotros ir – tú ser – yo volver – ellos dormir – tú encontrar – nosotros seguir – yo traducir – nosotros conducir – ellos repetir – yo hacer – vosotros venir – yo decir – tú venir – vosotros estar – yo dar

5 Más allá

5.1 Other irregularities

Some verbs simply have irregularities due to the spelling changes needed to preserve the sound.

 See Unit 2 Section 2.

5.1.1 Only in the first person

-ger, -gir > j
coger (*to get, to take, to grab*) **cojo, coges***
dirigir (*to direct*) **dirijo, diriges**
-guir > go
distinguir (*to distinguish*) **distingo, distingues**
-cer, -cir > zo
convencer (*to convince*) **convenzo, convences**

*In Latin America, use **tomar** instead.

5.1.2 In all persons (except 1st and 2nd plural)

-uir > uyo (add a 'y')
construir (*to build*) **construyo, construyes, construye, construimos, construís, construyen**

Other similar verbs:

destruir, incluir, influir.

5.1.3 Irregular in the first person

caber (*to fit in, to accommodate*): **<u>quepo</u>, cabes, cabe, cabemos, cabéis, caben**

5.2 Other uses of the present tense

5.2.1 The permanent or general present:

cinco y tres son ocho   *five and three are eight*

5.2.2 To say you've been doing something for a certain time

Enseña en la universidad desde 1999.	*He has been teaching (lit: teaches) at the university since 1999.*
Estudio español desde hace dos años.	*I've been studying (lit: I study) Spanish for two years.*

5.2.3 To express the past

This is mainly used in literary and journalistic language and to express historical events:

Antonio Banderas nace en 1960.	*Antonio Banderas was (lit: is) born in 1960.*

5.2.4

It can also be used in spoken language when telling something that has happened and that we want to emphasise by making the action more immediate:

El otro día me pasó algo horrible: Llego a casa, abro la puerta y encuentro a un ladrón.
The other day something awful happened to me. I arrive home, open the door and find a thief.

5.2.5

It can act as an imperative, to express an order or give instructions:

Tú vienes aquí ahora mismo.	*You come here right now.*
Tú te callas.	*You be quiet.*
Ahora pones el aceite y fríes la carne.	*Now you add the oil and fry the meat.*

5.2.6 Present in conditional sentences

 See Unit 32 on conditional sentences.

Si quieres, vamos al cine.	*If you like, we can go to the cinema.*
Si vienes pronto, iremos al cine.	*If you come early, we'll go to the cinema.*

6 Más práctica

24.6.1 Fill in the gaps using the following verbs in the present tense:
merendar, cenar, comer, tomar, levantarse, salir, volver, desayunar, acostarse

1. Generalmente, nosotros _____ en casa a mediodía.
2. La gente _____ a trabajar por la tarde, a las cuatro más o menos.
3. Los fines de semana, por la mañana, nosotros _____ más tarde y _____ a las once.

4. Por la noche vosotros _____ algo ligero.

5. A veces Ana y Luis _____ a cenar a un restaurante.

6. El fin de semana nosotros _____ muy tarde.

7. ¿Vosotros _____ café o té?

8. Mis hijos _____ chocolate con churros.

24.6.2 Housework. Write sentences using the given person of the present tense, then translate them into English.

1. yo hacer la cama
2. nosotros poner la mesa
3. vosotras quitar la mesa
4. ellos fregar los platos
5. mi madre fregar el suelo
6. tú limpiar el polvo
7. él pasar la aspiradora
8. vosotros planchar la ropa
9. nosotros barrer la cocina
10. yo sacar la basura

25 Reflexive verbs *Verbos reflexivos*

1 ¿Qué es?

Many everyday verbs are reflexive. They are formed when the subject and the object of the verb are the same, or when the verb is an action on the self. English equivalents are verbs like *to get up* (to get one**self** up), *to shower* (to give one**self** a shower), *to get dressed*. Although the reflexive element in English is absent, in Spanish it must always appear.

A: ¿A qué hora <u>te</u> levantas?　　*What time do you get up?*
B: <u>Me</u> levanto a las siete.　　　*I get up at seven.*
　　　　　　　　　　　　　　(lit: I get myself up at seven.)

A: ¿Cómo <u>se</u> llama?　　　　　*What's his name? (lit: What does*
　　　　　　　　　　　　　　　he call himself?)
B: <u>Se</u> llama Gustavo.　　　　　*He's called Gustavo.*

2 Form

2.1

One of the most commonly used reflexive verbs is **llamarse**. This literally means *to call oneself*, and is the verb we use to tell people who we are or to ask another person for his / her name.

A reflexive verb is identified by the reflexive pronoun **se** attached to the end of the infinitive form (**llamarse**).

The reflexive pronoun (**me, te, se, nos, os, se**) is placed in front of the conjugated form of the verb and agrees in person and number with the verb form, for example:

Yo <u>me</u> llamo Juan.　　　　　*I call myself Juan. / My name's Juan.*
Mi madre <u>se</u> llama　　　　*My mother is called (calls herself)*
　Pilar.　　　　　　　　　*Pilar.*

llamarse (present indicative)				
yo	<u>me</u> llamo	nosotros, nosotras	<u>nos</u> llamamos
tú	<u>te</u> llamas	vosotros, vosotras	<u>os</u> llamáis
usted	<u>se</u> llama	ustedes	<u>se</u> llaman
él, ella	<u>se</u> llama	ellos, ellas	<u>se</u> llaman

2.2

For the form of more regular reflexive verbs see **levantarse**, below.

Some common reflexive verbs are stem-changing verbs, e.g.:

despertarse: me despierto (*I wake up*); **vestirse: me visto** (*I get dressed*).

	levantarse	**despertarse**	**vestirse**
	(*to get up*)	(*to wake up*)	(*to get dressed*)
(yo)	me levanto	me despierto	me visto
(tú)	te levantas	te despiertas	te vistes
(él / ella / Vd)	se levanta	se despierta	se viste
(nosotros/as)	nos levantamos	nos despertamos	nos vestimos
(vosotros/as)	os levantáis	os despertáis	os vestís
(ellos / ellas / Vds)	se levantan	se despiertan	se visten

2.3

In the infinitive form the reflexive pronoun appears at the end of the verb:
levantarse:

La niña no quiere levantarse   *The girl doesn't want to get up*
  porque está cansada.   *because she is tired.*

2.4

In some cases, the pronoun can be separated from the infinitive when used colloquially or for effect with a verb like **querer**:

¿Quieres levantarte?   *Do you want to get up?*
¿Te quieres levantar?

2.5

When it is conjugated, the pronoun appears before the verb:

Me levanto tarde los domingos.   *I get up late on Sundays.*
¿Te levantas?   *Are you getting up?*

2.6

With the imperative and the gerund, the reflexive pronoun appears at the end of the verb:

¡Arréglate!   *Get (yourself) ready!*
¡Levántate!   *Get up!*
Juan está duchándose.   *Juan is having a shower.*

Note the addition of the accent in these cases in order to retain the stress on the second syllable.

 See Unit 10 Section 3.

3 Use

3.1

The reflexive verb **llamarse** (lit: *to call oneself*) can be contrasted with the non-reflexive verb **llamar** (*to call*):

Me llamo Juan.   *My name's Juan.(I call myself Juan.)*
Llamo a mis padres los fines de semana.   *I call my parents at the weekends.*

Also compare:

Me acuesto a las doce.   *I go to bed at twelve.*
      (lit: I put myself to bed at twelve.)
Acuesto a los niños a las ocho.   *I put the children to bed at eight.*

In the first example, the speaker is talking about himself / herself, and in the second about an action carried out on the children.

3.2

Common reflexive verbs are:

acostarse	*to go to bed*
arreglarse	*to get ready (to go out)*
bañarse	*to bathe*
caerse	*to fall over*
cambiarse	*to change (clothes)*
cortarse	*to cut oneself*
darse (un golpe)	*to give oneself (a bump)*
despertarse	*to wake up*
lavarse	*to get washed*
levantarse	*to get up*
llamarse	*to call oneself*
peinarse	*to comb (one's hair)*
romperse (la pierna)	*to break (one's leg)*
vestirse	*to get dressed*

3.3

Some common verbs can be used in the reflexive form to change the meaning slightly:

irse

The verb **ir** can be used in the reflexive form when we want to add emphasis to the person who is going:

¡Vete!   *Go!*
Me voy.   *I'm going.*

hacerse

Adding the reflexive pronoun to **hacer** gives it the meaning *to become*:

Voy a hacerme abogado.   *I'm going to be(come) a lawyer.*

 See Unit 41 on pronominal verbs.

4 Gramática práctica

 See Unit 10 for more exercises.

25.4.1 Complete the sentences with the given person of the verb.

Example: Yo (levantarse) pronto > Yo me levanto pronto.

1. Tú levantarse pronto.
2. Nosotros despertarse a las cinco de la mañana.
3. Ellos acostarse muy tarde.
4. Vosotros vestirse con el uniforme de trabajo.
5. La niña lavarse los dientes.
6. Ellos bañarse en la piscina.
7. Yo peinarse con una coleta.
8. Tú cambiarse de ropa para salir.
9. Nosotros arreglarse para la fiesta.

26 Gustar and similar verbs

1 ¿Qué es?

We use the verb **gustar** to talk about things we like or dislike.

Gustar literally means *to please*, so when we say:

Me gusta la paella. (*I like paella.*)

its literal meaning is *Paella pleases me*.

2 Form

This is a special construction which is formed in a different way from its English equivalent.

In the sentence **Me gusta la playa** (*I like the beach*), **la playa** is the subject and **me** is the object, so the literal translation is: *The beach pleases me*.

2.1 Gustar is always used in the 3rd person singular or plural

The singular form is used when we like one thing:

Me gusta el campo.   *I like the countryside.*

The plural form is used when we like more than one thing:

Me gustan las montañas.   *I like mountains.*

Gustar is always preceded by a personal pronoun and followed by a noun (the object or person we like) in the singular or plural: **la fruta, los plátanos** etc.

Personal pronoun	+ verb (gustar)	+ noun
me / te / le / nos / os / les	gusta	la playa
	gustan	las montañas

For example, if we want to say *I* like something we use **me** as the object pronoun.

If we say that *he* or *she* (or **usted**) *likes* something, we use **le** as the object pronoun:

Le gusta el arte.   *He likes art.*
Le gustan los deportes.   *He likes sports.*

2.2 Followed by the infinitive

If we want to say that we like doing something, as opposed to liking an object or a person, **gustar** is followed by the verb in the infinitive: **comer, salir** etc.

In this case **gustar** is always in the singular even if it's followed by more than one infinitive.

Personal pronoun	+ verb (gustar)	+ verb(s) in the infinitive
me / te / le / nos / os / les	+ gusta	nadar, jugar al fútbol y pasear

2.2.1 Note: sometimes it's possible to put the noun or the infinitive before gustar:

Los plátanos me gustan mucho.   (lit:) Bananas I like a lot.
Jugar al fútbol me gusta bastante.   (lit:) Playing football I like quite a lot.

2.3 Negatives

To form the negative we simply place **no** before the pronoun:

No me gusta la carne.   I don't like meat.
No le gusta jugar al tenis.   He doesn't like playing tennis.

2.4 Questions

If we want to ask someone if he / she likes something, we have to change the object pronoun:

¿Te gusta la paella?   Do you like paella?
                          (lit: Does paella please you?)

2.4.1

We can ask questions in the negative to express **Don't you like . . .?**:

¿No te gusta la leche?   Don't you like milk?
¿No les gusta la ópera?   Don't they like opera?

3

The following verbs are used in a similar way to **gustar**:

apasionar, apetecer, doler, encantar, faltar, importar, interesar, molestar, quedar.

Me encantan los deportes.   I love sport.
No me apetece salir esta noche.   I don't feel like going out tonight.
Le apasiona el arte.   Art impassions him.
                          (He's passionate about art)

Me duele la cabeza.   My head hurts.
Nos faltan dos días para ir   There are two days left before
   de vacaciones.   we go on holiday.
No me queda dinero.   I have no money left.
No me importa.   I don't mind.

4 Emphasis with pronouns

4.1 a + personal pronoun

In order to clarify or specify the person who likes something, or simply for emphasis, we can add the preposition **a** + a personal pronoun at the beginning of the sentence:

 See Unit 9 point 6.5.6 on personal pronouns used with prepositions.

A + personal pronoun + (prep.) (indirect object)			personal pronoun + verb (gustar) + what is liked	
A	+	mí	me	
		ti	te	
		él / ella / usted	le	gusta(n) encanta(n) / interesa(n), etc
		nosotros	nos	
		vosotros	os	
		ellos / ellas / ustedes	les	

A mí me gusta el cine.	*I like the cinema.*
A ti te gustan las películas de ciencia ficción.	*You like science fiction films.*
A él / ella / usted le encanta el mar.	*He / She / You love(s) the sea.*
A nosotros nos interesa la política.	*We are interested in politics.*
A vosotros os interesan los documentales.	*You're interested in documentaries.*
A ellos / ellas / ustedes les gusta pasear.	*They / You like walking.*

4.2

The 3rd person pronouns (**él, ella, ellos, ellas**) can be replaced by the name of the person:

A María le gusta el teatro.	*María likes the theatre.*
A Luisa y a José les interesa la historia.	*Luisa and José are interested in history.*

5 Questions and negatives

5.1 Questions

To ask a question you can simply use an affirmative sentence and change the intonation to make it into a question:

¿A ella le gusta el cine?   *Does she like the cinema?*

Or you can put **a ella** after the verb:

¿Le gusta a ella el cine?

5.2 Negatives

In the negative form, **no** always appears after **a mí / a ti / a él**, etc.

A mí no me gusta el cine.   *I don't like the cinema.*
A nosotros no nos gustan los deportes.   *We don't like sport.*

6 **Gustar** and similar verbs can be used in other tenses, following the same structure:

Antes me gustaba mucho correr.   *Before, I used to like running a lot.*
Me gustó mucho la película   *I liked the film we saw yesterday a*
   que vimos ayer.   *lot.*
¿Te ha gustado la cena?   *Did you enjoy dinner?*

7 Gramática práctica

26.7.1 Write sentences with the appropriate form of **gustar**.

Example: yo, la música > Me gusta la música.

1 ella, el teatro 2 tú, las revistas 3 yo, los deportes 4 ustedes, ver la televisión
5 nosotros, jugar al fútbol 6 usted, las películas cómicas 7 él, el cine
8 vosotros, ir de excursión 9 ellos, los pasteles

26.7.2 Write the sentences using an emphatic pronoun.

Example: (tú) / gustar / deporte > A ti te gusta el deporte.

1. (yo) / encantar / canciones románticas
2. (mis amigos) / gustar / salir a cenar
3. (mi amiga Ana) / gustar / bailar
4. (mis hermanas) / encantar / la música clásica
5. ¿ (vosotros) / gustar / las películas de misterio?
6. (tú) / encantar / los libros de historia
7. (nosotros) / no / gustar / la televisión
8. (mi madre) / interesa / el arte
9. (yo) / no / importar / trabajar / el fin de semana

8 Más allá

8.1 me gustaría

Gustar and some similar verbs follow the same pattern in the conditional form:

me gustaría, me interesaría, (no) me importaría.

They are always followed by an infinitive.

Me gustaría ir al cine.	*I would like to go to the cinema.*
Me encantaría comer chocolate ahora.	*I'd love to have chocolate now.*
Me interesaría trabajar en esta empresa.	*I'd be interested in working in this company.*
No me importaría pasar un año en esta ciudad.	*Spending a year in this city wouldn't bother me.*

8.2 Saying what you like more or less

When we want to say what we like doing *more* or *less* we use the following expressions with **gustar: me gusta más / menos:**

Me gusta más el rugby.	*I like rugby more.*
Me gusta menos el tenis.	*I like tennis less.*

8.3 lo que más and lo que menos

When we want to say what we like *most* or *least*, we use these expressions:

Lo que más me gusta es nadar.	*What I like most is swimming.*
Lo que más me gusta es el sol.	*What I like best is sunshine.*
Lo que más me gusta son las vacaciones.	*What I like best is holidays.*
Lo que menos me gusta es correr.	*What I like least is running.*
Lo que menos me gusta es el mal tiempo.	*What I like least is bad weather.*
Lo que menos me gusta son los problemas del tráfico.	*What I like least are the traffic problems.*

*Note that **lo** and **gusta** don't change.

9 Más práctica

26.9.1 Complete the dialogue with the following verbs in the correct form.

producir   encantar   dar   causar   importar   gustar   sentar   apetecer

Arturo: ¿Te _____ir a cenar a algún restaurante?
Carmen: No, no me _____. No me _____comer en los restaurantes,.
Arturo: ¿Te _____cenar en casa?
Carmen: Sí, me _____más cenar en casa.
Arturo: ¿Qué te _____cenar?
Carmen: Me _____ mucho pasta con salsa de carne. ¡Me _____la pasta!
Arturo: Pero la pasta me _____ dolor de estómago.

Carmen: Pues, no sé . . . ¿Te _____ un poco de jamón serrano y queso?

Arturo: No, el jamón por la noche me _____ mucha sed y el queso me _____ pesadillas.*

Carmen: ¿Te _____ más una paella?

Arturo: Sí, no me _____ cenar una paella. Es lo que más me _____ en este momento.

Carmen: Pero por la noche te _____ mal. Mejor no.

*pesadillas = *nightmares*

26.9.2 Write sentences as in the example. Use: **lo que más me gusta es / son**

Example: Yo / la paella > A mí lo que más me gusta es la paella.

1. él / patatas fritas **2.** nosotros / el pescado **3.** yo / el café solo **4.** tú / la verdura **5.** vosotros / la fruta **6.** ella / las naranjas **7.** yo / chocolate **8.** vosotros la tortilla de patata

27 Ser / Estar

1 ¿Qué es?

Ser and **estar** are two verbs meaning *to be* in English. But whereas English only uses the one verb to say, for example: *I am a student* and *I am in the park*,

Spanish uses **ser** in the first: **Soy estudiante**

and **estar** in the second: **Estoy en el parque**.

One or the other of these two verbs is used, depending on the concept and context. Sometimes the use of one or the other can change the meaning of a sentence completely, so it is important to make the right selection:

La señora es elegante.
La chica está muy elegante hoy.

The woman is smart. (always)
The girl is very smart today. (e.g. because she's going to a wedding)

But more generally, there are clearly defined situations and circumstances in which we use **ser** and **estar**, and these can be learnt separately so they cannot be confused. Some can even be learnt as fixed expressions.

2 Form

ser – present tense

yo soy; tú eres; él, ella, usted es; nosotros/as somos; vosotros/as sois; ellos, ellas, ustedes son

estar – present tense

yo estoy; tú estás; él, ella, usted está*; nosotros/as estamos; vosotros/as estáis; ellos, ellas, ustedes están

 For the full conjugation of these verbs see the Verb Tables.

*Note: be careful not to confuse **está**, **esta** and **ésta**:

está is the third person singular of the verb **estar**: **El niño está enfermo.** (*The child is ill.*)

esta is a demonstrative adjective: **esta falda** (*this skirt*)

ésta is a demonstrative pronoun: **me gusta ésta** (*I like this one*)

3 Uses of **ser**

3.1 Grammatical structures with **ser**

Ser is always used before the following:

3.1.1 a noun

A ¿Quién es?	Who is it?
B Es Ana.	It's Ana.

A ¿Qué es?	What is it?
B Es un libro.	It's a book.

3.1.2 a noun phrase

Es la mujer de mi hermano.	She is the wife of my brother.
Es el chico que va a clase conmigo.	He's the boy who goes to class with me.

3.1.3 a subject personal pronoun

A: ¿Eres tú?	Is it you?
B: Soy yo.	It's me.

3.1.4 possessives

Son mis padres.	They're my parents.
El piso es de mi hermano.	The flat is my brother's.

3.1.5 numerals

Son tres hermanos.	They are three brothers.

3.1.6 demonstratives

Mi amiga es esa chica rubia.	My friend is that blonde girl.

3.1.7 indefinites

A: ¿Es algo importante?	Is it anything important?
B: No, no es nada.	No, it's nothing.

A: ¿Es alguno de éstos?	Is it any of these?
B: No es ninguno de ésos.	No, it's none of those.

3.1.8 prepositions

Luis es de Madrid.	Luis is from Madrid.
La camisa es de algodón.	The shirt is made of cotton.
El regalo es para mi madre.	The gift is for my mother.
Esta muñeca no es para jugar.	This doll is not for playing with.

3.1.9 adverbs of time

Es tarde.	It's late.
Es hoy.	It's today.

 For **ser** + adjectives of quality see Section 5 below.

3.2 Functions and meaning of **ser**

We can use **ser** in the following cases:

3.2.1 To express identity, say who you and others are, give your name and title and talk about your family

Es Carmen.	*She's Carmen.*
Soy el señor González.	*I'm Mr Gonzalez.*
Es mi madre.	*She's my mother.*
¿Sois hermanos?	*Are you brothers?*

3.2.2 To say what something is, to identify something

Es una cartera de piel.	*It's a leather wallet.*
Es una película de terror.	*It's a horror film.*

3.2.3 To express profession or position

¿Eres profesora?	*Are you a teacher?*
Es pintor.	*He's a painter.*
El señor Martínez es el director de la empresa.	*Mr Martínez is the director of the company.*
Juan Carlos es el rey de España.	*Juan Carlos is the king of Spain.*

Note: Remember that the noun (or name of a profession, for example) follows the verb without the article **un / una**:

Soy profesor.	*I'm a teacher.*

 See Unit 5 point 3.2.1.

3.2.4 To say where you and others are from and to talk about nationalities

María es española.	*Maria is Spanish.*
Soy de Colombia.	*I'm from Colombia.*
Juan es andaluz, es de Málaga.	*Juan is Andalucian, he's from Malaga.*

3.2.5 To talk about religious, political or artistic affiliation

Mi primo es musulmán.	*My cousin is a Muslim.*
El presidente es socialista.	*The president is a Socialist.*
El cuadro es impresionista.	*The painting is an impressionist work.*

3.2.6 To express possession

La maleta es mía.	*The suitcase is mine.*
El bolso es de Ana.	*The bag is Ana's.*

 See Unit 12 for possessive pronouns.

3.2.7 To say times and dates

Es la una.	*It's one oclock.*
Son las diez y media.	*It's ten thirty.*
Es domingo.	*It's Sunday.*
Hoy es cinco de agosto.*	*Today is the fifth of August.*

*But note:

Estamos a cinco de agosto.	*We are at the fifth of August.*

 See point 4.2.3 below.

 See Unit 17 for telling the time.

3.2.8 Time expressions

3.2.8.1 With days of the week (using an impersonal construction)

Es lunes, mañana es martes.	*It's Monday, tomorrow is Tuesday.*

Note: There is no pronoun as in the English *it*.

3.2.8.2 Other time expressions

Levántate, es tarde.	*Get up, it's late.*
La clase de español es pasado mañana.	*The Spanish class is the day after tomorrow.*

Es mediodía.	*It's midday.*	**Es hoy.**	*It's today.*
Es medianoche.	*It's midnight.*	**Es de día.**	*It's daylight.*
Es tarde.	*It's late.*	**Es de noche.**	*It's dark.*
Es pronto.	*It's too soon.*	**Es mañana.**	*It's tomorrow.*
Es temprano.	*It's early.*	**Fue ayer.**	*It was yesterday.*
Es la madrugada.	*It's today.*		

La fiesta fue ayer.	*The party was yesterday.*

3.2.8.3 With the seasons

Es verano / primavera / otoño / invierno.*	*It's summer / spring / autumn / winter.*
Hace calor porque es verano.	*It's hot because it is summer.*

*Note the different, temporary meaning of:

Estamos en invierno.	*We are in winter.*
Hace frío pero es normal, ¡estamos en invierno!	*It's cold but it's to be expected, we're in winter.*

3.2.9 To express price, quantity and numbers

Son quince euros.	*That costs fifteen euros.*
Son cinco kilos.	*That's five kilos.*
Es mucho dinero.	*It's a lot of money.*
Es el segundo piso.	*It's the second flat.*

3.2.10 *To say what something is made of, and the colour*

Los guantes son de piel, el abrigo es de lana.	*The gloves are of leather, the coat is of wool.*
La chaqueta es de color gris.	*The jacket is a grey colour.*
La camisa es blanca.	*The shirt is white.*

 See Section 5 below for **ser** + adjectives.

3.2.11 *To say what something is for*

A: ¿Para qué son estas pastillas?	*What are these pills for?*
B: Estas pastillas son para la tos.	*These pills are for coughs.*

3.2.12 *To say where something is taking place:*

La comida de Navidad es en casa de mi hermana.	*Christmas dinner is at my sister's house.*

3.2.13 *In set expressions*

Es verdad / es mentira.	*It's true / it's a lie.*

3.3

En breve

We can use **ser** in the following cases:

To talk about:

name and title
family
profession or position
religious, political or artistic affiliation
nationalities
possession
days of the week
times and dates
time expressions and the seasons
price, quantity and numbers
colour

To say:

what something is
where you and others are from
what something is made of
what something is for
where something is taking place

---

4 Uses of **estar**

4.1 Grammatical structures with estar

Estar can be used:

4.1.1 before an adverb

Estoy bien.	*I'm fine*
Estoy mal.	*I'm unwell.*

4.1.2 before a preposition

Estoy en Madrid.	*I'm in Madrid.*
Está a la derecha.	*It's to the right.*
Estoy de vacaciones.	*I'm on holiday.*
Mi madre está con mi hermano.	*My mother is with my brother.*
Juan está por llegar.	*Juan is still to arrive.*
La película está para empezar.	*The film is about to start.*

4.1.3 with a personal pronoun (object)

A: ¿Qué tal me está la chaqueta?	*How is this jacket on me?*
B: Te está muy bien.	*It suits you very well.*

4.1.4

Estar can also be followed by the gerund to form continuous tenses, such as the Present Continuous:

A: ¿Qué estás haciendo?	*What are you doing?*
B: Estoy comiendo una manzana.	*I'm eating an apple.*

4.2 Functions and meanings of estar

We use **estar** in the following cases:

4.2.1 to say how we are or how something is, with the adverbs bien, mal, regular, fatal

A: ¿Qué tal estás?	*How are you?*
B: Estoy regular.	*I'm not bad.*
A: ¿Cómo está tu marido?	*How is your husband?*
B: Mi marido está mal.	*My husband is ill.*
A: ¿Qué tal está la película?	*What's the film like?*
B: Está muy bien.	*It's very good.*

4.2.2 to express location; to ask and say where something is, most commonly when asking and answering the question ¿Dónde está?

A: ¿Dónde está?	*Where is it?*
B: Está en el sur / cerca / lejos.	*It's in the south / near / a long way.*
A: ¿A cuántos kilómetros está?	*How far is it? (lit: at how many kilometres?)*

B: Está a cien kilómetros. — *It's a hundred kilometres away.*

A: ¿Dónde está la estación? — *Where is the station?*
B: Está al final de la calle. — *It's at the end of the street.*
Barcelona está en el noreste de España. — *Barcelona is in the north-east of Spain.*

Mi casa está en la plaza Mayor. — *My house is in Mayor Square.*

4.2.3 With dates, but only in the following structure

A: ¿A qué fecha estamos? — *(lit:) At what date are we?*
B: Estamos a quince de abril. — *(lit:) We are at the fifteenth of April.*

4.2.4 to express duration

A: ¿Cuánto tiempo estarás en la oficina? — *How long will you be in the office?*
B: Estaré cinco horas en la oficina. — *I'll be in the office for five hours.*

4.2.5

To express the meaning *it suits me* or *it fits me / you / him / her*, or to say something doesn't fit (e.g. it's too big, too small, etc.), accompanied by an object personal pronoun: *me, te, le* etc.:

Los pantalones me están grandes. — *The trousers are too big for me.*
Esa falda te está muy bien. — *That skirt fits / suits you.*

 See Unit 9 Section 6 for object pronouns.

4.2.6 with the preposition *para* meaning to be ready for

El vestido estará (listo) para las cinco. — *The dress will be ready for five o'clock.*

La comida estará (preparada) para las dos. — *Lunch will be ready / prepared for two o'clock.*

4.2.7 to express being accompanied, with the preposition *con*

Sara está con su amiga. — *Sara is with her friend.*
Los niños están con la profesora. — *The children are with the teacher.*

4.3 Set expressions with estar

All of the following give an impression of something temporary or of change.

4.3.1 *estar bien* (ok, that's ok)

Sí, está bien todo, gracias. — *Yes, everything is ok, thanks.*

4.3.2 *with the preposition de*

4.3.2.1

estar de vacaciones	*to be on holiday*
Estamos de vacaciones en Suiza.	*We're on holiday in Switzerland.*
estar de viaje	*to be travelling*
El director está de viaje.	*The director is on a trip.*

4.3.2.2

estar de acuerdo	*to be in agreement*
Estoy de acuerdo con esto.	*I'm in agreement (I agree) with this.*

4.3.2.3

estar de moda	*to be in fashion / fashionable*
Estos zapatos están muy de moda este año.	*These shoes are very fashionable this year.*

4.3.3 *with the preposition a in the following expressions*

estar a régimen	*to be on a diet*
Estoy a dieta.	*I'm on a diet.*

For **estar** + adjectives of quality see Section 5 below.

4.4

En breve
We use **estar** in the following cases:

To say:
how we are or how something is (with: **bien, mal**)
it suits me or *it fits me*
to be ready for

To express:
location
being accompanied, with **con**

and in various set expressions (see above).

---

5 Contrasting uses of **ser** and **estar** with adjectives of quality

We use **ser** or **estar** with an adjective of quality, depending on how we perceive that quality.

5.1 ser + adjective

This expresses an inherent quality and permanency: something that cannot change and has never changed. It is used to talk about:

5.1.1 Colours, shapes, stature

Es verde.	*It's green.*
Es cuadrado.	*It's square.*
Somos altos.	*We're tall.*

5.1.2 Personality and character (permanent qualities)

Mi hermano es inteligente y es simpático.	*My brother is intelligent and friendly.*
Los animales son buenos.	*Animals are good.*
Mi hija es muy cariñosa.	*My daughter is very affectionate.*

5.2 estar + adjective

This expresses a physical state or a psychological state or feeling that might change or is the result of a change.

Some adjectives always accompany **estar** as they express a temporary or changeable state:

contento, enfadado, cansado, agotado, vacío, lleno, seco, mojado, roto*, muerto*.

Ana estudia mucho y está cansada, pero está contenta.	*Ana studies a lot and is tired, but she is happy.*
La botella estaba llena ayer, pero hoy está vacía.	*The bottle was full yesterday, but today it's empty.*
Hace frío, la ventana está abierta.	*It's cold, the window is open.*
Llueve mucho y la ropa está mojada.	*It's raining a lot and the clothes are wet.*
Las plantas están secas porque no llueve.	*The plants are dry because it's not raining.*

*Important: with the adjectives **roto** (*broken*) and **muerto** (*dead*) we use **estar** because, although this state cannot change, it is the result of a change. Just as a glass is now broken but was not broken before, so someone has now died but was alive before.

La mesa está rota.	*The table is broken.*
La planta está muerta.	*The plant is dead.*

6 Gramática práctica

27.6.1 Fill the blanks with the correct form of the verb **estar** in the present tense.

1. Yo _____ triste.
2. María _____ cansada.
3. Tú _____ aburrido.

4. Julio _____ contento.
5. Nosotras _____ enfadadas.
6. Ellos _____ enfermos.
7. Ana _____ contenta.
8. Tú _____ enfermo.
9. Rosa _____ enferma.
10. Vosotros _____ contentos.

27.6.2 Complete the following sentences with the correct form of **ser** or **estar**.

1. ¿Qué país _____ éste? _____ Colombia.
2. ¿Cuál _____ la capital del país? _____ Bogotá.
3. ¿A cuántos kilómetros _____ de Medellín?
4. No sé a cuántos kilómetros _____.
5. Barcelona _____ en el este de España.
6. ¿Cómo _____ Barcelona?
7. _____ muy grande, pero también ____ muy bonita.
8. ¿_____ lejos de Madrid?
9. Sí, _____ muy lejos, _____ a más de seiscientos kilómetros.
10. ¿_____ éste tu pueblo? Sí, éste _____ mi pueblo.
11. Lisboa _____ en Portugal. _____ la capital del país.
12. Granada _____ en el interior del país.

27.6.3 Complete the text. Write **ser** or **estar** in the blanks.

Mi amigo Enrique tiene un apartamento en la playa que 1_____
muy grande y 2_____ muy viejo. El apartamento 3_____
muy limpio y ordenado. En el apartamento también hay una terraza que
4 _____ muy grande y 5_____ frente a la playa. Enrique y yo
por las noches 6_____ en la terraza hasta muy tarde porque el tiempo
7_____ muy bueno y las noches 8_____ muy calurosas. El
apartamento 9_____ muy bonito y 10 _____ muy bien cuidado. Las
casas 11 _____ típicas de la zona y todas 12_____ pintadas de blanco,
aunque algunas 13_____ azules. Yo 14_____ muy contento de pasar
unos días con Enrique porque me encanta la zona y la playa 15 _____
fantástica.

27.6.4 Join the words from List A with those of List B. Then add the correct form of **ser** or **estar** to make sentences.

List A

1. La puerta
2. El café
3. El pueblo
4. El árbol
5. La pelota
6. La taza
7. El documental
8. La camisa
9. Este plato
10. La televisión

List B

a) abierta
b) destruido
c) encendida
d) frío
e) interesante
f) muerto
g) redonda
h) roto
i) sucia
j) vacía

7 Más allá

7.1 More grammatical structures with **ser**

Ser is always used in the following contexts:

7.1.1 Before infinitives

Lo importante es estudiar.	*The important thing is to study.*

7.1.2 Impersonal expressions (in the 3rd person)

Es importante hablar español.	*It's important to speak Spanish.*
Es interesante estudiar la gramática.	*It's interesting to study grammar.*
Es bueno que hagas ejercicio.	*It's good that you do exercise.*

7.1.3 Passive constructions followed by a participle

Este palacio fue construido el siglo pasado.	*This palace was built last century.*

7.2 Other set expressions with **ser**

7.2.1

es igual	
es lo mismo	*it's ok, it doesn't matter*
eso es	*that's it / it's ok*

7.2.2

sea como sea	*whatever it is*

7.2.3 o sea

Used for explanation:

o sea	*that's to say . . .*

7.2.4 esto es

An expression at the beginning of a sentence to call attention to what we are talking about:

Esto es terrible.	*This is terrible.*
Esto es un problema.	*This is a problem.*

7.2.5 es que

Used for starting sentences which give an explanation or an excuse or add information; sometimes used instead of **porque** (*because*):

A: ¿No vienes al cine?	*Aren't you coming to the cinema?*
B: No, es que no tengo dinero.	*No, (it's that) I have no money.*

A: ¿Vas a hacer pescado para cenar?   *Are you going to do fish for dinner?*
B: No, es que no tenemos pescado.   *No, (because) we don't have any fish.*

A: ¿No compras la chaqueta?   *Aren't you going to buy the jacket?*
B: No, es que es muy cara.   *No, (because) it's very expensive.*

7.2.6 *Érase una vez . . . (lit:* There was once *. . .)*

Used at the beginning of (usually) a fairy story; the equivalent of *Once upon a time* in English:

Érase una vez una niña que   *Once upon a time there was (There*
   se llamaba Cenicienta . . .   *was once) a girl called Cinderella . . .*

7.3 More uses of estar

7.3.1

To talk about temporary situations, followed by the prepositions **de** or **con**:

Estaré de profesora en este instituto   *I'll be a teacher (I'll be teaching) in*
   durante tres meses.   *this school for three months.*
Estos pantalones están de moda   *These trousers are in fashion this*
   este año.   *year.*
Juan está con la gripe.   *Juan has flu. (lit: Juan is with the flu.)*

7.3.2

Estar is also used when we want to say that something is on the point of happening or being done. In this case it is followed by **por** or **para** or by the expression **a punto de**, plus an infinitive:

El trabajo está por terminar.   *The work is still to finish.*
El examen está para empezar.   *The exam is about to begin.*
El programa está a punto de terminar.   *The programme is about to finish.*

We can also say that someone is on the point of doing something:

El jefe está por llegar de un momento   *The boss is about to arrive*
   a otro.   *from one moment to the next.*
La mujer estaba para cruzar la calle   *The woman was about to cross the*
   cuando el coche la atropelló.   *street when the car ran her over.*
Los estudiantes están a punto   *The students are about to*
   de salir de clase.   *come out of class.*

7.4 Set expressions with estar

7.4.1

estar de pie   *to be standing up*
¿Por qué estás de pie?   *Why are you standing up?*

estar de rodillas   *to be down on one's knees (kneeling)*
Estaba de rodillas.   *He was on his knees.*

estar sentado   *to be seated / sitting*
Mis padres están sentados.   *My parents are sitting.*

7.4.2

estar de mal / buen humor	to be in a bad / good mood
Mi padre está de mal humor hoy.	My father is in a bad mood today.
Mi madre está de buen humor siempre.	My mother is always in a good mood.

estar de mal genio	to be in a bad temper
¿Por qué estás de mal genio?	Why are you in a bad temper?

7.4.3

estar al corriente	to be up to date
En su trabajo siempre estaba al corriente de las noticias.	In his work he was always up to date with the news.

7.4.4

estar de luto	to be in mourning
Murió su hermano. Está de luto toda la familia.	Her brother died. The whole family is in mourning.

7.4.5

estar en todo	to be everywhere (for children getting into mischief)
Esta chica siempre está en todo.	This girl, she's always into everything.

7.4.6

¡Ya está bien!	That's enough!
Por favor, ya te lo he dicho, ¡ya está bien!	Please, I've already told you, that's enough!

7.5 ser / estar: contrast and comparison

7.5.1

Ser and **estar** can be used with the same adjectives; the meaning of the sentence changes depending which verb is used. The choice of **ser** or **estar** depends on what the speaker wants to say, not on a grammatical rule.

Some adjectives accompany **estar** to express a temporary state but can accompany **ser** to express personality or status:

Juan es nervioso.	Juan is nervous. (he is a nervous man)
Juan está nervioso hoy.	Juan is nervous today. (he isn't always nervous, sometimes he's relaxed)

7.5.2

Ser is used for more objective statements; the meaning is permanent and as such is usually translated as *to be*.

Estar is used for more subjective statements where we perceive that the quality mentioned can change. In these cases **estar** can often be replaced by verbs like *to feel* or *to look*.

The choice of **ser** or **estar** is therefore subjective; the speaker can use one or the other to make a permanent quality temporary:

Ana es muy alta, es la más alta de la clase.	*Ana is very tall, she's the tallest in the class.*
Ana tiene cinco años, pero está muy alta.	*Ana is five years old, but she's very tall.*

or a temporary one permanent:

La niña está limpia, acabo de bañarla.	*The little girl is clean, I've just bathed here.*
La niña es muy limpia.	*The little girl is very clean.*

7.5.3

More examples:

El piso está limpio.	*The flat is clean.*
Pedro es muy limpio. (es una persona muy limpia)	*Pedro is a very clean person.*
Pedro es tranquilo.	*Pedro is calm* (he's a calm personality)
Pedro está tranquilo porque está de vacaciones.	*Pedro is (feels) calm (relaxed), because he's on holiday.*
María es muy amable / cariñosa.	*María is very friendly / affectionate* (it's her personality)
María está muy amable / cariñosa hoy.	*María is very friendly / affectionate today* (normally she is not)
Luis es fuerte.	*Luis is strong.*
Luis está fuerte, hace mucho ejercicio.	*Luis is (looks) strong because he does a lot of exercise.*
El gato es gordo y grande.	*The cat is fat and big.*
El gato está gordo porque come mucho.	*The cat is fat because he eats a lot.*
Ricardo es guapo.	*Ricardo is handsome.*
Ricardo está guapo con su traje nuevo.	*Ricardo looks handsome in his new suit.*

7.5.4

Note that when we use a temporary quality as a permanent one attributed to a person, it's possible to include **una persona** before the adjective:

La puerta está abierta.	*The door is open.*
María es abierta. / María es una persona muy abierta.	*María is open. / María is a very open person.*
La casa está ordenada.	*The house is tidy.*
Ana es ordenada. / Ana es una persona ordenada.	*Ana is tidy / Ana is a tidy person.*

7.5.5

The use of **ser** and **estar**, then, depends in many cases on the perception of the speaker. This happens especially with adjectives such as **delgado, gordo** or **calvo**; for example, if we meet someone who is thin we say: **Es delgado.**

But if we have met the same person before and he has lost weight we can say: **Está delgado.**

Again, if we meet Antonio and he is bald, we say: **Antonio es calvo.** But if we had already met Antonio when he had hair, we can say: **Antonio está calvo.**

7.5.6

But note that there are some exceptions to this rule: for example, when someone changes the colour of their hair:

Antes María era morena, ahora es rubia. *María was dark-haired before, now she is blonde.*

Hair colour is regarded as a permanent attribute, even though it changes with age (and with dyes!), so we use **ser**.

The same occurs with **pobre** (*poor*), **rico*** (*rich*), **feliz** (*happy*), **desgraciado** (*unhappy*), which are always used with **ser**.

There are other words in Spanish to express those feelings when they are temporary: **contento** (*happy*), **triste** (*sad*), **deprimido** (*depressed*), **animado** (*lively*).

* Note the use of **estar** with **rico** when we talk about food:

El pescado está rico. *The fish is nice (tasty). (not rich, though!)*

7.5.7 *estar or ser to express marital state*

Estar is used with **casado/a** (*married*), **soltero/a** (*single*), **separado/a** (*separated*), **divorciado/a** (*divorced*) or **viudo/a** (*widowed*). In this case these are adjectives:

Estoy casado.	*I'm married.*
Mi hermana está soltera.	*My sister is single.*
Elena está divorciada.	*She is divorced.*
La señora García está viuda.	*Mrs Garcia is widowed.*

But it is also possible to use the verb **ser**. In this case the words are nouns, and the meaning is different as it refers to status:

Luis es casado.	*Luis is a married man.*
Mi hermana es soltera.	*My sister is a single woman.*
Carmen es divorciada.	*Carmen is a divorced woman.*
Mi tío es viudo.	*My uncle is a widower.*

7.5.8

Some adjectives change their meaning completely depending on whether they are used with **ser** or with **estar**. Here are some examples:

Mi amiga es lista.	*My friend is clever.*
Mi amiga está lista para salir.	*My friend is ready to go out.*
Fernando es aburrido.	*Fernando is boring.*
Fernando está aburrido.	*Fernando is bored.*
Juan es rico.	*Juan is rich.*
El pollo está rico.	*The chicken is nice / tasty.*
Está seguro de eso.	*He is sure of it.*
La inversión es segura.	*The investment is safe.*

Other examples:

es atento / está atento	*he is polite / he is attending (to the speaker)*
es bueno / está bueno	*he / she / it is good / (the fish) is (tastes) good*
es malo / está malo	*he / she / it is bad / (the fish) is (tastes) bad*
es maduro / está maduro	*(the boy) is mature / (the apple) is ripe*
soy libre / estoy libre	*I'm free (independent) / I'm free (available)*

8 Más práctica

27.8.1 Write the correct form of **ser** or **estar**.

1. Ya _____ bien de hacer tonterías.
2. _____ importante trabajar en este proyecto.
3. Esto _____ algo interesante.
4. Mi profesor _____ de mal humor.
5. _____ aburrido, _____ que no sé qué hacer hoy.
6. Lo importante _____ descansar ahora.
7. _____ igual, no me importa lo que haces.
8. Yo _____ sentado, pero mi hermano _____ de pie.

27.8.2 Choose **ser** or **estar**.

1. No me gusta esta camisa porque es / está blanca, prefiero la azul.
2. La camisa es / está muy blanca, la he lavado con agua caliente.
3. Juan es / está moreno, ha tomado el sol.
4. Juan es / está moreno y tiene los ojos negros.
5. Pedro es / está débil, no tiene fuerza para trabajar.
6. Pedro es / está débil, necesita vitaminas.
7. María es / está muy joven, tiene 20 años.
8. Mi madre es / está muy joven, tiene 80 años, pero se cuida mucho.
9. El parque es / está muy bonito y tiene muchos árboles.
10. El parque es / está muy bonito en primavera.

11. La casa es / está oscura, tiene muy pocas ventanas.
12. La casa es / está oscura, las ventanas están cerradas.
13. El pescado es / está bueno para la salud.
14. El pescado es / está bueno con esta salsa.

27.8.3 Fill the gaps with **ser** or **estar** in the past tense. Use **era/eran**, **estaba/estaban**.

1. La casa de mi abuela _____ muy grande y _____ en el centro de la ciudad.
2. La catedral _____ muy bonita anoche con las nuevas luces que instalaron.
3. Mi casa antes _____ más pequeña, pero construyeron un ático y ahora es muy grande.
4. La comida que hiciste ayer _____ deliciosa.
5. El cuadro _____ muy sucio después de estar tantos años en el sótano.
6. El ascensor _____ estropeado y tuvimos que subir a pie.
7. Mis hermanos y yo _____ muy pequeños cuando murió nuestro padre.
8. Tu madre y la mía _____ muy amigas de pequeñas.
9. Juan _____ muy cansado ayer y no quiso salir.
10. Mi abuelo _____ un hombre muy activo cuando _____ joven.

28 The future tense *El futuro*

1 ¿Qué es?

The future is the tense we use to talk about what will happen or what we will do in the future.

In Spanish there are two ways to express the future:

ir + a + infinitive

Voy a visitar Madrid este verano.	*I am going to visit Madrid this summer.*

The future tense

Visitaré Madrid este año.	*I'll visit Madrid this summer.*

Note that these two forms of the future are interchangeable and there is very little difference in meaning between them.

1.1 ir + a + infinitive

This form of the future is formed by using the verb **ir + a** + the infinitive of the main verb. Although it is generally used when we talk about things that are going to happen nearer in time, it is often interchangeable with the future tense.

(yo)	voy a		I'm going	
(tú)	vas a		you are going	
(él / ella / Vd)	va a	estudiar	he / she / you is / are going	to study
(nosotros/as)	vamos a		we are going	
(vosotros/as)	vais a		you are going	
(ellos / ellas / Vds)	van a		they / you are going	

1.2 The future tense

The future tense is formed with the infinitive (the whole of the infinitive form of the verb) followed by the future endings, which are the same for the three conjugations:

-ar, -er, -ir.

Compare the endings of the present tense with those of the future tense and note how each is formed.

Infinitive: **cenar**
Present: **nosotros cen**amos
Future: **nosotros cenar**emos

1.3 Regular verbs

	-ar	-er	-ir
	cenar	comer	vivir
(yo)	cenaré	comeré	viviré
(tú)	cenarás	comerás	vivirás
(él / ella / Vd)	cenará	comerá	vivirá
(nosotros/as)	cenaremos	comeremos	viviremos
(vosotros/as)	cenaréis	comeréis	viviréis
(ellos / ellas / Vds)	cenarán	comerán	vivirán

1.4 Irregular future forms

There are very few irregular verbs in the future.

Note that the irregularity happens in the stem of the verb, but that the endings are the same as those of the regular verbs.

They can be grouped as follows:

1.4.1 Verbs which drop the -e or-i from the stem and add -d

tener (*to have*):   tendré, tendrás, tendrá, tendremos, tendréis, tendrán
salir (*to go out*):   saldré, saldrás, saldrá, saldremos, saldréis, saldrán
poner (*to put*):   pondré, pondrás, pondrá, pondremos, pondréis, pondrán
venir (*to come*):   vendré, vendrás, vendrá, vendremos, vendréis, vendrán

1.4.2 Verbs which drop the -e from the stem

poder (*to be able, can*)   podré, podrás, podrá, podremos, podréis, podrán
saber (*to know*)   sabré, sabrás, sabrá, sabremos, sabréis, sabrán
haber (*to have*)   habré, habrás, habrá, habremos, habréis, habran
caber (*to fit in*)   cabré, cabrás, cabrá, cabremos, cabréis, cabrán

1.4.3 Verbs which have completely irregular forms

ha**ce**r > é (drops **ce**)

quer**e**r > é (drops **e**)

de**c**ir > é (drops **ec**)

hacer *(to do)*   haré, harás, hará, haremos, haréis, harán
querer *(to want, to*   querré, querrás, querrá, querremos, querréis,
wish)   querrán
decir *(to say, to tell)*   diré, dirás, dirá, diremos, diréis, dirán

2 Uses of the future

2.1

The future is used to express an action that will take place at a later time than the present:

Mañana viajaré a México.   *Tomorrow I'll travel to Mexico.*

2.2

It can also be used to express the idea or meaning of probability:

A: **¿Quién llama?**   *Who's calling?*
B: **Será mi madre.**   *It'll be my mother.*

A: **¿Qué hora es?**   *What time is it?*
B: **No sé, serán las cinco.**   *I don't know, it'll be about five.*

2.3

It can expresses a promise or a prediction:

No te preocupes, jugarás en el   *Don't worry, you'll play in the game*
   partido del domingo.   *on Sunday.*

yo me casaré   *I will get married*
estudiaré   *I will study*
Tendré un trabajo muy bueno.   *I will have a very good job.*

3 Use of the present tense to refer to the future

When we are arranging to do something in the future with friends, we often use the present tense, as in the following examples:

¿Qué hacemos?   *What shall we do?*   *(lit: What do we do?)*
¿Adónde vamos?   *Where shall we go?*
¿Dónde quedamos?   *Where shall we meet?*
Quedamos en el cine.   *We'll meet at the cinema.*
Vengo a las cinco.   *I'll come round at five.*

4 Gramática práctica

28.4.1 Write the sentences in the **ir + a** + infinitive future.

Example: Yo trabajo para esta compañía. > Yo voy a trabajar para esta compañía.

1. Yo compro fruta y verdura.
2. Juan estudia mucho para el examen.
3. María trabaja en Madrid.
4. Nosotros viajamos a Francia.
5. Mis padres escriben a mis tíos.
6. ¿Vais al cine vosotros?
7. Mis hermanos limpian la casa.
8. Yo como en casa con mi familia.
9. Nosotros desayunamos en la cafetería.
10. Teresa vende ropa en el mercadillo

28.4.2 Now rewrite the sentences from 28.4.1 in the future tense.

Example: Yo trabajo para esta compañía. > Yo trabajaré para esta compañía.

28.4.3 Rewrite the sentences in the future tense.

Example: Yo no puedo venir. > Yo no podré venir.

1. Tú no puedes ayudarme.
2. Tú no quieres hacer nada.
3. Nosotros no hacemos nada.
4. El profesor pone muchos deberes.
5. Yo no salgo esta noche.
6. Mis amigos no vienen el fin de semana.
7. ¿Tienes bastante comida para todos?

> sabré   diré   pondremos   harán   querrán   cabrá   querréis
> habrá   vendré   tendrán   podremos   saldréis

8. No dice la verdad.
9. Hay mucho trabajo en la oficina.
10. Aquí no cabe nadie.
11. No sé cómo ir a su casa.

28.4.4 Complete the sentences with the verbs from the box.

1. Mis amigos _____ mucho trabajo el mes próximo.
2. Nosotros no _____ ir de vacaciones este verano.
3. ¿ _____ con nosotros mañana por la noche?
4. Yo _____ a verte mañana.
5. Los niños _____ los deberes antes de ir a jugar.
6. ¿ _____ venir a la piscina con nosotros?
7. Luego _____ las maletas en el coche.
8. Sin el mapa no _____ llegar a tu casa.
9. Mis hijos no _____ ir al cine con nosotros.
10. Este fin de semana _____ mucho tráfico en las carreteras.
11. No _____ toda la ropa en esta maleta.
12. No _____ nada porque es un secreto.

29 The preterite tense
El pretérito indefinido

1 ¿Qué es?

The **pretérito indefinido** or preterite is used to say what happened in the past.

2 Form

2.1

The preterite or simple past of regular verbs is formed by removing the endings from the infinitive and adding the preterite endings to the stem.

Regular verbs	-ar	-er	-ir
	desayunar	comer	escribir
(yo)	desayuné	comí	escribí
(tú)	desayunaste	comiste	escribiste
(él / ella / Vd)	desayunó	comió	escribió
(nosotros/as)	desayunamos	comimos	escribimos
(vosotros/as)	desayunasteis	comisteis	escribisteis
(ellos / ellas / Vds)	desayunaron	comieron	escribieron

Note that the the first person plural of **-ar** verbs is in the same form as for the present:

Desayunamos a las ocho.   *We have breakfast at eight.*
Desayunamos a las ocho.   *We had breakfast at eight.*

The endings of **-er** and **-ir** verbs are the same in the preterite.

2.2 Irregular forms in the preterite

2.2.1

Some of the most frequently used verbs in Spanish are irregular in the preterite. The following are the most common irregular verbs:

hacer (*to do/ to make*), **estar** (*to be*), **tener** (*to have*), **ir** (*to go*) and **ser** (*to be*).

	hacer	estar	tener
(yo)	hic<u>e</u>	estuv<u>e</u>	tuv<u>e</u>
(tú)	hic<u>iste</u>	estuv<u>iste</u>	tuv<u>iste</u>
(él / ella / Vd)	hiz<u>o</u>	estuv<u>o</u>	tuv<u>o</u>
(nosotros/as)	hic<u>imos</u>	estuv<u>imos</u>	tuv<u>imos</u>
(vosotros/as)	hic<u>isteis</u>	estuv<u>isteis</u>	tuv<u>isteis</u>
(ellos / ellas / Vds)	hic<u>ieron</u>	estuv<u>ieron</u>	tuv<u>ieron</u>

Note that the endings of irregular preterites are different from the regular endings, but they follow their own pattern. The exceptions are **ir** and **ser***, which are completely different: **fui, fuiste, fue, fuimos, fuisteis, fueron**.

*Note that **ir** and **ser** are placed together here as they have exactly the same preterite form.

2.2.2

Irregular preterites are also known as strong preterites, and the irregularities happen in the stem. The main difference is based on the stress: in the 1st and 3rd singular forms of regular verbs the stress is on the endings, whereas in irregular verbs it is on the stem:

com<u>í</u> / cen<u>é</u> / sal<u>í</u>
est<u>u</u>ve / h<u>i</u>ce / t<u>u</u>ve

A: **¿Qué hiciste anoche?**   *What did you do last night?*
B: **Tuve una fiesta.**   *I had a party.*

A: **¿Dónde estuviste ayer?**   *Where were you yesterday?*
B: **Estuve / estuvimos en casa.**   *I was / we were at home.*

2.2.3

> **En breve**
> There are five main groups of irregular preterites. Note that the endings of the following four are the same so you just have to remember the stems.
>
> **h<u>i</u>c-, qu<u>i</u>s-, d<u>ij</u>-, v<u>i</u>n-**
> **p<u>u</u>d-, p<u>u</u>s-, s<u>u</u>p-, h<u>u</u>b-**   +   **-e, -iste, -o, -imos, -isteis, -ieron**
> **t<u>u</u>v-, est<u>u</u>v-**
> **tra<u>j</u>-, d<u>ij</u>-**

2.3 Irregular preterites: the five groups

2.3.1 Verbs that change the root vowel to -i

An example is **hacer** (see above). Here are some others:

querer: quise, quisiste, quiso, quisimos, quisisteis, quisieron
Juan no quiso comer.   *Juan didn't want to eat.*

decir: dije, dijiste, dijo, dijimos, dijisteis, dijeron
¿Qué dijiste a María?   *What did you say to María?*

venir: vine, viniste, vino, vinimos, vinisteis, vinieron
No vinieron a la fiesta.   *They didn't come to the party.*

2.3.2 Verbs that change the stem vowel to -u-

poner: puse, pusiste, puso, pusimos, pusisteis, pusieron
Puso el libro encima de la mesa.   *He put the book on the table.*

poder: pude, pudiste, pudo, pudimos, pudisteis, pudieron
Intenté abrir la puerta pero no pude.   *I tried to open the door but I*
                                         couldn't.

saber: supe, supiste, supo, supimos, supisteis, supieron
No supo contestar a la pregunta.   *He didn't know how to answer the*
                                         question.

haber: hube, hubiste, hubo, hubimos, hubisteis, hubieron*
Hubo un accidente de tráfico.   *There was a traffic accident.*

*This is used as an impersonal form in the third person singular only: **hay >
hubo**.
It is also used as an auxiliary verb in the preterite compound tenses.

2.3.3 Verbs that add -uv- at the end of the stem: tener and estar

See the conjugation in point 2.2.1 above.

2.3.4 Verbs that add the consonant -j-

traer: traje, trajiste, trajo, trajimos, trajisteis, trajeron
¿Trajiste el libro?   *Did you bring the book?*

decir: dije, dijiste, dijo, dijimos, dijisteis, dijeron
No me dijo nada.   *He didn't say anything to me.*

2.4 ser / ir; dar, ver

These verbs are completely different and don't follow any of the patterns
above.

ser / ir (see point 2.2.1 above)

dar: di, diste, dio, dimos, disteis, dieron
¿Diste el paquete a tu madre?   *Did you give the package to your*
                                         mother?

ver: vi, viste, vio, vimos, visteis, vieron
Ayer vimos una película muy buena.   *Yesterday we saw a very good film.*

3 Use

3.1

This tense is used to express completed actions that happened in the past in relation to the moment of speaking.

Anoche fuimos a un restaurante.   *Last night we went to a restaurant.*

3.2

It also indicates the start of an action which began in the past but continues in the present:

Empecé a estudiar español el año pasado. *I started studying Spanish last year.*

3.3

It is used with adverbs and expressions of time such as:
ayer (*yesterday*), **el año pasado** (*last year*), **anoche** (*last night*), **anteayer** (*the day before yesterday*)

3.4

When forming a question, no extra words are required. The fact that it is a question is indicated by stress and intonation or by question marks in writing.

 See Unit 14 for questions.

Fue al partido.   *He went to the match.*
¿Fue al partido?   *Did he go to the match?*

3.5

When forming a negative, the word **no** is added:

No comí en el restaurante.   *I didn't eat in the restaurant.*

4 Gramática práctica

29.4.1 Write these sentences in the preterite.

1. En 1969 el primer hombre pisa la luna.
2. En 1936 empieza la guerra civil española.
3. En 1492 Cristóbal Colón llega a América.
4. Los árabes entran en España en el siglo ocho.
5. Los mayas forman un gran imperio en Centroamérica.

29.4.2 Answer the questions in complete sentences, using the prompts in brackets.

1. ¿A qué hora te levantaste? (8 de la mañana)
2. ¿Adónde fuiste? (centro ciudad)
3. ¿Qué hiciste? (ir de compras / ir al cine)

4. ¿Compraste muchas cosas? (comprar muchas cosas)

5. ¿Con quién fuiste al cine? (mi hermano)

6. ¿Qué hiciste por la noche? (cenar en casa / salir a un club / bailar hasta las 3 am)

7. ¿A qué hora te acostaste? (4 am)

8. ¿Lo pasaste bien? (muy bien)

29.4.3 Complete the sentences.

1. Hoy no llueve pero ayer _____ mucho.

2. El mes pasado _____ en la playa con mis padres, pero _____ mucho frío.

3. La semana pasada _____ de camping con mis amigos, pero ____ mucho viento.

4. Cuando _____ en Londres _____ muchos monumentos.

5. Juan, ¿_____ a la catedral? No, no _____ a la catedral.

6. Hoy no nieva, pero ayer _____ mucho y todo está blanco.

29.4.4 Write the correct preterite forms of the verbs in brackets.

1. Mis amigos y yo (ir) de excursión a la montaña.

2. Mis padres (estar) en Barcelona durante los Juegos Olímpicos del 92.

3. ¿Qué ciudades (visitar) vosotros cuando (ir) a Irlanda? Nosotros (visitar) Dublín.

4. Mi hermana y yo (hacer) un cursillo de windsurf cuando (estar) en la playa.

5. Mis primos (alquilar) un patín y (montar) en una lancha cuando (estar) en la playa.

6. Mis tíos (salir) por la noche, (ir) al cine y (ver) una película muy bonita.

5 Más allá

5.1

Some verbs that have a regular form in the preterite change slightly as a result of spelling conventions.

See Unit 2 Section 2.2.1.

The following changes only happen in the first person singular:

5.1.1

In verbs ending in **-car**, **c** changes to **qu**:

buscar > busqué
Busqué el bolígrafo.   *I looked for the pen.*

explicar > expliqué
Te lo expliqué ayer.   *I explained it to you yesterday.*

practicar > practiqué
Practiqué mucho.   *I practised a lot.*

5.1.2

In verbs ending in **-gar**, **g** changes to **gu** before **e**:

llegar > llegué
Llegué a casa a las nueve.   *I arrived home at nine.*

jugar > jugué
Jugué al fútbol ayer.   *I played football yesterday.*

pagar > pagué
Pagué la cuenta con tarjeta.   *I paid the bill by card.*

5.1.3

In verbs ending in **-zar**, **z** changes to **c** before **e**:

comenzar > comencé
Comencé en la universidad hace   *I started at the university*
  tres años.   *three years ago.*

cruzar > crucé
Crucé la calle en el semaforo.   *I crossed the street at the traffic lights.*

5.1.4

The following changes occur in the third person singular and plural.

In verbs ending in **-aer / -eer / -oír / -uir**, **i** changes to **y** between two vowels:

caer > cayó, cayeron
La chica se cayó.   *The girl fell over.*

creer > creyó, creyeron
Se lo dije pero no me creyeron.   *I told them but they didn't believe*
                                                         me.

leer > leyó, leyeron
Leyó un libro entero.   *He read a whole book.*

oír > oyó, oyeron
Les grité pero no me oyeron.   *I shouted at them but they didn't*
                                                         hear me.

construir > construyó, construyeron
Manuel construyó la caseta.   *Manuel built the shed.*

5.2 Stem-changing verbs (also known as radical-changing verbs)

5.2.1 e > i (in the 3rd persons singular and plural)

vestir: vestí, vestiste, <u>vistió</u>, vestimos, vestisteis, <u>vistieron</u>
Ana vistió a las niñas.   *Ana dressed the girls.*
Los chicos se vistieron solos.   *The boys got dressed themselves.*

preferir: preferí, preferiste, <u>prefirió</u>, preferimos, preferisteis, <u>prefirieron</u>
De los dos postres, Rosa prefirió   *Of the two desserts, Rosa preferred*
  el helado.   *the ice cream.*

Los niños prefirieron quedarse
  en la piscina.

*The children preferred to stay in the
  pool.*

pedir: pedí, pediste, **pidió**, pedimos, pedisteis, **pidieron**
El hombre pidió más tiempo.

The man asked for more time.

Los chicos pidieron caramelos.

The children asked for sweets.

5.2.2 *o > u (in the 3rd persons singular and plural)*

dormir: dormí, dormiste, **durmió**, dormimos, dormisteis, **durmieron**

María durmió toda la noche.

María slept all morning.

Los niños durmieron mucho.

The children slept a lot.

5.3 More irregular verbs

andar *(to walk)* **anduve, anduviste, anduvo, anduvimos, anduvisteis, anduvieron**

conducir *(to drive)* **conduje, condujiste, condujo, condujimos, condujisteis, condujeron**

5.4 The preterite contrasted with other tenses

For the difference in form and use between the preterite and the
imperfect see Unit 30 Section 5.

For the difference in form and use between the preterite and the
present perfect see Unit 31 Section 5.

6 Más práctica

29.6.1 Write sentences to say what Teresa did yesterday.

Teresa tener día aburrido – enferma por la mañana – y quedarse en casa
– estar en la cama toda la mañana – y leer un libro – levantarse – comer
un poco – acostarse otra vez – dormir la siesta hasta las seis – Por la tarde
vestirse – ir a casa amiga Carmen – llegar a su casa – y cenar con ella –
después volver a casa – y acostarse pronto

29.6.2 Complete these sentences with the preterite of the verbs in brackets.

1. Mis padres (llegar) a la ciudad el lunes, pero yo (llegar) ayer.
2. Yo (traer) mucha comida para la fiesta. ¿(traer) tus amigos las bebidas?
3. Mis tíos (venir) a vernos ayer, y nos (dar) muchos regalos.
4. Su abuelo (estar) muy enfermo y (morir) hace dos años.
5. Mi hermana se (caer) en la calle y se (romper) una pierna.
6. Yo (ver) a Enrique en la fiesta, ¿lo (ver) tú también?
7. David (beber) demasiado y no (conducir) a casa.
8. Nosotros no (poder) salir porque (hacer) mal tiempo.
9. El lunes yo me (caer), (pedir) ayuda, pero nadie me (oír).
10. Yo le (decir) la verdad), pero él no me (creer).

30 The imperfect tense
El pretérito imperfecto

1 ¿Qué es?

The imperfect is a past tense. We use it:

- to talk about what we used to do;
- to describe people, places and objects in the past;
- to say what we were doing or what was happening when something else occurred.

It is used in a different way from the preterite (**pretérito indefinido**).

 See point 5.7 below for examples of the contrast between the simple past and the imperfect.

2 Form

The imperfect is formed by dropping the infinitive endings and adding the endings of the imperfect to the stem of the verb.

2.1 Regular verbs

	-ar	-er	-ir
	cenar	comer	escribir
(yo)	cenaba	comía	escribía
(tú)	cenabas	comías	escribías
(él / ella / Vd)	cenaba	comía	escribía
(nosotros/as)	cenábamos	comíamos	escribíamos
(vosotros/as)	cenabais	comíais	escribíais
(ellos / ellas / Vds)	cenaban	comían	escribían

2.2 Other regular verbs

estar:	estaba, estabas, estaba, estábamos, estabais, estaban
estudiar:	estudiaba, estudiabas, estudiaba, estudiábamos, estudiabais, estudiaban
tener:	tenía, tenías, tenía, teníamos, teníais, tenían
vivir:	vivía, vivías, vivía, vivíamos, vivíais, vivían
haber (hay):	había

2.3

There are only two irregular verbs in the imperfect:

ir:	iba, ibas iba, íbamos, íbais, iban
ser:	era, eras, era, éramos, érais, eran

Note: **ver** is slightly irregular because it keeps the **e** from the infinitive ending, but the endings are regular.

ver: **veía, veías, veía, veíamos, veíais, veían**

3 Use

3.1 The imperfect tense with actions

3.1.1 Describing what we used to do in the past (habitual actions)

When we want to talk about actions that we did repeatedly or regularly in the past, we use the imperfect:

Todos los días jugaba al fútbol.	*Every day I played football.*
	I used to play football every day.
Por las mañanas contestaba el teléfono.	*In the mornings I answered the phone.*
	In the mornings I used to answer the phone.

We also use the imperfect to refer to something that happened or used to happen in the past without saying exactly when. We also use it when the action has not finished or the speaker is not interested in that aspect of the action.

A veces cenaba en casa.	*Sometimes I used to have dinner at home.*
Trabajaba como profesor.	*I worked (used to work) as a teacher.*

3.1.1.1

Note that if the number of times is specified, the preterite is used:

Comíamos en este restaurante a menudo.	*We ate in this restaurant often.*
Comimos en este restaurante tres o cuatro veces.	*We ate in this restaurant three or four times.*

3.1.1.2

Also note the difference between:

Fui a las montañas (el año pasado).	*I went to the mountains (last year).*
Iba a las montañas (cuando era joven).	*I used to go to the mountains (when I was young).*

3.1.2

It also expressses duration, and in this case is accompanied by the adverb **antes**:

Antes vivíamos en un pueblo pequeño.	*Before, we used to live in a small village.*

3.2 The imperfect in descriptions

3.2.1 *To describe objects, places, etc.*

The imperfect is used to describe objects, places, time, people and feelings in the past, and also to describe what something was like:

La mujer era baja y delgada, tenía el pelo largo y llevaba gafas.
The woman was short and thin, she had long hair and wore glasses.
La casa donde vivía mi abuela era grande y estaba en el campo.
The house where my grandmother lived was big and it was in the country.

3.2.2 *To describe what something was like over a period of time in the past*

Eran las seis de la tarde y ya estaba todo oscuro porque era invierno.
It was six in the afternoon and it was already dark because it was winter.
El gobierno español de los años cincuenta era una dictadura y había mucha censura de los medios de comunicación. No había elecciones ni parlamento.
The Spanish government of the fifties was a dictatorship and there was a lot of censorship of communications media. There were no elections, nor was there a parliament.

3.2.3 *To describe things or people that remain unchanged over a period of time*

Cuando era joven vivía en Barcelona.	*When I was young I lived (I used to live) in Barcelona.*
El hotel era moderno.	*The hotel was modern.*
El jardín tenía muchas flores.	*The garden had lots of flowers.*
Había un lago cerca de la casa.	*There was a lake near the house.*

3.2.4

The verbs used mostly for description in the past are:

era (ser), estaba (estar), tenía (tener), había (hay, haber).

Note that **había** means *there was / there were* and **era** means *it was*:

Había un parque.	*There was a park.*
Había árboles en las montañas.	*There were trees on the mountains.*
Había mucho tráfico.	*There was lots of traffic.*
El pueblo era pequeño.	*The town was small.*
La iglesia era muy bonita.	*The church was very pretty.*
Estaba muy enfadado.	*He was very angry.*
Yo estaba nervioso por el examen.	*I was nervous because of the exam.*

4 Gramática práctica

30.4.1 Last year you went on holiday. Say what you did every day.

Example: Me despertaba pronto y. . .

1. levantarse a las ocho	6. comer en el restaurante
2. desayunar	7. dormir la siesta
3. ir a la playa	8. salir de paseo
4. nadar en el mar	9. cenar en el hotel
5. tomar el sol un poco	10. acostarse

30.4.2 Write the complete sentences with a verb in the appropriate tense.

1. Antes mis hijos _____ al colegio, ahora _____ a la universidad.
2. Antes mi hijo_____cereales, ahora _____tostadas.
3. Antes mis padres_____ muchos problemas económicos, pero ahora _____mucho dinero.
4. Antes tú _____muchos refrescos, pero ahora _____sólo agua.
5. Antes vosotros _____ bastante gordos, ahora _____ muy delgados.
6. Antes Isabel _____ en una tienda, ahora _____ en una oficina.
7. Antes nosotros _____ en Barcelona, ahora _____ en Madrid.
8. Antes yo _____ a todas partes en coche, ahora _____ a pie.

30.4.3 Write sentences to describe the town in the past, using **haber, estar, ser, tener**.

1. En la ciudad _____ un parque grande.
2. La plaza _____ muy bonita.
3. El parque _____ muchos árboles.
4. La estación _____ en el centro de la ciudad.
5. El centro _____ muy tranquilo.
6. En el centro _____ una farmacia.
7. La ciudad _____ muchas tiendas.
8. La ciudad _____ cerca de las montañas.

5 Más allá

5.1

The imperfect is also used for background descriptions, or secondary actions and circumstances that surround the main action:

Ana paseaba por el campo con su hija, la niña cantaba y jugaba, cuando llegó el abuelo.	*Ana was walking in the country with her daughter, the child was singing and playing, when her grandfather arrived.*

5.2

It is used to say what was going on when something else happened:

Elena viajaba en el autobús cuando ocurrió el accidente.	*Elena was travelling in the bus when the accident occurred.*
Yo dormía cuando sonó el teléfono.	*I was sleeping when the telephone rang.*

5.3

We can use the imperfect to mean that someone was on the point of doing something or something was on the point of happening when something else happened:

Iba a salir cuando sonó el teléfono. *I was going to leave when the telephone rang.*

Yo llegaba cuando tú saliste. *I was just arriving when you left.*

5.4

To talk about two things that were happening at the same time. Note that these are linked by **mientras** (*while*):

Mi padre siempre veía la televisión mientras cenaba. *My father always watched the television while he had supper.*

5.5 Questions and requests

The imperfect is also used in formal questions and requests:

¿Qué quería? *What would you like?*
Quería comprar este libro. *I would like to buy this book.*

5.6 Reported speech

It is used in reported speech:

John: 'Estudio español.' > John dijo que estudiaba español.
  John said he studied Spanish.
Mi padre: 'Tengo dolor de cabeza.' > Mi padre dijo que tenía dolor de cabeza.
  My father said that he had a headache.

5.7 The simple past and the imperfect

Contrast these sentences and decide why each one uses the imperfect tense.

Antes vivíamos cerca de la playa. (1)
No íbamos de vacaciones porque la playa estaba muy cerca y era excelente. (1)
Un año fui de vacaciones a las montañas con mis padres. (2)
Todos los días me levantaba muy tarde y me acostaba muy tarde. (3)
Un día nos levantamos temprano y fuimos de excursión. (2)

1. The first of these two sentences refers to things that happened in the past without saying when. The second describes where the beach was and what it was like.
2. These sentences refer to things that happened once at a specific time and so use the preterite.
3. This sentence refers to things that happened again and again over a period of time.

6 Imperfect continuous

The imperfect continuous is formed with the imperfect forms of **estar** followed by the gerund, **-ando** for **-ar** verbs and **-iendo** for **-er** and **-ir** verbs, to say that something was happening or taking place when something else happened.

Yo estaba comiendo cuando
 llamaron a la puerta.

*I was eating when they knocked on
 the door.*

estaba, estabas, estaba, estábamos, estabais, estaban +

cenando
comiendo
escribiendo

 See Unit 36 on compound tenses.

7 The verb **soler**

The verb **soler** means *to be accustomed to (doing something)*. Its equivalent in the English present tense means *to usually do something*, and in the past, *used to do something*, as in the following:

Suelo ir al cine todos los sábados
por la noche.

*I usually go to the cinema every
Saturday night.*

Solía ir al cine todos los sábados
por la noche.

*I used to go to the cinema every
Saturday night.*

8 Más práctica

30.8.1 Write complete sentences.

Example: Teresa / pasear / por el parque / cuando / la tormenta / empezar >
Teresa paseaba por el parque cuando la tormenta empezó.

1. Juan / tocar / el piano / cuando / yo / entrar / en la habitación
2. María / limpiar / la casa / cuando / sus amigos / venir a verla
3. Yo / correr / hacia el autobús / cuando / me / caer
4. Nosotros / cruzar / la calle / cuando / ver / el accidente
5. Elena / hablar / con sus amigas / cuando / su marido / llegar
6. Yo / ver / la televisión / cuando / Felipe / me / llamar / por teléfono
7. Mi hermano / viajar / por Europa /cuando / se / poner / enfermo
8. Mi madre / prepar / la cena / cuando/ mi hermano / volver / del trabajo

30.8.2 Fill the gaps with verbs from the box in the appropriate tenses.
Note: some verbs appear more than once.

practicar	ser	vivir	nadar	jugar	trabajar	ir	conocer

1. En el pueblo donde yo _____ antes, _____ a muchas personas; en la ciudad donde _____ ahora no _____ a nadie.
2. Mi hermano _____ ingeniero antes, pero ahora _____ como profesor de matemáticas.
3. Cuando yo _____ pequeña _____ muchos deportes; ahora no _____ ninguno.
4. Todos los días tú _____ en la piscina, un día _____ en el río.
5. Los domingos nosotros _____ de excursión al campo. Dos o tres domingos _____ a la montaña.
6. Antes mis padres _____ en un pueblo pequeño, pero después _____ a trabajar a la ciudad.
7. Yo siempre _____ a clase en bicicleta, excepto dos veces que _____ en autobús.
8. Nosotros_____al baloncesto muchas veces, sólo _____al fútbol una vez.

31 The present perfect tense
El pretérito perfecto

1 ¿Qué es?

The present perfect is a compound past tense formed by an auxiliary verb, **haber**, followed by the participle of the conjugated verb, and used to describe recently completed actions.

He terminado mis deberes.   *I've finished my homework.*
Han llegado a tiempo.   *They have arrived on time.*
¿A qué hora has salido?   *What time did you leave?*

2 Form

This tense is formed with the present tense of the verb **haber** plus the past participle of the main verb. The **haber** part of the verb is conjugated; the participle remains constant and does not change.

2.1

The verb **haber** means *to have* but is mainly used as an auxiliary verb.

It also appears frequently in its impersonal form **hay** (**había**), meaning *there is, there are, there was* or *there were*. It is not to be confused with the verb **tener**, which means *to have* in the sense of possession.

haber: he, has, ha, hemos, habéis, han + past participle of verb

2.2 The participle form of regular verbs

This is as follows:

-ar   **-ado**   **trabajado**
-er   -ido   comido
-ir   -ido   vivido

			-ar > -ado	-er > -ido	-ir > -ido
(yo)	he				
(tú)	has				
(él / ella / Vd)	ha	+	trabaja<u>do</u>	com<u>ido</u>	viv<u>ido</u>
(nosotros/as)	hemos				
(vosotros/as)	habéis				
(ellos / ellas / Vds)	han				

He comprado comida.	*I have bought food.*
¿Has comido?	*Have you eaten?*
Ha salido.	*He has left.*
Hemos terminado.	*We've finished.*
¿Habéis estudiado mucho?	*Have you studied a lot?*
Han viajado mucho.	*They have travelled a lot.*

2.3

The two parts of a compound tense cannot be separated as they can in English:

Siempre <u>hemos ido</u> de vacaciones a la playa.	*We've always <u>gone</u> on holiday to the beach.*

2.4

Some verbs are irregular in their past participle form:

volver (*to come back*)	**vuelto**	**hacer** (*to do*)	**hecho**
escribir (*to write*)	**escrito**	**ver** (*to see*)	**visto**
poner (*to put*)	**puesto**	**decir** (*to say*)	**dicho**
romper (*to break*)	**roto**	**abrir** (*to open*)	**abierto**

Juan ha vuelto.	*Juan has come back.*
¿Qué has hecho?	*What have you done?*
He escrito una carta.	*I've written a letter.*
No he visto a María.	*I haven't seen Maria.*
¿Has puesto la mesa?	*Have you set the table?*
No me ha dicho nada.	*He hasn't said anything to me.*
He roto un plato.	*I have broken a plate.*
Han abierto una tienda nueva.	*They have opened a new shop.*

3 Use

3.1

We can use the present perfect tense in the same way as in English:

He comido pescado.	*I've eaten fish.*

3.2

But we can also use it to describe the recent past when we would use the simple past in English:

Compare:

Ha salido.	*He has left.*

with

Ha salido a las ocho.	*He left at eight.*

3.3

The present perfect tense is used to express actions that have happened in a period of time that has not yet finished. The action is finished, but the time in which the action took place is not: *this week, this month, this year, today, this morning / afternoon / evening.*

It is therefore used after expressions such as:

esta mañana	*this morning*
esta tarde	*this afternoon*
esta semana	*this week*
este mes	*this month*
hoy	*today*

Hoy no he ido al instituto y esta mañana me he levantado tarde.
I haven't been to school today and I got up late this morning.

The second half of this sentence is in the simple past in English because it is no longer *this morning*. In Spanish, we can still use the present perfect because it is a recently completed action that has happened today.

3.4

It is used to describe events that are important for the present or that have an effect on the present:

He estudiado mucho para el examen de hoy.   *I've studied a lot for today's exam.*

3.5

It can be used with time expressions such as **ya** and **todavía no**:

¿Todavía no has terminado?   *Haven't you finished yet?*

3.6

In many parts of Latin America and some areas of Spain the preterite is more commonly used than the present perfect:

¿Llegaste ahora?   *Did you just arrive?*
¿Has llegado ahora?   *Have you just arrived?*

4 Gramática práctica

31.4.1 Write these sentences using the present perfect.

1. ¿Tú (visitar) este museo? No, yo no (visitar) este museo.
2. ¿Vosotros (estar) en Granada? No, nosotros no (estar) en Granada.
3. ¿Tú (comer) chorizo? No, yo no (comer) chorizo nunca.
4. ¿Vosotros (probar) el turrón? No, nosotros no (probar) el turrón.
5. ¿Ellos (ir) a la oficina? No, ellos no (ir) a la oficina.
6. ¿Tú (estudiar) la lección? No, yo no (estudiar) la lección.
7. ¿Vosotros (comprar) comida? No, nosotros no (comprar) comida.
8. ¿Los niños (beber) toda la leche? No, los niños no (beber) toda la leche.

31.4.2 Write complete sentences in the present perfect.

Example: (yo) salir con mis amigos > He salido con mis amigos.

1. (nosotros) comer pizza.
2. (ellos) escribir un email.
3. (vosotros) conocer a mi hermano.
4. (tú) enviar el paquete.
5. (mi hijo) romper el jarrón chino.
6. (Javier) decir que viene a la fiesta.
7. (sus padres) hablar con el profesor.
8. (nosotros) ver esta película.
9. (yo) hacer todos los ejercicios.
10. (nosotros) ir a cenar al restaurante.
11. (yo) volver muy tarde a casa.

5 Más allá

5.1 With **alguna vez** (*ever*), **nunca** (*never*)

¿Has comido calamares alguna vez?   *Have you ever eaten squid?*
No he comido nunca calamares.   *I've never eaten squid.*

5.2 With **hace***

Hace media hora que se ha ido.   *He went half an hour ago.*
                                            (lit: It makes half an hour that he
                                            has gone.)

 * See also point 5.6.2 below.

5.3 With pronouns

Pronouns always go before the present perfect:

La he visto esta mañana.   *I've seen her this morning.*
                                            I saw her this morning.

5.4

Reflexive verbs in the present perfect always have the pronoun before the verb.

Unlike in English, we use the definite article (**el / la / los / las**) to refer to parts of the body when describing an accident, and we use a pronoun to refer to the person: **me / le / te** etc.:

Me he roto la pierna.   *I have broken my leg. (<u>not</u> he roto mi pierna)*

Me he quemado.   *I have burnt myself.*
Me he quemado la mano.   *I have burnt my hand.*
¿Te has hecho daño?   *Have you hurt yourself?*
Se ha cortado el dedo.   *She has cut her finger.*

5.5 Differences between the preterite and the present perfect

5.5.1

Often the preterite and the present perfect are interchangeable, and their use depends on the intention of the speaker. If the speaker wants to emphasise the distance from the past action the preterite is used; but if we want to bring the action nearer to the present, the present perfect is used.

Su hermano ha muerto. / Su hermano murió. *His brother has died / died.*

5.5.2

If there is a time barrier (the night, the weekend, etc.) the preterite is used:

La semana pasada fuimos al cine.	*Last week we went to the cinema.*
Esta semana hemos ido al cine.	*This week we have been to the cinema.*

5.6 ¡Es diferente!

The present perfect is not used in the following cases:

5.6.1

To say the equivalent of the English *I have just done something*.
In Spanish we use **acabar de** + infinitive, rather than the present perfect:

Acabamos de comer. *We have just eaten.*

The verb **acabar** literally means *to finish*:

Acabo la clase a las doce. *I finish the class at twelve.*

5.6.2

To say you have been doing something for a period of time.
In Spanish we use **hace** + the present tense:

Hace dos años que estudio español. *I have studied Spanish for two years. (lit: It makes two years that I study Spanish.)*

or the present tense + **desde**:

Vivo en Málaga desde 2008. *I've lived in Malaga since 2008.*

6 Más práctica

31.6.1 Combine the sentence halves.

List A

1. Me he quemado
2. Me he cortado
3. Me he dado un golpe
4. Me he roto el brazo.

List B

a) con un cuchillo
b) con la plancha
c) y no puedo escribir
d) en la cabeza

5. He tomado el sol demasiado
6. Me he torcido el tobillo.
7. Me han salido unos granos

e) y no puedo andar.
f) y me escuece la espalda
g) por toda la cara

31.6.2 Translate the completed sentences into English.

31.6.3 Put the verbs in brackets into the present perfect form.

1. Juan (romperse) el brazo esta semana.
2. María y Luisa (acostarse) muy tarde.
3. Nosotros (bañarse) en la playa esta mañana.
4. Yo (torcerse) el tobillo.
5. Mi perro (romperse) la pata.
6. Mi madre (cortarse) con un cuchillo.
7. Esta mañana yo (ducharse) con agua fría.
8. Y tú, ¿cómo (romperse) la pierna?
9. Yo (romperse) la pierna esquiando.
10. Mi padre ha tenido un accidente y (darse) un golpe muy fuerte en la cabeza.

32 The conditional *El condicional*

1 ¿Qué es?

This tense is the equivalent of *would do* or *could do* something in English.

Me encantaría visitar Buenos Aires.   *I would love to visit Buenos Aires.*
Yo podría hacerlo.   *I could do it.*

2 Form

The conditional is formed in a similar way to the future tense, as the endings for both tenses are added to the infinitive form of the verb.
The verb endings are the same for the three conjugations: **-ar, -er, ir**.
The regular form of the conditional is formed by adding the endings **-ía, -ías, -ía, -íamos, -íais, -ían** to the infinitive. These endings are the same as those of the imperfect for **-er** and **-ir** verbs.

 See Unit 30 for the imperfect tense.

2.1 Regular verbs

	-ar	**-er**	**-ir**
	jugar	comer	escribir
(yo)	jugaría	comería	escribiría
(tú)	jugarías	comerías	escribirías
(él / ella / Vd)	jugaría	comería	escribiría
(nosotros/as)	jugaríamos	comeríamos	escribiríamos
(vosotros/as)	jugaríais	comeríais	escribiríais
(ellos / ellas / Vds)	jugarían	comerían	escribirían

2.2 Irregular verbs

These are formed in a similar way to the irregular verbs in the future, in that the irregularity occurs in the stem of the verb (although the endings are the same as those of the regular verbs). They can be grouped as follows:

2.2.1 Verbs which drop the -e from the stem and add -d:

tener (*to have*) **tendría, tendrías, tendría, tendríamos, tendríais, tendrían**

salir (*to go out / leave*) **saldría, saldrías, saldría, saldríamos, saldríais, saldrían**

poner (*to put*) **pondría, pondrías, pondría, pondríamos, pondríais, pondrían**

venir (*to come*) **vendría, vendrías, vendría, vendríamos, vendríais, vendrían**

2.2.2 Verbs which drop the -e

poder (*to be able, can*) **podría, podrías, podría, podríamos, podríais, podrían**

saber (*to know*) **sabría, sabrías, sabría, sabríamos, sabríais, sabrían**

haber (*to have*) **habría, habrías, habría, habríamos, habríais, habrían**

2.2.3 Verbs which have completely irregular forms

ha**ce**r (*to do*) drops **ce**:
haría, harías, haría, haríamos, haríais, harían

de**c**ir (*to say, to tell*) drops **ec**:
diría, dirías, diría, diríamos, diríais, dirían

quer**e**r (*to want, to wish*) drops **e**:
querría, querrías, querría, querríamos, querríais, querrían

3 Use

3.1

The conditional is used to express the equivalent of the *could* or *would* form of the verb in English.

Compraría la casa, pero es muy cara.   *I would buy the house but it's very expensive.*

3.2

It is used to say what we would like to do (**gustaría**).

When we want to say what we would like to do or to be, we use the verb **gustar** in the conditional form **gustaría** and follow it with another verb in the infinitive:

¿Te gustaría venir al cine conmigo?   *Would you like to go to the cinema with me?*

Sí, me gustaría mucho.   *Yes, I would.*

¿Dónde te gustaría vivir?   *Where would you like to live?*

Me gustaría vivir en un pueblo.   *I'd like to live in a village.*

¿Qué te gustaría ser?   *What would you like to be?*

Me gustaría ser piloto.   *I would like to be a pilot.*

3.2.1

It's also used with verbs similar to **gustar** in expressions such as:

me encantaría	*I would love*
me interesaría	*I would be interested*
Me encantaría visitar Buenos Aires.	*I'd love to go to Buenos Aires.*
Me interesaría leer este libro.	*I'd be interested in reading this book.*

3.2.2

It is used in polite questions and requests:

¿Podría abrir la ventana, por favor?	*Could you open the window please?*
¿Querrían (ustedes) cenar con nosotros?	*Would you wish / like to have dinner with us?*

4 Gramática práctica

32.4.1 Translate into Spanish.

1. Would you like to come to the cinema with me?
2. I would love to go to the cinema with you.
3. Would you be interested in visiting the museum?
4. I would like to visit the museum.
5. Could you open the door, please?
6. Would you wish to live here?

32.4.2 Write sentences from the prompts.

Example: yo salir / pero no poder > Yo saldría, pero no puedo.

1. nosotros comer / pero no tener hambre
2. él escribirte un email / pero no tener tu dirección
3. ellos venir a tu casa / pero ser tarde
4. yo comprar un coche / pero no tener dinero
5. nosotros poder ir al cine / pero preferir ir al teatro
6. Juan ponerse la camisa / pero estar sucia
7. tú tener más dinero / pero gastar mucho
8. yo saber más matemáticas / pero no estudiar

5 Más allá

5.1

The conditional is used to give advice and suggestions:

Deberías hacer más ejercicio.	*You should do more exercise.*
Podríamos ir al cine.	*We could go to the cinema.*
Yo iría al médico.*	*I would go to the doctor.*

*Note the sentences:

Yo que tú iría al médico.	*If I were you I'd go to the doctor.*
Si yo fuera tú iría al médico.	

5.2

It is used in reported speech:

'Trabajaré más.' > Me dijo que trabajaría más.	*'I'll work more.' > He told me he would work more.*

5.3

It is also used to express probability or uncertainty in the past:

Estaría aquí unos veinte minutos.	*He was here about twenty minutes. (lit: He would be here about twenty minutes.)*
Serían las tres cuando salió.	*It would be three o'clock when he left.*

5.4

It is used in conditional constructions, where one clause begins with **si** (*if*).

Note that the verb after **si** is in the imperfect subjunctive form:

➡ **See Unit 39 on the imperfect subjunctive.**

Si la casa fuera más barata, la compraría.	*If the house were cheaper I'd buy it.*
Iría a la playa si hiciera sol.	*I'd go to the beach if it were sunny.*

This type of conditional, known as the second conditional, is used for events that are unreal or unlikely:

Si fuera primera ministra, terminaría con la violencia.	*If I were prime minister I would end violence.*
Si fuera a una isla desierta, llevaría un libro.	*If I went to a desert island I would take a book.*
¿Qué harías si te tocara la lotería?	*What would you do if you won the lottery?*
Viajaría y compraría una casa.	*I would travel and I would buy a house.*

6 Más práctica

32.6.1 Fill the gaps with the verbs from the box.

deberíamos   compraría   deberían   sería   deberías   tendrías   haría   tendríais

1. Tú _____ comer menos carne.
2. Yo _____ un coche más pequeño.
3. Yo _____ más amable con él.
4. Tú _____ que estudiar más.
5. Yo _____ los deberes ahora.

6. Vosotros _____ que salir más.

7. Nosotros _____ comprar pan.

8. Ellos _____ asistir a clase.

32.6.2 Put the verbs in brackets into the conditional form.

Example: Yo (tener) más vacaciones en otro trabajo > Yo tendría más vacaciones en otro trabajo.

I. Nosotros (venir) a verte todas las semanas, pero vives muy lejos.

2. Tú (tener) más amigos aquí.

3. Nosotros (cuidar) niños para ganar dinero extra.

4. Yo (salir) esta tarde, pero no puedo.

5. ¿(poner) tú este cuadro aquí?

6. ¿(ser) usted tan amable de explicarme esto?

32.6.3 Complete the sentences with the correct conditional form.

I. Si no hiciera frío (yo / ir) a la playa.

2. Si vinieras (nosotros / cenar) en el restaurante.

3. Si estudiaras más (tú / aprobar) el examen sin problemas.

4. Si tuviera coche (él / viajar) por el país.

5. Si comieras más fruta (tú / estar) más sano.

6. Si tuviérais más dinero (vosotros / comprar) un piso.

7. Si compraras un piso (tú / vivir) más cómodo.

8. Si trabajaran más (ellos / tener) más dinero.

33 The infinitive *El infinitivo*

1 ¿Qué es?

The Spanish infinitive is the basic form of the verb. All of the verb's forms come from the infinitive form. It is the form of the verb that we find in the dictionary and is the equivalent of the *to* form of the verb in English (*to speak*).

Grammatically, we can say that the infinitive expresses the meaning of the verb without indicating person, tense or number.

trabajar	*to work*
beber	*to drink*
escribir	*to write*

2 Form

2.1

The Spanish infinitive shows that there are three different types of verb, each of which is conjugated in a slightly different way:

-ar	**-er**	**-ir**
trabaj-ar	**beb-er**	**escrib-ir**

2.1.1

The compound infinitive is **haber** + past participle of the conjugated verb:

haber trabajado	*to have worked*
haber bebido	*to have drunk*
haber salido	*to have left / gone out*

3 Use of the infinitive

3.1

It is used to express the future in the following construction:

ir + a + infinitive

Voy a comprar un coche.	*I'm going to buy a car.*
Vamos a salir esta noche.	*We are going to go out tonight.*

3.2

It is also used with the construction **tener + que** + infinitive:

Tengo que trabajar mañana.   *I have to work tomorrow.*

 For its use with other similar constructions see Unit 42 on phrasal verbs.

3.3

It is used after the following modal verbs:

deber	*should, ought to, must*
poder	*can, could, may, might, be able to*
querer	*want, would like*
saber	*know, know how to, be able to*
soler	*usually, used to*

No puedo ir al cine hoy.   *I can't go to the cinema today.*
No sé nadar.   *I can't swim.*

 For the use of the infinitive with modal verbs see Unit 43.

3.4

Note that in constructions with the infinitive the pronouns are usually placed after it:

Quiero comprarlo.   *I would like to buy it.*
Me gusta verlas.   *I like seeing them.*
Necesito hablarte.   *I need to talk to you.*

 For the use of personal pronouns with the infinitive see Unit 9.

3.5 ¡Es diferente!

Note that in Spanish, **gustar** (*to like*) and similar verbs are followed by the verb in the infinitive, while English uses the gerund: *I like doing.*

Me gusta <u>estudiar</u> español.   *I like <u>studying</u> Spanish.*

 For constructions like **gustar** + the infinitive see Unit 26.

---

4 Gramática práctica

33.4.1 Add the infinitive endings in the following sentences.

1. Tienes que termin- los deberes.
2. No puedo comprend- a mis hijos.

3. Quiero compr- un coche.
4. Voy a viv- en Madrid.
5. Vamos a pon- la mesa para com-.
6. Mi padre va a dirig- una empresa muy importante.

5 Más allá

5.1 Infinitive with prepositions

After some prepositions the infinitive is used in some common expressions:

5.1.1 *Adjective + de + infinitive*

Es fácil de hacer. | *It's easy to do.*

5.1.2 *al + infinitive*

This refers to a specific point in time:

Al terminar su trabajo volvió a casa. | *As soon as he finished work he returned home.*

This has the same meaning as:
Cuando terminó su trabajo volvió a casa.

5.1.3 *a / para + infinitive*

This expresses the purpose of an action:

Fui a darle el dinero. | *I went to give him the money.*
Vino para devolverte el libro. | *She came to return your book.*

5.1.4 *de + infinitive*

This is used to indicate the conditional:

De haber sabido eso no habría venido. | *If I had known that I wouldn't have come.*

5.1.5 *por + infinitive*

This indicates an unfinished action:
La casa nueva está por terminar aún. | *The new house still has to be finished.*

5.1.6 *¡Es diferente!*

After certain prepositions Spanish uses the infinitive while English uses the gerund (*-ing* ending):
antes de, sin, después de + infinitive

Te llamaré antes de salir. | *I'll call you before leaving.*
Salió sin decir adiós. | *He left without saying goodbye.*
Iremos al cine después de comer. | *We'll go to the cinema after eating.*

5.2 The infinitive used as imperative

5.2.1

The infinitive has an imperative meaning in notices, instructions and advertisements:

Girar a la derecha.   *Turn right.*

5.2.2 The infinitive preceded by *a*

¡A comer!	*Let's eat!*
¡A dormir!	*Time for bed! / Go to sleep!*

5.3 ¡Es diferente!

As well as its more common use as a verb, some infinitives can be used as a noun to describe a concept.

Note that in English we use a gerund (*-ing* ending) in these cases, where Spanish uses the infinitive:

Descansar es importante para nosotros.   *Relaxing is important for us.*

5.3.1

The infinitive used as a noun can also be accompanied by an article:

El viajar es un placer.   *Travel (travelling) is a pleasure.*

Note that, in this usage, the infinitive is always masculine.

6 Más práctica

33.6.1 Match the sentence halves.

List A

1. El libro es difícil
2. Hacer deporte es bueno
3. Compró el billete una semana
4. Fuimos de compras
5. Fue a casa de su madre
6. La casa que compré aún está
7. Tiene que estudiar otro año
8. Se puso enfermo
9. No podemos limpiar
10. Juan fue con sus amigos

List B

a) por terminar
b) después de comer el pescado
c) a sacar entradas para el teatro
d) de encontrar
e) al salir de la oficina
f) antes de terminar la carrera
g) sin ordenar las cosas antes
h) para la salud
i) para celebrar su cumpleaños
j) antes de viajar

33.6.2 Translate the completed sentences into English.

34 The gerund *El gerundio*

1 ¿Qué es?

The gerund (or present participle) is an invariable verb form. The equivalent in English is the *-ing* form of the verb.

The gerund is mainly used with the verb **estar** to form the present continuous tense.

Juan está nadando.   *Juan is swimming.*

It can also have an adverbial meaning:

Pedro vino corriendo.   *Pedro came running.*

2 Form

2.1

The gerund form for each of the three verb types is as follows:

-ar > -ando	-er > -iendo	-ir > -iendo
cenar > cenando	comer > comiendo	escribir > escribiendo
tomar > tomando	beber > bebiendo	salir > saliendo

Note how the gerund of the following verbs is formed:

dar *(to give)*	>	**dando**
ser *(to be)*	>	**siendo**
ver *(to see)*	>	**viendo**

Juan está cenando con sus amigos.   *Juan is having dinner with his friends.*
Los niños están comiendo fruta.   *The children are eating fruit.*
Estoy escribiendo un correo a   *I am writing an email to my*
  mi hermano.   *brother.*

2.2 Verbs with irregularities

2.2.1 Changes in the ending from -i- to -y-

leer *(to read)*	>	**leyendo**	**caer** *(to fall)*	>	**cayendo**
construir *(to build)*	>	**construyendo**	**oír** *(to hear)*	>	**oyendo**
traer *(to bring)*	>	**trayendo**	**ir** *(to go)*	>	**yendo**

Mis hermanos están construyendo una   *My brothers are building a house*
  casa en el campo.   *in the country.*
Estoy oyendo ruidos.   *I'm hearing noises.*

2.2.2 *Changes in the stem*

e > i

decir (*to say*)	>	diciendo	sentir (*to feel*)	>	sintiendo
venir (*to come*)	>	viniendo	reír (*to laugh*)	>	riendo
pedir (*to ask for*)	>	pidiendo	sonreír (*to smile*)	>	sonriendo

Estoy diciendo la verdad.   *I'm telling the truth.*
Están pidiendo el segundo plato.   *They're ordering the main course.*
Marta siempre está sonriendo.   *Marta is always smiling.*

o > u

dormir (*to sleep*) > durmiendo   poder (*to be able to*) > pudiendo

La niña está durmiendo.   *The little girl is sleeping.*

3 Use

The gerund is used in the following ways:

3.1

To talk about what you are doing at the moment of speaking by using **estar** plus the gerund. This is the same as the *to be doing* form in English:

¿Qué estás haciendo?   *What are you doing?*
Estoy estudiando.   *I'm studying.*
Está comiendo.   *He / She is eating.*
Estamos leyendo.   *We're reading.*
¿Estáis escribiendo?   *Are you writing?*
Están viendo la televisión.   *They're watching television.*

3.2

The gerund is also used to express the duration of an action:

Paso el fin de semana limpiando la casa.   *I spend all weekend cleaning the house.*

Trabaja escuchando la radio.   *He works while listening to the radio.*

3.3

The simple present tense is often used in place of the present continuous, especially with verbs such as **ir** and **venir**:

Luis va al colegio ahora.   *Luis is going to school now.*

is more common than:
Luis está yendo al colegio ahora.

Juan viene por la calle.   *Juan is coming along the street.*

is more usual than
Juan está viniendo por la calle.

4 The gerund with pronouns

4.1

If the gerund is accompanied by an object pronoun, this is usually placed after the verb.

 See Unit 9 Section 6.5.2.

A: ¿Estás preparando la cena?	*Are you preparing dinner?*
B: Sí, estoy preparándola.	*Yes, I am preparing it.*

A: ¿Está escuchando las noticias?	*Is he listening to the news?*
B: Sí, está escuchándolas.	*Yes, he's listening to it.*

4.2

But sometimes, especially in speech, the pronoun is placed before the conjugated verb:

A: ¿Estáis viendo la televisión?	*Are you watching the television?*
B: Sí, la estamos viendo.	*Yes, we're watching it.*
(Sí, estamos viéndola.)	

¿Estás llamando a tu hermano?	*Are you calling your brother?*
Sí, lo estoy llamando.	*Yes, I'm calling him.*
(Sí, estoy llamándolo.)	

4.3

The rule also applies to reflexive verbs, which always have a pronoun with them:

María está duchándose.	*María is having a shower.*
María se está duchando.	

Yo estoy bañándome en la piscina.	*I'm bathing in the pool.*
Yo me estoy bañando en la piscina.	

5 Gramática práctica

34.5.1 Transform the verbs in brackets using **estar** + gerund.

1. Nosotros (estudiar) para un examen.
2. Mi madre (trabajar) ahora.
3. ¿Qué (hacer) Pedro?
4. María y yo (terminar) los deberes de español.
5. Juan (desayunar) aún y va a llegar tarde a clase.
6. Nosotras (comer) con unos amigos.
7. Yo (tomar) café con mis padres.
8. Nosotros (jugar) al tenis.
9. Ricardo (beber) un café con leche.
10. Yo (escribir) unos emails.

34.5.2 Write the complete response using the present continuous with a pronoun.

Example: ¿Estás tomando la leche? Sí, estoy tomándola ahora.

1. ¿Ha comido el niño la sopa? No, (comer) ahora.
2. ¿Has leído este libro? No, (leer) ahora.
3. ¿Han terminado los deberes todos los estudiantes? No, pero (terminar) ahora.
4. ¿Has planchado la ropa? No, (planchar) en este mismo momento.
5. ¿Habéis fregado los platos? No, (fregar) ahora.
6. ¿Has limpiado tu cuarto? No, (limpiar) ahora.
7. ¿Se han bañado los niños? No, (bañarse) ahora.
8. ¿Ha dado los ejercicios el profesor? No, (dar) ahora.
9. ¿Has hecho la cena? No, (hacer) ahora.
10. ¿Has escuchado las noticias? No, (escuchar) ahora.

6 Más allá

6.1

With two object pronouns the rule is the same as with one:

A: ¿Está comprando la pulsera para su novia?	*Is he buying the bracelet for his girlfriend?*
B: Sí, está comprándosela.	*Yes, he's buying it for her.*
A: ¿Estuviste explicando los verbos a los estudiantes?	*Were you explaining the verbs to the students?*
B: Sí, estuve explicándoselos.	*Yes, I was explaining them to them.*

Note that the indirect object pronoun forms **le / les** change to **se** in all cases when they are paired with direct object pronouns, as in the above examples.

 See Unit 9 point 6.3.3.

6.2 The gerund as an adverb

The gerund can have an adverbial function; this means it can act as an adverb in the sentence and modify the main verb:

Pedro viene corriendo.	*Pedro is coming, running.*
María entró sonriendo.	*Maria came in smiling.*
Pedro aprende leyendo en voz alta.	*Pedro learns by reading aloud.*

 For the use of the gerund with other verbs and structures see Unit 42 on phrasal verbs.

7 Más práctica

34.7.1 Answer the questions using the present continuous with two pronouns.

Example: ¿Estáis comprando las botas para Julio? > Sí, estamos comprándoselas.

1. ¿Estás comprando los pantalones a tu hijo?
2. ¿Estáis preparando la cena para vuestros amigos?
3. ¿Están escribiendo los emails a sus hijos?
4. ¿Estás preparando los documentos para mí?
5. ¿Estás dando la comida al bebé?
6. ¿Estás leyendo el libro a la niña?
7. ¿Estáis comprando el regalo para vuestra madre?
8. ¿Estás buscando el libro para mí?
9. ¿Estáis preparando la cena para nosotros?
10. ¿Estás haciendo el desayuno para mí?

35 The participle *El participio*

1 ¿Qué es?

The participle (past participle) is the verb form that follows the auxiliary **haber** in compound tenses, and it is also used in passive constructions. The participle can also act as an adjective.

He comido ensalada.	*I have eaten salad.*
El ladrón fue detenido por la policía.	*The thief was arrested by the police.*
Estoy cansado.	*I'm tired.*

2 Forms

2.1

The participle is formed by removing the infinitive endings and adding its own endings:

-ar > -ado	**trabajar > trabajado**
-er > -ido	**comer > comido**
-ir > -ido	**vivir > vivido**

Note that the forms for **-er** and **-ir** verbs are the same.

He trabajado mucho esta semana.	*I've worked a lot this week.*
Hoy he comido con mis padres.	*Today I've had lunch with my parents.*
Ha vivido muchos años en Barcelona.	*He has lived in Barcelona for many years.*

2.2 Irregular participles

hacer (*to do*)	>	**hecho**	**poner** (*to put*)	>	**puesto**
escribir (*to write*)	>	**escrito**	**abrir** (*to open*)	>	**abierto**
ver (*to see*)	>	**visto**	**romper** (*to break*)	>	**roto**
volver (*to return*)	>	**vuelto**	**cubrir** (*to cover*)	>	**cubierto**
decir (*to say*)	>	**dicho**	**morir** (*to die*)	>	**muerto**

2.3

Some participles have a regular form when they act as verbs and an irregular form when they act as adjectives.

despertar (*to wake up*)	>	**despertado**	>	**despierto**
freír (*to fry*)	>	**freído**	>	**frito**
confundir (*to confuse*)	>	**confundido**	>	**confuso**
soltar (*to let go*)	>	**soltado**	>	**suelto**
hartar (*to get fed up*)	>	**hartado**	>	**harto**

Me he despertado a las seis de la mañana. Estoy despierto.
I woke up at 6 in the morning. I'm awake.

He freído las patatas. Las patatas están fritas.
I've fried the potatoes. The potatoes are fried.

3 Use

3.1 Compound tenses

The participle is used to form compound tenses and it follows the auxiliary verb **haber**. In this case the participle form doesn't change.

 See Units 31 (present perfect) and 36 (compound tenses).

María ha salido de casa.
María has left the house.

Manolo ha llegado tarde al trabajo.
Manolo has arrived late at work.

Mis padres han venido a mi casa.
My parents have come to my house.

Nosotros hemos ido al cine.
We have been to the cinema.

3.2 Adjectives

If the participle is used as an adjective its form changes in gender and number as adjectives do.

 See Unit 6.

Compare:

Ana está cansada.
Ana is tired.

Ana se ha cansado.
Ana has got tired. (lit: Ana has tired herself.)

El vaso está roto.
The vase is broken.

El pollo ya está asado.
The chicken is roasted now.

La puerta está abierta.
The door is open.

Las niñas están invitadas a la fiesta.
The girls are invited to the party.

Los niños están cansados.
The boys are tired.

4 Gramática práctica

35.4.1 Answer the questions following the example:

¿Vas a limpiar la casa? > Ya he limpiado la casa.

1. ¿Vais a comprar el pan?
2. ¿Vais a terminar el trabajo?
3. ¿Vas a estudiar?
4. ¿Van a salir?
5. ¿Vas a comer?
6. ¿Vais a pasear por el parque?

35.4.2 Fill the gaps with the participles of the verbs in the box.

cubrir hacer caer poner gustar oír llover decir ver volver engañar
empezar morir abrir acostar romper pasar poner

1. El cielo se ha _____ completamente y ha _____
2. El niño ya ha _____ los deberes y se ha _____
3. No me has _____ la verdad, me has _____
4. No me han _____ la puerta, pero los he _____ dentro.
5. El jarrón se ha _____ y se ha _____
6. No me he _____ el abrigo y he _____ mucho frío.
7. No han _____ aún del cine y hemos _____ a cenar.
8. Ya hemos_____ esta película y no nos ha _____
9. Mi gato se ha _____ y nos hemos _____ muy tristes.

5 Más allá

5.1 Forms

-er and **-ir** verbs with the stem ending in a vowel add an accent to the **i** in
-ido, except when the vowel is **-u**, e.g.: **destruido**.

 See Unit 2.

traer > **traído** (*brought*)
leer > **leído** (*read*)
caer > **caído** (*fallen*)
oír > **oído** (*heard*)
reír > **reído** (*laughed*)

But note: **La casa está destruida. El desayuno está incluido.**

5.2 he comprao

In spoken colloquial Spanish the **-d-** of the participle of verbs in **-ar** is often
dropped: **comprado** > **comprao**, **cenado** > **cenao**

He comprado un abrigo azul. > He comprao un abrigo azul.
He cenado pollo con patatas fritas. > He cenao pollo con patatas fritas.

5.3

The participle is often used as an adjective with the verb **to be estar**.

This usage should not be confused with **ser** + participle; if the participle is used with **ser** it is to form a passive sentence (see point 5.4 below).

Compare:

Las patatas están cocinadas.	*The potatoes are cooked. (i.e. not raw)*
Las patatas son cocinadas por mi madre.	*The potatoes are cooked by my mother.*

5.4 The passive

The participle also forms part of the passive; this is constructed with the verb **ser** + participle forms. In this case the participle is variable; it changes in gender and number depending on the passive subject:

Los cuadros han sido llevados al museo.	*The pictures have been taken to the museum.*
Este cuadro fue pintado por Picasso.	*This picture was painted by Picasso.*
Esta bolsa ha sido encontrada en el autobús.	*This bag has been found on the bus.*
Mis hermanas no fueron invitadas a la fiesta.	*My sisters weren't invited to the party.*

 See Unit 44.

5.5 Absolute participle

This is used mainly in written and literary style. It often begins the sentence and it's variable, like an adjective.

Terminada la clase salieron de compras.	*The class having finished, they went shopping.*

5.6 The adjectival present participle

This acts as an adjective. Although the English equivalent is the *-ing* form, the adjectival participle should not be confused with the gerund, which is used for continuous tenses.

The forms are:

-ar > -ante	preocupar > preocupante
-er > -ente or -iente	proceder > procedente
-ir > -ente or -iente	sonreír > sonriente

El AVE procedente de Madrid llegará a las cuatro.	*The AVE (coming) from Madrid will arrive at four o'clock.*

6 Más práctica

35.6.1 Complete the sentences with the participles of the verbs in brackets. Remember that in the passive voice the participles change in number and gender.

Example: Las ventanas fueron (abrir) por la mañana. > Las ventanas fueron <u>abiertas</u> por la mañana.

 1. Este cuadro fue (pintar) por Goya.
 2. Esta escultura fue (hacer) por un escultor francés.
 3. Los papeles fueron (encontrar) en un taxi.
 4. María no fue (invitar) a la boda.
 5. Los ladrones fueron (ver) en un barrio de las afueras.
 6. La mujer fue (poner) en libertad.
 7. Los estudiantes fueron (examinar) por un tribunal.
 8. Los cuadros fueron (exponer) en el museo nacional.
 9. La casa ha sido (comprar) por una familia con niños.
10. El paquete fue (devolver) porque no estabas en casa.

35.6.2 Translate the sentences from 35.6.1 into English.

36 Compound tenses of the indicative
Tiempos compuestos del modo indicativo

1 ¿Qué es?

Compound tenses are formed by two verbs: the auxiliary verb **haber** and the participle of the main verb, e.g.: **He comprado** (*I have bought*).

The auxiliary verb can be conjugated, and indicates the different tenses and persons. The main verb, the participle, gives the meaning to the sentence.

Note that the participle does not vary in gender or number in Spanish.

A: ¿Habéis estudiado la lección?   *Have you studied the lesson?*
B: Sí, ya hemos estudiado la lección.   *Yes, we have studied the lesson.*
A: ¿Habías visitado antes la ciudad?   *Had you visited the city before?*
B: No, no había visitado nunca la ciudad.   *No, I had never visited the city.*

2 The indicative compound tenses

The following are the compound tenses of the indicative in Spanish:

2.1 El pretérito perfecto (*The present perfect*)

El profesor se ha enfadado porque   *The teacher got angry because I*
  he llegado tarde a clase.   *arrived late to class.*

2.2 El pretérito pluscuamperfecto (*The pluperfect*)

Cuando llegaste al restaurante   *When you arrived at the restaurant*
  ya habíamos comido.   *we had already eaten.*

2.3 El pretérito anterior (*The past anterior*)*

Cuando todo el público hubo   *When all the people had entered the*
  entrado empezó el concierto.   *concert began.*

* This tense is never used in spoken Spanish.

2.4 El futuro perfecto (*The future perfect*)

Cuando vengas ya habremos   *When you come we will already have*
  preparado la comida.   *prepared the meal.*

2.5 El pasado condicional (*The past conditional*)

Yo habría estado solo todo el día si   *I would have been on my own all*
  no hubieras venido a visitarme.   *day if you hadn't come to visit me.*

 See the full forms in the Verb tables.

See also Unit 35 on Participles.

The forms and uses of each of the tenses are studied below.

Note: all compound tenses except the present perfect belong to the **Más allá** section (higher level).

 To study the compound tenses of the subjunctive see Unit 39.

3 The present perfect

This is the most commonly used of the compound tenses. It is formed with the present tense of the verb **haber** plus the participle of the conjugated verb:

yo + he + cenado / comido / salido

He empezado mi nuevo trabajo.   *I have started my new job.*

 See Unit 31 on the present perfect.

4 Más allá

4.1 The pluperfect

4.1.1

This is formed with the imperfect of the auxiliary verb **haber** and the participle of the conjugated verb:

yo + había + cenado / comido / salido

More examples:

yo había entrado, tú habías venido, él había salido, nosotros habíamos hablado, vosotras habíais terminado, ellas habían estudiado

4.1.2

The pluperfect refers to events that happened before other events in the past. In other words it is the past of the past. In English it corresponds to **someone had done something** or **something had happened**.

La tienda había cerrado cuando llegamos.	*The shop had closed when we arrived.*
Había terminado de comer cuando me llamaste.	*I had finished eating when you called me.*
Cuando llegó la policía el hombre había desaparecido.	*When the police arrived, the man had disappeared.*

4.2 The past anterior

4.2.1

It is never used in spoken Spanish and is mainly found in literary texts.

The past anterior is formed with the preterite or simple past of the auxiliary verb **haber** and the participle of the conjugated verb:

yo + hube + cenado / comido / salido

4.2.2

It expresses an action completed just before another past action. It is usually preceded by the time adverb **apenas**:

Apenas hube llegado, empezó la conferencia.	*I had hardly arrived when the conference began.*

4.3 The future perfect

4.3.1

This is formed with the future of the auxiliary verb **haber** and the participle of the conjugated verb:

yo + habré + cenado / comido / salido

4.3.2

It expresses a future action which will happen before another future action. It is translated as **will have done something**:

Cuando lleguemos mi madre habrá preparado la comida.	*By the time we arrive my mother will have already prepared dinner.*

4.3.3

It is also used to express probability in the past:

Ana habrá salido ya.	*Ana will have left already.*

4.4 The past conditional

4.4.1

It is formed with the conditional of the auxiliary verb **haber** and the participle of the conjugated verb:

yo + habría + cenado / comido / salido

4.4.2

It corresponds to the English **would have done something** or **something would have happened**:

Luis dijo que cuando vinieras él ya habría salido.	*Luis said that by the time you arrived he would already have left.*

4.4.3

It is mostly used in past conditional sentences in the following construction:

if + the pluperfect subjunctive + past conditional

Si hubieras llamado habría salido contigo.

If you had called I would have gone out with you.

5 Gramática práctica

36.5.1 Complete the sentences with the correct form of the pretérito pluscuamperfecto.

Example: Cuando yo llegué, Pedro ya (salir) > Cuando yo llegué, Pedro ya había salido.

1. Cuando Marta entró en casa, sus padres ya (cenar)
2. Cuando entramos en el cine, ya (terminar) la película.
3. Cuando salimos de casa, ya (empezar) a llover.
4. Cuando la niña fue a coger el pastel, su hermano ya se lo (comer)
5. Cuando fui a comprar la falda, la dependienta ya la (vender)
6. Cuando llegó la policía, los ladrones ya se (escapar)
7. Cuando llegué a la tienda, aún no (abrir)

36.5.2 Underline the tenses that you have studied in this section and say which tense each one is.

1. Teresa habrá terminado ya sus exámenes.
2. El programa había terminado cuando puse la tele.
3. Si hubieras estudiado, habrías sacado buenas notas.
4. Cuando venga el jefe, nosotros ya habremos terminado el proyecto.
5. Mis hermanos no han cenado aún.
6. Cuando ocurrió el accidente, yo aún no había llegado.
7. Cuando lleguemos, ya habrán limpiado el apartamento.
8. No he salido de casa desde hace una semana.

36.5.3 Translate the sentences in 36.5.2 into English.

37 The imperative *El imperativo*

1 ¿Qué es?

The imperative is a verb form that is used to give instructions, advice and orders.

2 Form

The imperative has four forms in Spanish: two for the familiar or informal **tú** and **vosotros** and two for the formal **usted** and **ustedes**.

	Informal		Formal	
	Singular	**Plural**	**Singular**	**Plural**
Verb	tú	vosotros	usted	ustedes
tomar	tom<u>a</u>	tom<u>ad</u>	tom<u>e</u>	tom<u>en</u>
comer	com<u>e</u>	com<u>ed</u>	com<u>a</u>	com<u>an</u>
escribir	escrib<u>e</u>	escrib<u>id</u>	escrib<u>a</u>	escrib<u>an</u>

Note that the **vosotros** form replaces the final **-r** of the infinitive with **-d**.

2.1

The informal or familiar **tú** form is the same as the 3rd person singular of the present indicative tense.

Compare:

Ana come un plátano todas las mañanas. *Ana eats a banana every day.*
Ana, come un plátano, está muy bueno. *Ana, eat a banana, it's good.*

2.2

The formal **usted** and **ustedes** forms and the negative forms of the imperative (both formal and informal) are the same as the present subjunctive forms.

 For the present subjunctive, see Unit 38.

Tome (usted) la calle a
   la derecha.
Miren (ustedes) los cuadros.

Take the street on the right.
   (formal sing.)
Look at the pictures. (formal plural)

No escribas (tú) en el libro.	*Don't write in the book. (informal singular)*

2.3 Irregular imperatives (informal singular: tú)

poner	>	pon	tener	>	ten
salir	>	sal	decir	>	di
hacer	>	haz	ir	>	ve
venir	>	ven	ser	>	sé

 For irregulars in the **usted / ustedes** forms and the negative imperative see the subjunctive forms in Unit **38** and the Verb tables.

To help you remember: **pon, sal, haz** are like the 3rd person singular of the verb but without the final -e: **sale > sal, pone > pon, hace > haz**

or simply drop the infinitive endings: **venir > ven, tener > ten**

Pon el libro en la mesa.	*Put the book on the table.*
Sal de casa ahora.	*Leave the house now.*
Haz los deberes.	*Do the homework.*
Ven aquí.	*Come here.*
Ten cuidado.	*Take care, be careful.*
Di la verdad.	*Tell the truth.*
Ve a casa ahora.	*Go home now.*
Sé bueno.	*Be good.*

3 Use

3.1 Informal and formal

3.1.1

We use the informal form of the imperative if we are talking to a member of the family or a friend.

We use the formal form of the imperative if we are talking to someone we don't know well, or someone in authority, or in any kind of formal situation, for example giving directions in the street.

 See Unit 9 point 5.6 on **tú** and **usted**.

Verb	Informal	Formal	
seguir	sigue	siga (la calle)	*carry on along (the street)*
tomar	toma	tome (la primera calle)	*take (the first street)*

Compare these examples of the same directions; the first is informal, the second is formal:

English:
Cross the street and carry straight on, take the first on the right, go up that street, pass the supermarket and it's there.

Informal:
Cruza la calle y sigue todo recto, toma la primera a la derecha, sube por esa calle, pasa el supermercado y allí está.

Formal:
Cruce la calle y siga todo recto, tome la primera a la derecha, suba por esa calle, pase el supermercado y allí está.

3.1.2 *Many everyday expressions are imperatives*

Informal	Formal	
Oye	Oiga	*Excuse me* (lit: *Listen, hear*)
Perdona	Perdone	*Pardon me, Excuse me*
Perdóname	Perdóneme	*Sorry!*
Cuida	Cuide	*Careful!*
Mira	Mire	*Look!*
Ven aquí	Venga aquí	*Come here!*

3.1.3

The following expressions use the formal form but are used as fixed expressions in all situations, formal and informal:

Diga, Dígame   *Hello (on the phone)*
                        (lit: Speak, speak to me)

¡Venga!   *Come on!*
¡Vaya!   *Well! (surprise, disappointment)*

3.1.4

Imperatives are also used in many everyday situations, often adding **por favor** at the end or beginning of the sentence:

tú	usted		
Dame	Deme	un kilo de tomates	*(Can you) give me a kilo of tomatoes.*
Ponme	Póngame	dos kilos de peras	*give* (lit: *put*) *me two kilos of pears.*
Cóbrame	Cóbreme	los cafés, por favor	*take (the money) for the coffees please.*

Note how many of these add a personal pronoun at the end to form one word.

Note also that words formed in this way, which are of three or more syllables, often require an accent, as in **póngame, cóbreme.**

  See Unit 2 Section 3.

Note also that the personal pronoun must always go after the imperative.

See Unit 9 point 6.5.3. See also point 5.1.1 in **Más allá** below.

3.1.5

The informal form is widely used in Spain, and even becomes acceptable in many fairly formal situations simply by adding *please*: **por favor**:

In a bar, talking to a younger waiter:

Dame una cerveza, por favor.   *(Could you) give me a beer, please.*

But this is not the case in Latin America, where the forms **tú** and **vosotros** are not used at all. Latin American Spanish prefers the forms **usted** and **ustedes** even when talking to family, friends and children.

Pase, por favor.   *Come in, please.*
Niños, empiecen el examen ahora.   *Children, start the exam now.*

3.1.6

Often in the imperative, the **usted** form is replaced by **poder** (*to be able*) + infinitive:

Abra la puerta.   *Open the door.*
¿Puede abrir la puerta?   *Can you open the door?*

3.1.7 The vocative

When we use the imperative to address someone, the person addressed often appears at the beginning of the sentence, followed by a comma; this is called a **vocativo** (*vocative*)

María, ven aquí.   *Maria, come here.*
Mamá, compra pan.   *Mum, buy some bread.*

4 Gramática práctica

37.4.1 Rewrite the sentences in the imperative (**tú** or **usted**).

Example: Tiene(s) que tomar las pastillas > Toma / Tome las pastillas.

 1. Tienes que tomar menos café.
 2. Tienes que escribir a tu amigo.
 3. Tiene que comer en ese restaurante.
 4. Tiene que pasar por esta calle.
 5. Tienes que hablar con tu hermano.
 6. Tienes que comprar un regalo para tu madre.
 7. Tiene que abrir la tienda.
 8. Tiene que mandar el paquete.
 9. Tienes que vender el coche.
10. Tiene que subir al segundo piso.

37.4.2 Give the plural imperatives of the sentences in 37.4.1.

Example: Toma / Tome las pastillas > Tomad / Tomen las pastillas.

37.4.3 Complete the sentences using the imperative of the verbs: **tener**, **poner**, **hacer**, **salir**, **decir**, **ir**, **venir**, **ser**

1. _____ la mesa, vamos a comer.
2. ¡_____ a casa ahora mismo!
3. _____ ahora de casa o perderás el tren.
4. _____ a ver esta película, te gustará.
5. _____ cuidado con el tráfico.
6. _____ los deberes.
7. _____ tu nombre en voz alta.
8. _____ bueno con tus hermanos.

5 Más allá

5.1 Imperatives + personal pronouns

5.1.1

As we have seen above (point 3.1.4) the imperative is always followed by the personal pronoun. This is also the case when there are two pronouns:

Haz la comida para ellos.>	*Make lunch for them. >*
Házsela.	*Make it for them.*
Compra un regalo para mí. >	*Buy a gift for me. >*
Cómpramelo.	*Buy me it.*
Decid el problema a él. >	*Tell him the problem. >*
Decídselo.	*Tell him it.*

5.1.2

The **vosotros** imperative plural loses the final **-d** of its ending when it is followed by the personal pronoun **os** (2nd person plural: **you**):

levantad + os > levantaos

Niños, levantaos, son las ocho.   *Kids, get up, it's eight.*

lavad + os > lavaos

Lavaos bien las manos.   *Wash your hands properly.*

5.1.3

Note that you might hear some Spanish speakers using the infinitive instead of the imperative plural **vosotros** form, especially when followed by a pronoun:

pasad > pasar
Terminad los deberes. > Terminar los deberes.

This way of formulating the imperative is not considered grammatically correct.

 For the use of pronouns with the negative imperative see Unit 38 on the Subjunctive.

5.2 Double imperative

It is possible to repeat an imperative or to use two different imperatives combined for emphasis or for greater effect.

Often one of the imperatives is an exclamative: **venga** or **anda**.

Invitation:

A: ¿Puedo pasar? *Can I come in?*
B: Sí, claro, pasa, pasa. *Yes of course, come in, come in.*

Anda, entra, que te están esperando. *Go on, go in, they're waiting for you.*

Urgency:

Corre, corre, que se va el autobús. *Hurry up, hurry up, the bus is going.*

5.3 ¡Vamos!

The first person plural can take an imperative meaning, although it is not an imperative form in itself. The equivalent in English is *Let's (go)*, and it is used to make suggestions:

Llegamos tarde, ¡vamos! *We'll arrive late, let's go!*
Vamos al cine. *Let's go to the cinema.*

6 Más práctica

37.6.1 Complete the sentences with the appropriate imperatives and pronouns.

1. Sra González, (sentarse) en este sillon, estará más cómoda.
2. Juan, (levantarse) de la cama, vas a llegar tarde.
3. Luis, (dar a mí) el libro que está sobre la mesa.
4. Jorge, (ponerse) esta camisa, ésa está sucia.
5. María, (irse) ahora y así llegarás antes.
6. Niños, (lavarse) las manos.
7. Luis, (llamar a tu madre) por teléfono mañana.
8. Sres pasajeros, (abrocharse) los cinturones.
9. (Darse) prisa, que llegaréis tarde a clase.

37.6.2 Turn the questions into imperatives.

Example: ¿Me lo das? > Dámelo.

1. ¿Me lo compras?
2. ¿Nos la das?
3. ¿Se lo come?
4. ¿Se los cobras?
5. ¿Me las pasas?
6. ¿Se la pone?
7. ¿Te las tomas?
8. ¿Me lo vende?
9. ¿Os los bebéis?
10. ¿Me los prestan?

38 The subjunctive I (present)
El subjuntivo I (presente)

1 ¿Qué es?

In Spanish, the indicative mood (**modo indicativo**) of verbs expresses actions that are either real or certain or believed to be real or certain by the speaker in the different tenses.

But there is another mood called the subjunctive (**modo subjuntivo**), which is a parallel system which expresses possibility, uncertainty or unreality.

The speaker uses the subjunctive mode to express his or her feelings and personal attitudes such as wishes, doubts, orders, annoyances, and fears. An easy way to remember when to use the subjunctive is to consider it as a subjective action or idea, as seen from the perspective of the speaker. Compare the following examples:

Juan estudia para los exámenes.   *Juan is studying for his exams.*

In this example, we know Juan is studying and therefore we use the indicative mood in the present. Now look at the following:

Quiero que Juan estudie para   *I want Juan to study for his*
los exámenes.   *exams.*

In this example the speaker expresses a wish that Juan should study for his exams. So here the subjunctive mood in the present is used, reflecting the context and attitude of the speaker.

There are various tenses in the subjunctive, but first we'll study the present.

2 Forms

2.1 The present subjunctive: regular verbs

	-ar (tomar)	-er (comer)	-ir (escribir)
(yo)	tom<u>e</u>	com<u>a</u>	escrib<u>a</u>
(tú)	tom<u>es</u>	com<u>as</u>	escrib<u>as</u>
(él / ella / Vd)	tom<u>e</u>	com<u>a</u>	escrib<u>a</u>
(nosotros/as)	tom<u>emos</u>	com<u>amos</u>	escrib<u>amos</u>
(vosotros/as)	tom<u>éis</u>	com<u>áis</u>	escrib<u>áis</u>
(ellos / ellas / Vds)	tom<u>en</u>	com<u>an</u>	escrib<u>an</u>

Note: Verbs that end in **-er** take the same forms as those that end in **-ir**.

The subjunctive is formed in the same way as the first person of the present indicative tense, but with a different ending; for example: **tom_o_** becomes **tom_e_, com_o_** becomes **com_a_**:

Normalmente tomo café a las ocho.	*I have coffee at eight.*
No creo que tome café hoy.	*I don't think I'll have coffee today.*

Learning tip:

Apart from the first person singular, the endings of the verbs in **-ar** in the subjunctive are the same as those of the indicative for the verbs in **-er** and **-ir**.

Similarly, for **-er** and **-ir** verbs, apart from the first person singular the endings are the same as those of the verbs in **-ar** in the indicative.

So we have the indicative:

¿No desayun_as_ hoy?	*Aren't you having breakfast today?*

and the subjunctive:

Mejor que no desay un_es_ hoy.	*It's best if you don't have breakfast today.*

and

¿No com_e_?	*Isn't he having lunch?*
No creo que com_a_ hoy.	*I don't think he's having lunch today.*

2.2 The present subjunctive: irregular verbs

2.2.1 Present subjunctive of stem-changing verbs

If the verb has an irregular form in the first person singular of the present simple, it uses the same form to make the subjunctive for all persons:

	Infinitivo	1ª p. pres. indic.	Pres. Subj.
Example:	**poner >**	**pong_o_ >**	**pong_a_**

¿Pongo la mesa?	*Shall I set the table?*
Es mejor que ponga la mesa ¿verdad?	*It's best if I set the table, isn't it?*
¿No pones la mesa?	*Aren't you going to set the table?*
Es mejor que pongas la mesa.	*It's best if you set the table.*

The subjunctive form of stem-changing verbs is as follows:
hacer: haga, hagas, haga, hagamos, hagáis, hagan
poner: ponga, pongas, ponga, pongamos, pongáis, pongan
venir: venga, etc.
salir: salga, etc.
tener: tenga, etc.
decir: diga, etc.
oír: oiga, etc.
seguir: siga, etc.

2.2.2

Present subjunctive of verbs that have vowel stem changes:

e > ie; o/u > ue

In these verbs, the first and second persons plural have a regular stem, as in the present indicative:

querer: quiera, quieras, quiera, queramos, queráis, quieran
poder: pueda, puedas, pueda, podamos, podáis, puedan
volver: vuelva, vuelvas, vuelva, volvamos, volváis, vuelvan

Note that **dormir** (*to sleep*) changes the **-o** to **-u**: **duerma > durmamos**;
sentir and **mentir** change the **-e** to **-i**: **sienta > sintamos; mienta > mintamos**.

But in verbs that change **-e** to **-i** the irregularity is kept in the first and second persons plural of the present subjunctive:

pedir: pida, pidas, pida, pidamos, pidáis, pidan
seguir: siga, sigas, siga, sigamos, sigáis, sigan

 See Unit 24 for stem-changing verbs in the present.

2.2.3 Major irregular verbs

ir (voy > vaya); dar (doy > dé); haber (he > haya); saber (sé > sepa);

2.2.4 Other subjunctive forms in the present

estar (estoy > esté)

 For full conjugations see Verb tables.

3 Use

The present subjunctive is used to talk about both the present and the future. It can be used in independent sentences, such as commands or invitations:

¡Entre!	*Go in!*
Vaya por aquí.	*Go this way.*
Pase, por favor.	*Please come in.*

and also in subordinate clauses. In this case the sentence is introduced and usually linked to the main sentence by **que**:

Quiero que compres este coche.   *I'd like you to buy this car.*

The use of the subjunctive depends on what we say in the main clause. Study the following examples; the first one uses the indicative and the second the subjunctive.

Estoy seguro de que Juan   *I'm certain Juan will pass*
  aprobará el examen.   *the exam.*

No estoy seguro de que Juan apruebe el examen.	*I'm not sure whether Juan will pass the exam.*

The first one expresses a reality; the speaker is sure it's going to happen.

The second one expresses a doubt; the speaker is not sure the action is going to happen and therefore he / she uses the subjunctive.

Note that the subject of the main clause (which has the verb in the indicative) must be different from the subject of the subordinate clause in order to have a subjunctive, as in this example:

Yo quiero que Juan apruebe el examen.	*I want Juan to pass the exam. (lit.: I want that Juan passes the exam.)*

The subject of the main clause is **yo** (*I*) and the subject of the subordinate clause is Juan.

If both clauses have the same subject we use the infinitive in the second clause:

Yo quiero aprobar el examen.	*I want to pass the exam.*

The subject of both clauses, *want* and *pass*, is **yo** (*I*).

The subjunctive is used in the following cases:

3.1 To give instructions and orders

3.1.1 As a formal positive imperative, in independent sentences

The forms of the subjunctive are used for the formal imperative **usted**: **(usted) tome, coma, escriba, compre, salga** etc.

¡Pase!	*Come in!*
¡Dígame!	*Tell me! (used when answering the phone)*
Tome la derecha, cruce, siga todo recto.	*Take the right hand turning, cross, carry straight on.*

3.1.2 Negative imperative

If the instructions, orders or advice are in the negative, we use the present subjunctive form of the verb for both the informal (**tú**):

no comas	*don't eat*
no escribas	*don't write*

and formal (**usted**):

no salga	*don't leave*
no venga	*don't come*

Note: To give instructions and orders in the negative, use the same subjunctive form but with the word **No** at the beginning of the sentence.

Examples for **tú / vosotros** (informal):

tirar

No tires / No tiréis papeles al suelo.   *Don't throw litter on the floor.*

utilizar

No utilices / No utilicéis insecticidas.   *Don't use insecticides.*

comprar

No compres / No compréis botellas   *Don't buy plastic bottles.*
   de plástico.

Examples for **usted / ustedes** (formal):

cruzar

No cruce (usted) / No crucen   *Don't cross the street.*
   (ustedes) la calle.

salir

No salga (usted) / No salgan (ustedes).   *Don't leave / go out.*

 For the familiar affirmative imperative (**tú**) see Unit 37.

3.1.3 *After main clauses with verbs of ordering, forbidding, allowing*

mandar, ordenar, prohibir, dejar, permitir (te mando que . . .,

le ordeno que . . ., os prohíbo que . . ., nos deja que . . ., les permiten que . . .)

Te prohíbo que vayas allí.   *I forbid you to go there.*
En el camping no permiten que entren coches después de las doce de la noche.
In the campsite they don't allow cars to enter after midnight.

3.1.4 *To express an order or a strong suggestion the following structure is used frequently*

que + (no) subjunctive:

¡Que pase!   *Tell him / her to come in.*
     (lit: that he /she should come in)

¡Que venga ahora!   *He should come now.*

Notice that although it's an exclamatory phrase, **que** has no accent because it is the equivalent of *that*. Think of such sentences as orders with the main verb (e.g. *tell*) understood but not expressed.

3.2 To give advice

3.2.1 *As an imperative (see point 3.1 above for instructions)*

Tomen más sopa, está muy buena.   *Have more soup, it's very nice.*
     (Speaking formally to more than one person)

No salgas ahora, está lloviendo.   *Don't go out now, it's raining.*
     (Speaking informally to one person)

3.2.2 *After verbs of advice*

aconsejar que
Te aconsejo que le compres
  este libro.

*I advise you to buy him /
  her this book.*

recomendar que
Te recomiendo que alquiles
  el apartamento.

*I recommend that you rent
  the apartment.*

sugerir que
Sugiero que vayamos al cine.

I suggest we go to the cinema.

3.2.3 *After expressions of advice (impersonal)*

es mejor que
Es mejor que le compres el rojo.

It's better if you buy him the red one.

es aconsejable que
Es aconsejable que pongas la comida
  en el frigorífico.

*It's advisable to put the food in
  the fridge.*

es recomendable que
Es recomendable que
  vayas ahora.

*It's to be recommended that
  you go now.*

3.3 To say that it is necessary or important to do something

es importante que
Es importante que ayudemos
  en campañas ecologistas.

*It's important that we help
  ecological campaigns.*

es necesario que
Es necesario que usemos
  menos electricidad.

*It's necessary that we use
  less electricity.*

conviene que / es conveniente que
Conviene / Es conveniente
  que salgas temprano.

*It's convenient that you
  leave early.*

3.4 To express possibility, probability or doubt with verbs and expressions such as

dudar que
Dudo que trabajemos todos en casa.

I doubt if we will all work at home.

no estar seguro de que
No estoy seguro de que tengamos suerte.

I'm not sure that we'll be lucky.

no creer que
No creo que lleguemos a tiempo.

I don't think we'll arrive on time.

es posible que
Es posible que venga mañana.

It's possible that he'll come tomorrow.

es probable que
Es probable que llueva hoy.   *It'll probably rain today.*

puede ser que
Puede ser que traiga manzanas.   *He might bring some apples.*

3.5 To express possibility, probability or doubt

3.5.1 *After adverbs and expressions such as* quizá / quizás, tal vez, seguramente, probablemente, posiblemente

Notice that these are not followed by **que**.

Quizás termine el trabajo esta semana.   *Maybe I'll finish the work this week.*
Tal vez vaya a verte   *Maybe I'll come and see*
  mañana.   *you tomorrow.*

3.5.2

But note that with these expressions and especially with **seguramente**, **probablemente**, **posiblemente**, we can use either the subjunctive or the indicative, depending on the level of possibility. If something is perceived as very probable or certain the indicative can be used; if not we might use the subjunctive:

Probablemente Pedro llegará mañana. (Pedro will almost certainly come tomorrow)
Probablemente Pedro llegue mañana. (it is possible but not definite)

3.5.3 *A lo mejor*

This expression indicates doubt, and is much used; but, curiously, it does <u>not</u> take the subjunctive but the indicative:

A lo mejor viene mañana.   *He'll probably come tomorrow.*

3.6 Positive and negative opinions

When we want to express a positive opinion or say that we are sure about something, the indicative is used after **creer que, decir que, opinar que, pensar que, es verdad que, es cierto que**:

Creo que la reunión   *I think the meeting is*
  es mañana.   *tomorrow (certain).*

But when we express an opinion in the negative or express any doubt, or say we are not sure about something, we use the subjunctive after **no creer que, no decir que, no opinar que, no pensar que, no es verdad que, no es cierto que**.

No creo que la reunión sea mañana.   *I don't think the meeting is tomorrow.*

Notice the differences:

Pienso que su idea es excelente.   *I think his idea is excellent.*
No pienso que su idea sea excelente.   *I don't think his idea is excellent.*

Estoy seguro de que Luis vendrá.   *I'm sure that Luis will come.*
No estoy seguro de que Luis venga.   *I'm not sure whether Luis will come.*

3.7 To express desire, interest, likes, hope, fear

3.7.1

After verbs such as: **querer, desear, gustar, encantar, interesar, esperar, temer, tener miedo de**:

Quiero que vengas con nosotros.   *I'd like you to come.*
Desea que le acompañemos.   *He would like us to accompany him.*
Me encanta que comáis con nosotros.   *I'm so pleased you can eat with us.*
Espero que ganes.   *I hope you win.*
Tengo miedo de que me lo pida.   *I'm frightened that he'll ask me for it.*

3.7.2

Also for dislikes or annoyance:

enfadar (me enfada que . . .), molestar (me molesta que . . .), no gustar (no me gusta que . . .) odiar (odio que . . .), fastidiar (me fastidia que . . .):

Me enfada que dejen   *It makes me angry that they leave*
  los platos.   *their plates.*
Me molesta que sean tan vulgares.   *It annoys me that they are so vulgar.*

3.7.3

Golden rule:
If we want to say: *I want to do something*: **Yo** quiero hacer (infinitive).
But: *I want **you** to do something*: **Yo** quiero **que tú** hagas (subjunctive).

3.8 In independent sentences with the expression Ojalá

¡Ojalá vengas a verme!   *Let's hope you come to see me.*

Notice that **que** is not normally used after **Ojalá** and that usually the sentence is written with exclamation marks:

¡Ojalá haga sol mañana!   *Please let it be sunny tomorrow.*

It is sometimes possible to include **que** after **Ojalá**:

¡Ojalá que tengas un buen viaje!   *Let's hope you have a good journey!*

3.9 To express wishes with ¡Que + subjunctive!

There are many expressions which use this form:

¡Que seas feliz!   *I hope you'll be happy!*

 See point 3.1.4 above about strong suggestions.

¡Que tengas suerte!   *I hope you're lucky!*
    (lit: that you should have luck)

¡Que tengas un buen viaje!	*Have a good journey.*
¡Que cumplas muchos más (años)!	*Many happy returns.*
¡Que vaya bien!	*I hope all goes well.*

Note: **que** can be replaced by **ojalá**, and is a kind of shorter form of **espero que** . . . (*I hope that* . . .):

¡Que tengas suerte! = ¡Ojalá tengas suerte! = Espero que tengas suerte.

The expressions with **que** and **ojalá** have a stronger meaning and are said to give a greater impact than **espero que**. . . and therefore add exclamation marks in their written form.

3.10 In future time expressions

After the following:

cuando, hasta que, mientras que, antes de que, en cuanto, tan pronto como:

Cuando termine el instituto iré a la universidad.	*When I finish secondary school I'll go to university.*
Cuando termine la universidad trabajaré como profesor.	*When I finish university I'll work as a teacher.*
Trabajarán hasta que sea de noche.	*They'll work till it gets dark.*
Tan pronto como llegues, llámame.	*As soon as you arrive, call me.*

3.11 To express purpose or intention or finality

After:

para que, a fin de que, con la intención de que:

Trabaja mucho para que sus hijos estudien en la universidad.	*He works hard so that his children can study at university.*

3.12 To express *although, despite*

After:

aunque, a pesar de que, por mucho que.

In this case the subjunctive is only used when the action is in the future:

Aunque llueva, iremos al campo.	*Even if it rains we'll go to the country.*

But:

Aunque llueve, iremos al campo.	*Even though it's raining now, we'll still go to the country.*

Compare:

Por mucho que estudie no sacará buenas notas.	*It doesn't matter how much he might study, he won't get good results.*

with

Por mucho que estudia no saca buenas notas.	*It doesn't matter how much he studies, he never gets good results.*

3.13 After other expressions

3.13.1 *result, purpose, manner*

de manera que, de modo que, sin que:

Te daré la llave de modo que
   puedas entrar.

I'll give you the key so that
   you can get in.

3.13.2 *condition*

a condición de que, con tal de que, siempre y cuando:

Te doy el dinero siempre y cuando
   termines el trabajo.

I'll give you the money only
   when you finish the work.

3.14 After como

Hazlo como quieras

Do it as you like.

Note that **como quieras** is an expression used on its own to respond to a suggestion or an invitation:

A: ¿Salimos ya?

Shall we go out now?

B: Como quieras.

As you like.

3.15 With relative clauses

The subjunctive is used when the subject of the main sentence is not known, usually after: **el que, no hay quien, lo que**:

El que llegue primero, ganará el premio.   *Whoever arrives first wins the prize.*
No hay quien entienda esto.   *No-one can understand this.*
Haremos lo que tú digas.   *I'll do whatever you say.*

3.16 In some set expressions with lo que

sea lo que sea
Dame la noticia, sea lo que sea.   *Give me the news, whatever it is.*

pase lo que pase
Te ayudaré siempre, pase
   lo que pase.

I'll always help you,
   whatever happens.

digas lo que digas*
Digas lo que digas, no te
   harán caso.

You can say what you like, they
   won't take any notice.

haga lo que haga*
Haga lo que haga, siempre lo
   hago mal para él.

Whatever I do, I always do it badly
   as far as he's concerned.

trabaje lo que trabaje*
Trabaje lo que trabaje, nunca
   tendrá dinero.

It doesn't matter how hard he works,
   he'll never have any money.

*In these cases, the form of the verb can change:

Hagamos lo que hagamos . . .   *Whatever we do . . .*

4 Gramática práctica

38.4.1 Put the verbs in brackets into the appropriate form of the subjunctive.

1. Es importante que tú (poner) más baja la calefacción.
2. Es necesario que la gente (viajar) más en transporte público.
3. Es importante que nosotros (ir) en bicicleta por el centro de la ciudad.
4. Es esencial que las fábricas (contaminar) menos.
5. Es mejor que la gente (dejar) el coche en casa.
6. Es necesario que todos (ahorrar) energía eléctrica.
7. Es importante que (haber) menos tráfico.
8. Es mejor que tú (usar) menos agua caliente.

38.4.2 Transform the advice using the verbs in brackets.

Example: Tienes que tomar las pastillas (aconsejar) > Te aconsejo que tomes las pastillas.

1. Tienes que estudiar la lección. (es mejor)
2. Debes probar el pescado, está muy bueno. (recomendar)
3. Tienes que ir al médico. (es importante)
4. Compra la camiseta negra, es más bonita. (es mejor)
5. Debes darte crema bronceadora. (aconsejar)
6. Tienes que escribir a tus padres. (es importante)
7. Toma la sopa, es exquisita. (recomendar)
8. Ven pronto. (es mejor)
9. Debes ponerte el abrigo, hace frío. (aconsejar)
10. Coge el paraguas, va a llover. (es mejor)

38.4.3 Transform the sentences following the example.

Tienes que hablar más alto > Es necesario que hables más alto.

> Es necesario que. . . / Es importante que. . . + subjuntivo

1. Debes estudiar más.
2. Tienes que leer más libros en español.
3. Debes tener cuidado con la pronunciación.
4. Haz todos los deberes.
5. Tienes que organizar tu horario.
6. Debes pasar el examen.
7. Debes practicar con tus amigos españoles.
8. Tienes que aprender bien la gramática.

38.4.4 Write complete sentences, starting with '**Yo quiero. . .**'. Some will need the subjunctive and others not.

> Querer + infinitive: Quiero ir al cine
> Querer + subjunctive: Yo quiero que tú vayas al cine.

1. Yo / ir de vacaciones
2. Mi hermano / comprar una moto

3. Mi padre / venir a verme
4. Yo / aprobar los exámenes
5. Mis amigos aprobar los exámenes también
6. Yo / dar una fiesta
7. Mi madre / regalarme una moto
8. Tú / venir a mi fiesta
9. Mis amigos / traer muchos regalos
10. Yo / salir a dar una vuelta

38.4.5 Complete the sentences following the example.

Example:

A: ¿Qué opinas de la moda actual?
B: Yo creo que está bien.
A: Yo no creo que esté bien.

1 **A:** ¿Qué opinas de la ciudad?
B: Limpia
A: No / limpia

2 **A:** ¿Qué opinas de este libro?
B: Interesante
A: No / interesante

3 **A:** ¿Qué opinas de este tema?
B: Fácil de entender
A: No / fácil de entender

38.4.6 Indicative or subjunctive? Write the verbs in brackets in the correct form.

1. Es necesario que tú (levantarte) temprano.
2. Deberías (salir) de casa pronto.
3. Es mejor que María (ir) al médico hoy.
4. No debemos (llegar) tarde.
5. Cuando (venir) a mi casa, haremos los deberes.
6. Cuando (venir) a verme me pongo muy contenta.
7. Me gusta (practicar) deporte.
8. Me encanta que mis hijos (practicar) tanto deporte.
9. Quiero (salir) contigo.
10. Quiero que tú (salir) conmigo.

39 The subjunctive II (other tenses)
El subjuntivo II (otros tiempos)

1 The imperfect subjunctive

1.1 Form

The imperfect subjunctive is unique in that it has two possible endings that mean exactly the same.

This tense is formed by adding the endings to the stem of the preterite tense indicative. All the irregularities of the preterite are the same in the imperfect subjunctive.

 See Unit 29 for verbs in the preterite.

The first form is as follows:

	-ar	**-er**	**-ir**
	(tomar)	(comer)	(escribir)
(yo)	tom<u>ara</u>	com<u>iera</u>	escrib<u>iera</u>
(tú)	tom<u>aras</u>	com<u>ieras</u>	escrib<u>ieras</u>
(él / ella / Vd)	tom<u>ara</u>	com<u>iera</u>	escrib<u>iera</u>
(nosotros/as)	tom<u>áramos</u>	com<u>iéramos</u>	escrib<u>iéramos</u>
(vosotros/as)	tom<u>arais</u>	com<u>ierais</u>	escrib<u>ierais</u>
(ellos / ellas / Vds)	tom<u>aran</u>	com<u>ieran</u>	escrib<u>ieran</u>

Note how these relate to the 3rd person plural of the preterite

tom<u>aron</u> > tom<u>ara</u>; com<u>ieron</u> > com<u>iera</u>; escrib<u>ieron</u> > escrib<u>iera</u>

The second form is as follows:

	-ar	**-er**	**-ir**
	(tomar)	(comer)	(escribir)
(yo)	tom<u>ase</u>	com<u>iese</u>	escrib<u>iese</u>
(tú)	tom<u>ases</u>	com<u>ieses</u>	escrib<u>ieses</u>
(él / ella / Vd)	tom<u>ase</u>	com<u>iese</u>	escrib<u>iese</u>
(nosotros/as)	tom<u>ásemos</u>	com<u>iésemos</u>	escrib<u>iésemos</u>
(vosotros/as)	tom<u>aseis</u>	com<u>ieseis</u>	escrib<u>ieseis</u>
(ellos / ellas / Vds)	tom<u>asen</u>	com<u>iesen</u>	escrib<u>iesen</u>

The **-ara**, **-iera** endings are more commonly used. The **-ase**, **-iese** endings are used in more formal registers.

1.2 Irregular verbs

Infinitive	preterite (indicative)	imperfect (subjunctive)	
dar	di /dieron	diera	diese
hacer	hice / hicieron	hiciera	hiciese
haber	hube / hubieron	hubiera	hubiese
saber	supe / supieron	supiera	supiese

1.3

Ir and **ser** have the same form for the preterite and therefore for the imperfect subjunctive. The endings for this verb are **-era, -ese** instead of **-iera, -iese**:

Infinitive: **ser / ir**   preterite (indicative): **fue / fueron**
imperfect (subjunctive): **fuera / fuese**

1.4

Note: the endings of verbs with **-j-** or **-y-** (**decir, construir**) are **-era, -ese** instead of **-iera, -iese**:

dijera, dijese; construyera, construyese

2 Use

2.1

The imperfect subjunctive is widely used in very formal exchanges, using the verb **querer**, as in:

Quisiera comprar esta camisa.   *I was wanting to buy this shirt.*

2.2

The imperfect subjunctive is used in the same cases as the present but, whereas when the main sentence is in the present or the future tense it is followed by a present subjunctive, when the main sentence is in the past (preterite, imperfect) or in the conditional, the imperfect subjunctive is used.

Me gusta que vengas a verme.   *I like it when you come and see me.*
Me gustaría que vinieras a verme.   *I would like it if you came to see me.*

Te aconsejo que estudies más.   *I advise you to study more.*
Te aconsejé que estudiaras más.   *I advised you to study more.*

Es mejor que salgas pronto.	*It's better that you leave early.*
Sería mejor que salieras pronto.	*It would be better if you left early.*

2.3

In reported speech in the past:

Ven.	*Come.*
Me dijo que viniera.	*He told me to come.*
No salgas.	*Don't leave.*
Me dijo que no saliera.	*He told me not to leave.*
Compra fruta.	*Buy fruit.*
Me pidió que comprara fruta.	*He asked me to buy fruit.*

2.4

In independent expressions it is used to express unreality in the past or the remote possibility that something might have happened, had happened or would / could happen:

Quizás viniera, pero no me di cuenta.	*Maybe he came but I didn't realise.*
¡Ojalá vinieras a verme!	*I wish you would come to see me.*

2.5

The imperfect subjunctive is used in conditional sentences after **si**, equivalent to the English *if I had / were . . . I would . . .*:

Si + imperfect subjunctive + conditional

Si hiciera buen tiempo iríamos a la playa.	*If the weather were good we'd go to the beach.*
Si tuviera dinero compraría un apartamento.	*If I had some money I'd buy an apartment.*

 See Unit 32 on conditional sentences.

3 Compound forms in the subjunctive

These are the present perfect (**pretérito perfecto**) and the pluperfect (**pluscuamperfecto**).

3.1 Present perfect subjunctive

The present perfect subjunctive is formed with the present subjunctive of the auxiliary verb **haber** plus the participle of the conjugated verb.

		-ar	**-er**	**-ir**
(yo)	haya			
(tú)	hayas			
(él / ella / Vd)	haya	+ -ado (cenado)	-ido (comido)	-ido (salido)
(nosotros/as)	hayamos			
(vosotros/as)	hayáis			
(ellos / ellas / Vds)	hayan			

 See Unit 35 on participles.

3.1.1 Use

Dudo que mis amigos hayan salido.	*I doubt that my friends have gone out.*
¡Ojalá me haya comprado un regalo!	*Let's hope he's bought me a gift.*
Espero que haya llegado pronto a la oficina.	*I hope she's arrived early at the office.*

3.2 The pluperfect subjunctive

The pluperfect subjunctive is formed with the imperfect subjunctive of the auxiliary verb **haber** plus the participle of the conjugated verb. Remember that the imperfect subjunctive of all verbs has two possible endings.

		-ar	**-er**	**-ir**
(yo)	hubiera / hubiese			
(tú)	hubieras / hubieses			
(él / ella / Vd)	hubiera / hubiese	+ -ado (cenado)	-ido (comido)	-ido (salido)
(nosotros/as)	hubiéramos / hubiésemos			
(vosotros/as)	hubierais / hubieseis			
(ellos / ellas / Vds)	hubieran / hubiesen			

3.2.1 Use

3.2.1.1

It can be used after clauses with the verb in the simple or compound past and conditional tenses:

Me habría gustado que hubieras venido a verme.	*I would have liked it if you had come to see me.*
Nunca pensé que hubiera* hecho eso.	*I never thought he would have done that.*

*habriá could also be used here

But the most common usage is in past conditional sentences after **si**, the equivalent of the English *if I had (done / had, bought, written, etc.) I would have . . .*:

Si hubieras llegado antes habríamos ido al teatro.	*If you had arrived earlier we would have gone to the theatre.*
Si hubiéramos comprado la casa nos habríamos quedado en la ciudad.	*If we had bought the house, we'd have stayed in the city.*

4

En breve

There is a correlation between the tenses of the indicative and those of the subjunctive.

Present indicative	Present subjunctive
Creo que Juan llega hoy.	**No creo que Juan llegue hoy.**
Present perfect	Present perfect subjunctive
Creo que Juan ha llegado hoy.	**No creo que Juan haya llegado hoy.**
Preterite / imperfect / conditional	Imperfect subjunctive
Creía que Juan llegaba/llegaría/llegó ayer.	**No creía que Juan llegara ayer.**

5 Gramática práctica

39.5.1 Transform the sentences.

Example: No hables tan rápido > Me dijo que no hablara tan rápido.

1 No compres ese coche.
2 No bebas tanto café.
3 No discutas siempre con los amigos.
4 No uses el coche para todo.
5 No comas demasiados pasteles.
6 No abras la puerta a personas extrañas.
7 No entres a la oficina.
8 No escribas tan mal.

39.5.2 Más ecología. Put the verbs in brackets into the subjunctive.

Example: Sería importante que tú (poner) más baja la calefacción. > Sería importante que tú pusieras más baja la calefacción.

1. Sería necesario que la gente (viajar) más en transporte público.
2. Sería importante que nosotros (ir) en bicicleta por el centro de la ciudad.
3. Sería mejor que las fábricas (contaminar) menos.

4. Sería mejor que la gente (dejar) el coche en casa.
5. Sería necesario que todos (ahorrar) energía eléctrica.
6. Sería importante que (haber) menos tráfico.
7. Sería mejor que tú (usar) menos agua caliente.

39.5.3 Change the sentences.

Example: me gustaría / mis padres darme dinero > Me gustaría que mis padres me dieran dinero.

1. Me gustaría / todas las personas / ser simpáticas
2. Me encantaría / mis amigas / llamar por teléfono
3. Me gustaría / mis amigos / visitarme
4. Me encantaría / tú / poner la música que me gusta
5. Me encantaría / mis amigos / regalarme muchas cosas para mi cumpleaños.
6. Me gustaría / mi hermano / hacer bien sus exámenes
7. Me gusta / tú / invitarme al cine

39.5.4 Put the verbs in brackets into the present perfect subjunctive..

1. No creo que tú (levantarte) temprano.
2. Dudo que Juan (salir) de casa pronto.
3. No creo que María (ir) al médico hoy.
4. Dudo que mi hermano (llegar) tarde.
5. No creo que mis amigos (ir) a mi casa.
6. Dudo que Juan (practicar) mucho deporte recientemente.
7. No creo que Luis (salir) con Sara.
8. No creo que vosotros (empezado) ya.
9. Dudo que nosotros (tomar) la ruta más directa.
10. No creo que ustedes (ver) esa película.

40 Impersonal verbs *Verbos impersonales*

1 ¿Qué es?

Impersonal verbs are those which are only used in the third person (*it*), e.g.:
llueve, *it rains*.

Note though that they can be used in different tenses:
llovió, *it rained*; **lloverá**, *it will rain*.

2 Verbs and use

2.1 Impersonal weather and time expressions

llover	
llueve, llovía	*it rains / it's raining, it was raining*
nevar	
nieva, nevó	*it snows / it's snowing, it snowed*
amanecer	
amanece, amanecerá	*it gets light / it's getting light,* *it will get light.*
anochecer	
anochece, anocheció	*it gets dark / it's getting dark,* *it got dark*
hacer	

hace calor / hacía frío / hará niebla /
   hizo buen tiempo / ha hecho
   mal tiempo
	it's hot / it was cold / it'll be foggy /
	   it was nice weather / the weather
	   has been bad

haber	
hay niebla / hubo hielo	*it's foggy / it was icy*
ser	
es primavera / era otoño	*it's spring / it was autumn*

2.2

Haber (hay) and **ser** are also impersonal in other circumstances.

2.2.1 haber

The impersonal form of **haber** in the present is **hay**, used for singular and
plural. The equivalent in English is *there is / there are*:

En la ciudad hay una catedral muy antigua, hay muchos monumentos y muchos parques.
In the city there is a very old cathedral, there are many monuments and many parks.

The impersonal **haber** can be used in different tenses, but always in the singular:

Había mucha gente.	*There were lots of people.*
Hubo muchos problemas.	*There were many problems.*
Mañana habrá una fiesta.	*Tomorrow there'll be a party.*

2.2.2 hay que

It expresses necessity and it is followed by an infinitive:

Hay que comprar comida **para la fiesta.**	*It's necessary to buy food for the party.*
Hay que pagar el alquiler.	*We need to pay the rent.*
Habrá que comprarle un regalo **a tu hermano.**	*You'll have to buy a gift for your brother.*

2.2.3 ser (es)

This means *it is . . .* and can be used in expressions of time:

es la una y media*	*it's one thirty*
es pronto	*it's early*
es temprano	*it's early*
es tarde	*it's late*
es de día	*it's daylight*
era de noche	*it was night time*

*Note: **son las dos**

3 Gramática práctica

40.3.1 Translate into Spanish.

1. In Paris it's raining.
2. In London it was foggy.
3. In Dublin it will be cold.
4. In Moscow it will snow.
5. In Rome it was windy.
6. In Barcelona it's hot.
7. In Madrid it will be sunny.
8. In Berlin it was overcast.
9. In Athens it's stormy.

40.3.2 Now describe tomorrow's weather in the same countries. Use the future tense.

1. En París hacer viento.
2. En Londres llover.
3. En Dublín estar cubierto.
4. En Moscú hacer mucho frío.
5. En Roma hacer sol.

6. En Barcelona haber tormentas.
7. En Madrid haber niebla.
8. En Berlín nevar.
9. En Atenas hacer calor.

4 Más allá

4.1 hace

4.1.1 In expressions of time

4.1.1.1 hace + time + que + verb to mean for, since and ago

Hace dos años que trabajo aquí.	*I've been working here for two years. (lit: it makes two years that I work here.)*
Hace tres meses que llegué a esta ciudad.	*I arrived in this city three months ago. (lit: it makes three months that I arrived in this city.)*

4.1.1.2 desde hace (for, since)

Estudio español desde hace tres años.	*I've been studying Spanish for three years. (lit: I study Spanish since three years ago.)*

4.1.2 hacer falta

No hace falta reservar un asiento en el autobús.	*It's not necessary to reserve a seat in the bus.*
No hace falta que vengas.	*It's not necessary for you to come.*

4.2 Other impersonal constructions

es mejor	*it's better*
es peor	*it's worse*
es importante	*it's important*
fue necesario	*it was necessary*
seriá aconsejable	*it would be advisable*

All these expressions can be used in main clauses followed by **que** and a clause in the subjunctive:

Es mejor que te levantes pronto.	*It's better if you get up early.*
Es importante que hagas el exámen bien.	*It's important that you do the exam well.*

 See Unit 38 on the subjunctive.

4.3 Impersonal constructions with other verbs

4.3.1 *faltar*

There is a singular form **falta**, and a plural form **faltan**:

Falta una hora para llegar.	*There's an hour (to go) before we arrive.*
Faltan dos días para tu examen.	*There are two days left before your exam.*
Sólo falta limpiar la cocina.	*All that's left is to clean the kitchen.*

It is possible to add a personal pronoun to **faltar**:

Me faltan dos horas para llegar a casa.	*I've got two hours before I arrive home.*

4.3.2 *valer*

Used in the expression **más vale que** followed by a subjunctive. It means *It's better that . . .*:

Más vale que llegues pronto.	*It's better that you get there early.*

4.3.3 *parecer*

Parece interesante.	*It seems interesting.*

4.3.3.1 *parece que*

This means *it seems that . . .* or *it looks as though . . .* and is followed by the indicative:

Parece que va a hacer frío mañana.	*It looks as though it'll be cold tomorrow.*
Parece que van a comprar una casa en el campo.	*It seems they're going to buy a house in the country.*

4.3.3.2

It is possible to add a personal pronoun to **parecer**:

me parece bien	*it seems OK to me*
le parece mal	*he thinks it's bad*
Me parece que no voy a ir al cine.	*I don't think I'll go to the cinema.*

4.4 Impersonal expressions with se

Se prohíbe fumar	*No smoking*

 See Unit 44 point 2.4.1.

4.5 Impersonal expressions using the 3rd person plural of the verb

Construyeron una casa allí.	*A house was built there. (Lit: They built a house there)*

See Unit 44 point 2.2.

5 Más práctica

40.5.1 Fill the gaps with **falta** or **faltan**.

1. _____ una silla, ¿puedes traerla?
2. _____ dos vasos, están en el armario.
3. No tengo bastante dinero para el autobús, me _____ dos euros.
4. _____ un libro, ¿quién lo tiene?
5. Hoy _____ tres estudiantes en clase.

40.5.2 Complete the sentences with the words and phrases from the box.

hay que   es mejor   es importante   son   es tarde
faltan   es pronto   hace   falta   hay   hace falta

1. En el pueblo _____ un supermercado.
2. Estos días _____ mucho frío y llueve.
3. _____ una hora para la fiesta.
4. Para aprobar el examen _____ estudiar más.
5. No _____ pagar aquí.
6. Los niños tienen que acostarse porque _____.
7. _____ para ir a la playa.
8. _____ viajar en tren.
9. _____ dos años que estudio español.
10. _____ dos horas para la clase.
11. Vamos a comer, _____ las dos.
12. _____ llegar a tiempo.

41 Pronominal verbs *Verbos pronominales*

1 ¿Qué es?

Pronominal verbs are verbs which are accompanied by a reflexive pronoun or a personal object pronoun which is the same as the subject of the sentence.

Me llamo Carmen. *My name is Carmen.*
Me visto para salir. *I'm getting dressed to go out.*

There are many different kinds of Spanish pronominal verbs. Pronouns are sometimes used with verbs even when they are not necessary:

Me voy a la oficina. *I'm going to the office.*
Se comió toda la ensalada. *She ate all the salad.*

2 Form

The pronouns used by these pronominal verbs are the reflexive pronoun forms, **me, te, se, nos, os, se**, even when the verbs are not themselves reflexive.

Note: The third person singular and plural pronoun that is used in pronominal verbs is **se**, <u>not</u> **le** or **les**.

This **se** is therefore different from the **se** that replaces **le** or **les** as a personal indirect object pronoun.

Marta <u>se</u> levanta a las ocho de la mañana. (reflexive se)	*Marta gets up at eight in the morning.*
A las nueve <u>se</u> va a la oficina. (pronominal se)	*At nine he goes to the office.*
A: ¿Le das el libro al niño?	*Will you give the book to the boy?*
B: Sí, <u>se</u> lo doy. (personal indirect object se)	*Yes, I'll give it to him.*

 See Unit 10 for reflexive pronouns and Unit 9 section 6 for personal object pronouns.

Examples of various pronominal verbs:

Yo <u>me</u> levanto a las siete.	*I get up at seven.*
¿<u>Te</u> has puesto enfermo esta mañana?	*Did you get ill this morning?*
Manuel <u>se</u> hizo profesor el año pasado.	*Manuel became a teacher last year.*
Nosotros <u>nos</u> conocimos en la playa.	*We met each other at the beach.*
¿Por qué no <u>os</u> vais de vacaciones?	*Why aren't you going on holiday?*
Mis amigos no <u>se</u> marcharon hasta muy tarde.	*My friends didn't leave till very late.*

3 Types of verbs and uses

3.1 Reflexive verbs

Reflexive verbs are accompanied by a reflexive pronoun and are therefore considered to be pronominal verbs. They are studied in their own unit, but the following is a reminder.

 See Unit 25 for reflexive verbs and also Unit 10 on reflexive pronouns.

They are used in sentences in which the subject carries out and also receives the action, literally when we do things to ourselves like *I wash myself, I get myself up*, etc. The nearest English equivalent is expressions using *get*, as in *get dressed, get washed*, etc.

Me ducho por la mañana.	*I have a shower in the morning.* *(lit: I shower myself.)*

3.2 Reciprocal verbs

We use a reciprocal verb when an action or feeling refers back to the person(s) concerned. It is similar to saying *each other* in English.

Los amigos se encontraron en la calle.	*The friends met each other in the street.*
Luis y Alicia se enamoraron en París.	*Luis and Alicia fell in love with each other in Paris.*

Other verbs that can be reciprocal: **casarse, divorciarse, separarse, conocerse, enfadarse, mirarse, hablarse**.

3.3 Other verbs with a pronominal form

3.3.1

Several verbs can be used with or without the reflexive to mean slightly different things:

Acostaré a los niños y luego me acostaré yo.	*I'll put the children to bed and then I'll go to bed myself.*

3.3.2

Some verbs have both forms, which have completely different meanings:

cambiar	*to change*
cambiarse	*to get changed*
Alfonso cambió las fechas de sus vacaciones.	*Alfonso changed the dates of his holiday.*
Alfonso se cambió antes de salir.	*Alfonso got changed before going out.*
aburrir	*to bore*
aburrirse	*to get / be bored*

| molestar | to bother |
| molestarse | to be bothered |

3.4 Pronominal verbs with special meanings

3.4.1 *hacerse*

This means *to become*, but in a professional, political or religious context. It implies voluntary change:

| **hacerse profesor** | *to become a teacher* |

3.4.2 *ponerse* (to become, to get)

This is used with adjectives to indicate changes of a temporary nature. They are often used instead of a more formal verb which means the same thing.

ponerse enfermo (enfermar)
Se puso enfermo. *He got ill.*

ponerse triste (entristecer)
María siempre se pone triste en otoño. *Maria always gets sad in the Autumn.*

3.5 Verbs which use the pronoun as intensifier

Some Spanish verbs do not need a reflexive pronoun, but have adopted one for the purpose of emphasis. The verb is made stronger in this way.

3.5.1

The most common case occurs with the verb **ir** (*to go*), which is mostly used with a pronoun in spoken Spanish:

Me voy a casa. *I'm going home.*
Javier se fue de vacaciones a Málaga. *Javier went to Malaga on holiday.*

3.5.2 *It also happens with verbs that mean eating and drinking: comerse, beberse, tomarse*

**Se bebió un vaso de vino y se
  comió el jamón.** *He drank a glass of wine and
  ate the ham.*

4 Gramática práctica

41.4.1 Put the verbs into the correct form.

1. Mis hermanos (acostarse) siempre muy tarde.
2. Mi amiga (irse) de vacaciones ayer.
3. Espera un momento, yo (ponerse) el abrigo y voy contigo.
4. Tú (beberte) siempre toda la leche.
5. Arturo y yo no (hablarse).
6. Vosotros (ponerse) contentos con la noticia.
7. Mi hermano y mi marido no (conocerse).
8. Yo (cambiarse) de ropa para salir.

5 Más allá

5.1 More on reflexives

5.1.1

Many verbs have only a pronominal form, but are not reflexive:

arrepentirse	*to repent*
quejarse	*to complain*
atreverse	*to dare*

Mis padres se quejaron de la comida en el restaurante.	*My parents complained about the food in the restaurant.*

5.1.2

With some verbs the reflexive element can mean to have something done for you instead of doing it yourself:

Ana se corta el pelo en la peluquería de su madre.	*Ana has her hair cut at her mother's hairdresser's.*
Juan se construyó una casa grande.	*Juan had a big house built.*

5.1.3

Sometimes there can be ambiguity; two meanings are possible in this example:

Carmen se va a hacer un sombrero para la boda.

This could mean that Carmen is going to make the hat herself or that she is going to have it made for her.

Note that the subject pronoun plus **mismo** or **solo** are sometimes added to avoid this confusion:

Carmen se va a hacer un sombrero ella misma.	*Carmen is going to make a hat herself.*

5.2 More on reciprocal verbs

The following phrases are sometimes added to expressions with reciprocal meaning for clarity:

el uno al otro	*each other*
los unos a los otros	*each other (plural)*

Se miraron el uno al otro.	*They looked at each other.*

5.3 More pronominal verbs with special meanings

5.3.1 *volverse*

This means *to become, to go* and indicates psychological change. It is used when we want to describe something more permanent than **ponerse**:

volverse loco	*to go mad*
volverse agresivo	*to become aggressive*

It also means a change in circumstances:

La situación se ha vuelto difícil.	*The situation has become difficult.*

5.3.2 *convertirse en*

This means *to become* in the sense of *to turn into*:

El chico se ha convertido en el héroe de la zona.	*The boy has become the hero of the area.*

5.3.3 *quedarse*

This means *to remain, to be left, to end up*:

quedarse viudo	*to be left a widower*
quedarse solo	*to remain alone*

Note: **quedarse** can also have other meanings:

Me quedaré en casa.	*I'll stay at home.*

5.4 More verbs which use the pronoun as intensifier

5.4.1 *Verbs of motion:* **marcharse, subirse, bajarse, escaparse, caerse**

Mañana me marcho al campo.	*Tomorrow I'm going to go to the country.*
Los sábados se sube a la montaña.	*On Saturdays he goes up the mountains.*

5.4.2 *With verbs that indicate perception and knowledge*

¿Te sabes la lección?	*Do you know the lesson?*
Sí, me la he aprendido enseguida.	*Yes, I learnt it in no time.*

5.4.3 *Miscellaneous verbs:* **comprarse, creerse, olvidarse, reírse, morirse**

Me compré una chaqueta muy bonita.	*I bought a very nice jacket.*
Me creí todo lo que me dijo.	*I believed everything he told me.*
Me olvidé de cerrar la puerta con llave.	*I forgot to lock the door.*
Se ríe mucho.	*He laughs a lot.*

Note that **morirse** means to die a natural death. Compare:

Juan se murió el año pasado.　　　*Juan died last year.*
Juan murió en un accidente.　　　*Juan died in an accident*

 For other pronominal constructions, especially with se, see Unit 25 on reflexive verbs and Unit 44 on the passive.

6 Más práctica

41.6.1 Put the verb and its pronoun into the correct form.

Note: remember to put the pronoun after the verb with the infinitive and the gerund.

　1. El bebé (reírse) mucho.
　2. No debes (creerse) todo lo que te dice.
　3. Elena (cortarse) el pelo en la peluquería.
　4. (Marcharme) al campo con mi hermana.
　5. Mis padres (divorciarse) el año pasado.
　6. Tú siempre estás (quejarse) de todo.
　7. Nosotros (comerse) ayer toda la comida.
　8. El año pasado tú (hacerse) mecánico, ¿verdad?
　9. Vosotros (olvidarse) de hacer los ejercicios esta mañana, ¿verdad?
10. Tú no debes (ponerse) triste por eso.
11. Yo voy a (hacerse) un vestido para la boda de mi hermana.

41.6.2 Translate the sentences in the exercise above into English.

41.6.3 Put the correct pronoun in the correct place in the following sentences, if one is needed.

　1. Yo aburro mucho en mi trabajo.
　2. Juan y Pedro encuentran en el bar por la tarde.
　3. Como pescado los viernes.
　4. Yo cambié el vestido por otro más grande.
　5. El pescado que comí ayer estaba muy bueno.
　6. Esta película es malísima, aburre a cualquiera.
　7. Yo quedaré aquí hasta mañana.
　8. Ricardo y Teresa casan mañana.
　9. Mis padres han comprado una casa en el campo.
10. Mi hermana murió en un accidente de tráfico.
11. ¿Vosotros cambiáis de casa mañana?
12. Margarita encontró a sus amigos en la calle.

42 Phrasal verbs *Perífrasis verbales*

1 ¿Qué es?

Phrasal verbs are expressions formed with a verb followed by either an infinitive, a gerund or a participle. In many cases these constructions also include a preposition.

1.1

> **En breve**
>
> Verb (conjugated) + preposition + infinitive
>
> **Voy a salir esta noche.**   *I'm going out tonight.*
>
> Verb (conjugated) + gerund
>
> **Estoy comiendo en casa.**   *I'm eating at home.*

1.2

The conjugated verb, which comes first in the sentence, gives the information about the tense, person and number.

The infinitive gives the meaning:

María acaba de llegar.	*María has just arrived.*
Los niños acabaron de comer.	*The children (just) finished eating.*

2 Form and use of phrasal verbs

2.1 Phrasal verbs with the infinitive

2.1.1 *ir a + infinitive*

Used to express the immediate future or an intention to do something in the future. It is often interchangeable with the future form:

Voy a cenar esta noche con mi hermana.	*I'm going to have dinner tonight with my sister.*
Voy a ir a Mallorca la semana próxima.	*I'm going to Mallorca next week.*

2.1.2 *acabar de* + infinitive

Used to express an action which has just happened, or one in the immediate past:

El avión acaba de aterrizar. *The plane has just landed.*
Tú acababas de salir cuando llegué. *You had just left when I arrived.*

2.1.3 *volver a* + infinitive

Used to express repetition or the idea of doing something again:

Esto está mal, vuelve a empezar. *This is wrong, start again.*
(= empieza otra vez)

2.1.4 *empezar a* + infinitive

Used to express the start of an action in either the present, the future or the past.

Fernando empezó a trabajar en mi *Fernando started to work in my*
empresa el mes pasado. *company last month.*

2.1.5 *terminar de* + infinitive

Used to express the end of an action in either the present, the future or the past.

Termina de hablar, tenemos que irnos. *Finish talking, we have to go.*

2.2 Phrasal verbs with the gerund (-*ing* form)

Used to express the present continuous, to say that someone is doing something or that something is happening:

estar + gerund (**cenando, comiendo, viviendo**)

Está estudiando. *He is studying.*

 See Unit 34 on the gerund and the present continuous.

---

3 Gramática práctica

42.3.1 Link the phrases from list A with those of list B to make sentences.

List A

1. No tengo hambre porque
2. María no terminó el curso y
3. Mis amigos y yo
4. Enrique y yo fuimos de compras
5. Isabel no puede ponerse al teléfono porque
6. María llegó, dejó sus maletas y
7. Llegas tarde, el tren
8. Cuando tenía cinco años

List B

a) acaba de salir.
b) vamos a estudiar español.
c) acabo de comer.
d) empecé a tocar el piano.
e) cuando terminamos de trabajar.
f) ha vuelto a empezar.
g) volvió a salir.
h) está durmiendo.

42.3.2 Translate the sentences from the exercise into English.

4 Más allá

4.1 More phrasal verbs with the infinitive

Important: Note how in many of these cases the gerund form (*-ing*) is used in English instead of the infinitive.

4.1.1 *ponerse a + infinitive*

Used to express the beginning of an action:

Cada noche se pone a leer en la cama, pero se duerme en cinco minutos.
Every night he starts reading in bed, but he goes to sleep in five minutes.

4.1.2 *echar / echarse a + infinitive*

Used to express the beginning of a sudden action.

La mujer se enfadó y echó a gritar.	*The woman got angry and started shouting.*

4.1.3 *quedar en + infinitive*

It means to agree to do something:

Quedamos en encontrarnos a las cinco.	*We arranged to meet at five.*
He quedado con Luis a las siete.	*I have arranged to meet Luis at seven o'clock.*
	(lit: I have agreed with Luis to meet at seven.)

It can also express commitment:

Juan quedó en venir, pero no está aquí.	*Juan agreed to come, but he is not here.*

4.1.4 *dejar de and parar de + infinitive*

It means to stop doing something.

He dejado de comer carne.	*I've given up eating meat.*
¡Para de hacer tonterías!	*Stop doing silly things!*

4.1.5 *llegar a + infinitive*

It means to end up doing something:

Carlos siempre habla de sus cosas y llega a aburrir a todos.	*Carlos is always talking about himself and ends up boring everybody.*

4.2 More phrasal verbs with the gerund

4.2.1 *seguir / continuar + gerund*

This expresses continuity of action:

Luis sigue estudiando en la universidad.	*Luis continues to study at university.*
Continúo trabajando en la misma empresa.	*I continue to work in the same company.*

Note that English uses the infinitive in these cases.

4.2.2 *llevar + gerund*

Used to express a temporary action that started in the past and continues in the present:

Llevo dos años viviendo en Barcelona.	*I've been living in Barcelona for two years.*

4.2.3 *quedarse + gerund*

Used to express duration and continuity of an action:

Se quedó estudiando todo el fin de semana.	*He stayed studying all weekend.*

5 Más práctica

42.5.1 Complete the sentences with the words from the box.

continúan dejamos llegué llevan para pone pongo	
quedamos quedaron seguimos	

1. Mi madre siempre se _____ a limpiar la casa hasta mediodía.
2. Mi prima y yo nos _____ hablando hasta muy tarde.
3. No _____ a terminar el examen porque era muy largo.
4. Mis padres _____ viviendo en la misma casa desde hace cuarenta años.
5. Pedro y yo _____ de salir juntos hace un mes.
6. El niño no nos deja dormir, no _____ de llorar.
7. Juan y Luis _____ en encontrarse en la puerta del cine.
8. Nosotros _____ viviendo en Sevilla.
9. Yo me _____ a trabajar ahora mismo.
10. Mis amigos _____ tres años viviendo en Londres.

42.5.2 Translate the sentences from 42.5.1 into English.

43 Modal verbs

1 ¿Qué es?

Modal verbs are used to express intentions or opinions. They are followed by an infinitive. Usually the infinitive and the main verb share the same subject. In Spanish modal verbs can be used in all tenses.

2 Form

The most frequently used modal verbs are:

deber / tener que / hay que	*must / have to / should / ought to*
poder	*can / be able to*
querer	*want / would like to*
saber	*know*

Luis debe trabajar.	*Luis must / has to / should / ought to work.*
Tengo que trabajar.	*I must / have to / should / ought to work.*
Hay que trabajar.	*One must / should / ought to work.*
María puede venir mañana.	*María can / is able to come tomorrow.*
Ana quiere estudiar Historia.	*Ana wants / would like to study History.*
El niño sabe nadar.	*The child knows how to swim.*

The above examples are all in the present, but these verbs can be used in all tenses and persons:

Deberías hacer más ejercicio.	*You should do more exercise.*
Tuve que limpiar la cocina.	*I had to clean the kitchen.*
¿Podrás venir conmigo?	*Will you be able to come with me?*

3 Use

3.1 deber + infinitive

Used to express obligation:

Debes llegar más temprano.	*You should arrive earlier.*

3.1.1

Don't confuse it with **deber de** + infinitive, which expresses a probability, supposition or assumption:

Mi hijo debe de estar ya en casa.	*My son must be at home already.*

Note the difference:

Debe ganar mucho dinero.	*He should earn a lot of money.*
Debe de ganar mucho dinero.	*He must earn a lot of money.* *(I assume so)*

However, **de** is sometimes dropped in spoken Spanish, and you have to guess the meaning by the context.

3.2 tener que + infinitive

Similar to **deber**; it expresses obligation or necessity:

Tengo que escribir una carta.	*I have to write a letter.*

3.3 haber que

It is only used in the third person as the impersonal form **hay que**. It also expresses obligation:

Hay que estudiar más.	*One must study harder.*

3.4 querer

Expresses a wish or a request:

Quiero ir al cine.	*I want to go to the cinema.*
Quiero comprar esta camiseta, por favor.	*I'd like to buy this T-shirt, please.*

Note: **Quisiera** and **querría** are polite forms of **querer**, also used when expressing a request, for example when ordering food or drink or when buying something.

Quisiera tomar ensalada.	*I would like to eat salad.*
¿Querrías venir conmigo?	*Would you like to come with me?*

Remember though that **quiero** is also used as a polite request, especially if followed by **por favor**.

Quiero vino, por favor.	*I'd like wine, please.*

3.5 saber and poder

3.5.1

Saber means *to know* and is used to express the ability to do something such as play the piano, speak Spanish or drive:

Sé tocar el piano.	*I can play the piano.*
María no sabe nadar.	*María cannot swim.*
No saben conducir.	*They don't know how to drive.*

3.5.2 poder

It means *can, may, could, be able to.*

¿Puedes salir ahora?	*Can you go out now?*
No, no puedo.	*No, I can't.*

3.5.2.1

Note: **podría** can be used in more formal situations, although **puede** is also used as a polite form, especially if followed by **por favor**.

¿Podría decirme dónde está	*Could you tell me where the*
la estación?	*station is?*
¿Puede decirme dónde está el banco,	*Could you tell me where the bank*
por favor?	*is, please?*

3.5.2.2 se puede (can, may one / I / we)

This impersonal form is often used to ask for information about what one can or cannot do:

¿Se puede aparcar aquí?	*Can one park here?*

3.5.2.3 Poder

Poder has different meanings, but cannot be used to express knowledge. It can, though, express a physical ability with the meaning *to be able to:*

Puedo nadar una hora sin parar.	*I can swim an hour without stopping.*

Compare:

Sé nadar, pero hoy no puedo nadar	*I know how to swim, but today I can't*
porque el agua está demasiado fría.	*swim because the water is too cold.*

4 Gramática práctica

43.4.1 Put the correct form of the verbs from the box in the sentences.

> tengo querrías tienes sabe tuvo debe podréis podemos deberías
>
> sé podría quiero quisiera debe hay

1. Juan nadar muy bien.
2. Pepe trabajar más.
3. Yo que levantarme muy pronto mañana.
4. que cortar la hierba del jardín.
5. No estudiar el año próximo.
6. Nosotros no correr tan rápido.
7. Tú comer menos.
8. Ana que quedarse en casa ayer.
9. ¿encontrarnos en la puerta del cine?
10. El tren de llevar retraso.

43.4.2 Translate the sentences from 43.4.1 into English.

44 The passive *La voz pasiva*

1 ¿Qué es?

The passive voice means that the subject doesn't do the action but receives it; in other words, something is done <u>to</u> the subject.

In Spanish there are various ways of expressing the passive.

2 Form

2.1 The passive form with the verb **ser** (*to be*)

The passive is formed with the verb **ser** (*to be*) and the past participle of the conjugated verb:

La casa fue construida por la empresa.   *The house was built by the company.*

In this example **la casa** is the passive subject and the action of building was done to it by the company, **la empresa**, which is known as the agent. It is preceded by **por** (*by*).

The past participle agrees in number and gender with the subject of the sentence. In the example above, **construida** agrees with **casa**, which is a feminine singular noun. Compare this with:

Las casas fueron construidas   *The houses were built by the*
   por la empresa.   *company.*

This form of the passive is more normally used in written and formal language than in everyday spoken language. It is also more normally used in speech in Latin American Spanish.

2.2 The impersonal form with passive meaning

When the agent is unknown, the passive form is often replaced by the third person plural of the verb: **ellos / ellas** (*they*). The pronoun is not normally used:

(Ellos) construyeron   *The house was built.*
   la casa.   *(lit: They built the house.)*
Operaron a mi hija en   *My daughter was operated*
   este hospital.   *on in this hospital.*
                           (lit: They operated on my daughter in
                           this hospital.)

2.3 Passive constructions with se

When we place the emphasis on the action itself and are less interested in who carries out the action (the agent), the tendency is to use the pronoun **se** followed by the third person of the verb in the singular or plural, depending on the subject.

The agent is not included in the sentence in these cases.
The subject can appear either before or after the verb with **se**.

Este cuadro se pintó en el siglo quince.	*This picture was painted in the 15th century.*
Se pintó este cuadro en el siglo quince.	
Estos coches se fabrican en Alemania.	*These cars are made in Germany.*
Se fabrican estos coches en Alemania.	

Note that this construction can be replaced by the actual passive form (see 2.1 above):

Este cuadro fue pintado en el siglo quince.
Estos coches son fabricados en Alemania.

2.4 Impersonal se

2.4.1

This is the same construction as shown in 2.3 above, but with the difference that, as we don't know the identity of the agent, it cannot appear in the sentence. It is often seen on public signs:

Se prohíbe el paso.	*No entry. (lit: Access is prohibited)*
Se vende apartamento.	*Apartment for sale.*
Se alquila.	*For rent.*

In this case the construction cannot be replaced by the passive form.

2.4.2

Most verbs followed by an infinitive don't change:

Se prohíbe aparcar coches en esta calle.   *Parking is prohibited in this street.*

2.4.3

Note that this is not the case with the following verbs:

querer, poder, deber, tener que, acabar de

which can change to the plural form if the subject is plural:

Se quieren limpiar los parques.	*They want to clean the parks.*
Se pueden comprar varios litros de aceite.	*You can buy several litres of oil.* *(lit: Several litres of oil can be bought.)*

2.4.4

The construction with **se** cannot be used in combination with other verbs that have **se** as part of themselves, i.e. reflexive and pronominal verbs. In this case we can use **uno**:

En esta casa se come uno todo lo que le dan.	*In this house you eat everything they give you.*

2.4.5 Some constructions with se

se dice que	*they say that*
se ve que	*you can see that*
se espera que	*it is hoped that / it is thought that / they think that*
se cree que	*it is believed that*
Se espera que mañana haya tormenta.	*They expect there's going to be a storm tomorrow. (A storm is expected tomorrow.)*
Se dice que esta cantante vendrá a la ciudad.	*They say that this singer will come to the city.*

2.4.6

The impersonal sense is often achieved by using indefinite pronouns:

uno, alguien, alguno, la gente etc.,

followed by the third person singular or plural of the verb. Another possibility is to use the first person plural.

For example, the sentence **Se toma buen café en España** can also be written as:

Uno toma buen café en España.	*One has good coffee in Spain.*

or:

Tomamos buen café en España.	*We have good coffee in Spain.*

3 Gramática práctica

44.3.1 ¿Qué hicieron en el pueblo? Write sentences using the third person plural impersonal.

Example: Construir muchas casas > Construyeron muchas casas.

1. Derribar los edificios viejos
2. Plantar muchos árboles
3. Instalar fábricas
4. Poner más autobuses
5. Abrir muchas tiendas
6. Hacer una autopista

44.3.2 Transform the sentences, beginning with **se**.

Example: viajamos mucho > se viaja mucho.

En España. . .
1. desayunamos café
2. comemos a las dos
3. tomamos el aperitivo
4. merendamos chocolate con churros
5. cenamos tarde
6. salimos a pasear

44.3.3 Write these sentences with **se** and the verbs in the preterite.

1. Este traje (diseñar) en los años cincuenta.
2. Estos coches (fabricar) en Japón.
3. El banquete de la boda (celebrar) en el restaurante Barcelona.
4. La fiesta (organizar) con poco dinero.
5. Los partidos (suspender) a causa de la lluvia.
6. La catedral (construir) en el siglo quince.
7. Los conciertos (cancelar) por la enfermedad del cantante.

44.3.4 Rewrite the sentences from 44.3.3 in the passive.

Example: Este traje (diseñar) en los años cincuenta > Este traje se diseñó en los años cincuenta > Este traje fue diseñado en los años cincuenta.

44.3.5 Translate into Spanish. Begin with **se** or **no se**.

1. This house is for sale.
2. This apartment is for rent.
3. Noise is forbidden.
4. Playing ball is not allowed..
5. No talking in class.
6. No trespassing.
7. Cash only.

Verb tables

Regular verbs

Conjugation of verbs ending in -ar

Example: **hablar** (*to speak*)

PRESENT	IMPERFECT	PRETERITE
(yo) hablo	hablaba	hablé
(tú) hablas	hablabas	hablaste
(él / ella / Vd) habla	hablaba	habló
(nosotros/as) hablamos	hablábamos	hablamos
(vosotros/as) habláis	hablabais	hablasteis
(ellos / ellas / Vds) hablan	hablaban	hablaron

FUTURE	CONDITIONAL
hablaré	hablaría
hablarás	hablarías
hablará	hablaría
hablaremos	hablaríamos
hablaréis	hablaríais
hablarán	hablarían

PRESENT SUBJUNCTIVE	IMPERFECT SUBJUNCTIVE
hable	hablara / hablase
hables	hablaras / hablases
hable	hablara / hablase
hablemos	habláramos / hablásemos
habléis	hablarais / hablaseis
hablen	hablaran / hablasen

PAST PARTICIPLE	hablado
GERUND	hablando

IMPERATIVE (tú) habla, (vosotros) hablad, (usted) hable, (ustedes) hablen

Conjugation of verbs ending in -er

Example: **comer** (*to eat*)

PRESENT	IMPERFECT	PRETERITE
(yo) como	comía	comí
(tú) comes	comías	comiste
(él / ella / Vd) come	comía	comió
(nosotros/as) comemos	comíamos	comimos
(vosotros/as) coméis	comíais	comisteis
(ellos / ellas / Vds) comen	comían	comieron

FUTURE	CONDITIONAL
comeré	comería
comerás	comerías
comerá	comería
comeremos	comeríamos
comeréis	comeríais
comerán	comerían

PRESENT SUBJUNCTIVE	IMPERFECT SUBJUNCTIVE
coma	comiera / comiese
comas	comieras / comieses
coma	comiera / comiese
comamos	comiéramos / comiésemos
comáis	comierais / comieseis
coman	comieran / comiesen

PAST PARTICIPLE	comido
GERUND	comiendo

IMPERATIVE (tú) come, (vosotros) comed, (usted) coma, (ustedes) coman

Conjugation of verbs ending in -ir

Example: **vivir** (*to live*)

PRESENT	IMPERFECT	PRETERITE
(yo) vivo	vivía	viví
(tú) vives	vivías	viviste
(él / ella / Vd) vive	vivía	vivió
(nosotros/as) vivimos	vivíamos	vivimos
(vosotros/as) vivís	vivíais	vivisteis
(ellos / ellas / Vds) viven	vivían	vivieron

FUTURE	CONDITIONAL
viviré	viviría
vivirás	vivirías
vivirá	viviría
viviremos	viviríamos
viviréis	viviríais
vivirán	vivirían

PRESENT SUBJUNCTIVE	IMPERFECT SUBJUNCTIVE
viva	viviera / viviese
vivas	vivieras / vivieses
viva	viviera / viviese
vivamos	viviéramos / viviésemos
viváis	vivierais / vivieseis
vivan	vivieran / viviesen

PAST PARTICIPLE	vivido
GERUND	viviendo

IMPERATIVE (tú) vive, (vosotros) vivid, (usted) viva, (ustedes) vivan

Compound tenses

They are formed with the past participle of the verb preceded by the auxiliary verb **haber**, conjugated.

The past participle is formed from the infinitive, dropping the infinitive endings and adding the past participle endings **-ado, -ido, -ido**:

Ha llegado tarde.   *He has arrived late.*

- The perfect tense is formed with the present tense of **haber** plus the past participle:

comprar	comer	vivir
-ado	**-ido**	**-ido**
he comprado	he comido	he vivido
has comprado	has comido	has vivido
ha comprado	ha comido	ha vivido
hemos comprado	hemos comido	hemos vivido
habéis comprado	habéis comido	habéis vivido
han comprado	han comido	han vivido

- The past perfect is formed with the imperfect tense of **haber** plus the past participle:

comprar	comer	vivir
-ado	**-ido**	**-ido**
había comprado	había comido	había vivido
habías comprado	habías comido	habías vivido
había comprado	había comido	había vivido
habíamos comprado	habíamos comido	habíamos vivido
habíais comprado	habíais comido	habíais vivido
habían comprado	habían comido	habían vivido

- The future perfect is formed with the future tense of **haber** plus the past participle:

comprar	comer	vivir
-ado	**-ido**	**-ido**
habré comprado	habré comido	habré vivido
habrás comprado	habrás comido	habrás vivido
habrá comprado	habrá comido	habrá vivido
habremos comprado	habremos comido	habremos vivido
habréis comprado	habréis comido	habréis vivido
habrán comprado	habrán comido	habrán vivido

- The conditional perfect is formed with the conditional tense of **haber** plus the past participle:

comprar	comer	vivir
-ado	**-ido**	**-ido**
habría comprado	habría comido	habría vivido
habrías comprado	habrías comido	habrías vivido
habría comprado	habría comido	habría vivido
habríamos comprado	habríamos comido	habríamos vivido
habríais comprado	habríais comido	habríais vivido
habrían comprado	habrían comido	habrían vivido

- The past anterior is formed with the preterite of **haber** plus the past participle:

comprar	comer	vivir
-ado	**-ido**	**-ido**
hube comprado	hube comido	hube vivido
hubiste comprado	hubiste comido	hubiste vivido
hubo comprado	hubo comido	hubo vivido
hubimos comprado	hubimos comido	hubimos vivido
hubisteis comprado	hubisteis comido	hubisteis vivido
hubieron comprado	hubieron comido	hubieron vivido

- The perfect subjunctive is formed with the present subjunctive of **haber** plus the past participle:

comprar	comer	vivir
-ado	**-ido**	**-ido**
haya comprado	haya comido	haya vivido
hayas comprado	hayas comido	hayas vivido
haya comprado	haya comido	haya vivido
hayamos comprado	hayamos comido	hayamos vivido
hayáis comprado	hayáis comido	hayáis vivido
hayan comprado	hayan comido	hayan vivido

- The past perfect subjunctive is formed with the imperfect subjunctive of **haber** plus the past participle:

comprar	comer	vivir
-ado	**-ido**	**-ido**
hubiera comprado	hubiera comido	hubiera vivido
hubieras comprado	hubieras comido	hubieras vivido
hubiera comprado	hubiera comido	hubiera vivido
hubiéramos comprado	hubiéramos comido	hubiéramos vivido
hubierais comprado	hubierais comido	hubierais vivido
hubieran comprado	hubieran comido	hubieran vivido

Irregular verbs

Note: there are many other irregular verbs. The following are the most common ones. Note that many verbs are irregular in some tenses and regular in others.

dar (*to give*)

PRESENT	IMPERFECT	PRETERITE	FUTURE
doy	daba	di	daré
das	dabas	diste	darás
da	daba	dio	dará
damos	dábamos	dimos	daremos
dais	dabais	disteis	daréis
dan	daban	dieron	darán

CONDITIONAL	PRESENT SUBJUNCTIVE	IMPERFECT SUBJUNCTIVE
daría	dé	diera / diese
darías	des	dieras / dieses
daría	dé	diera / diese
daríamos	demos	diéramos / diésemos
daríais	deis	dierais / dieseis
darían	den	dieran / diesen

PAST PARTICIPLE dado
GERUND dando
IMPERATIVE (tú) da, (vosotros) dad, (usted) dé, (ustedes) den

decir (*to say, tell*)

PRESENT	IMPERFECT	PRETERITE	FUTURE
digo	decía	dije	diré
dices	decías	dijiste	dirás
dice	decía	dijo	dirá
decimos	decíamos	dijimos	diremos
decís	decíais	dijisteis	diréis
dicen	decían	dijeron	dirán

CONDITIONAL	PRESENT SUBJUNCTIVE	IMPERFECT SUBJUNCTIVE
diría	diga	dijera / dijese
dirías	digas	dijeras / dijeses
diría	diga	dijera / dijese
diríamos	digamos	dijéramos / dijésemos
diríais	digáis	dijerais / dijeseis
dirían	digan	dijeran / dijesen

PAST PARTICIPLE dicho
GERUND diciendo
IMPERATIVE (tú) di, (vosotros) decid, (usted) diga, (ustedes) digan

estar (*to be*)

PRESENT	IMPERFECT	PRETERITE	FUTURE
estoy	estaba	estuve	estaré
estás	estabas	estuviste	estarás
está	estaba	estuvo	estará
estamos	estábamos	estuvimos	estaremos
estáis	estabais	estuvisteis	estaréis
están	estaban	estuvieron	estarán

CONDITIONAL	PRESENT SUBJUNCTIVE	IMPERFECT SUBJUNCTIVE
estaría	esté	estuviera / estuviese
estarías	estés	estuvieras / estuvieses
estaría	esté	estuviera / estuviese
estaríamos	estemos	estuviéramos / estuviésemos
estaríais	estéis	estuvierais / estuvieseis
estarían	estén	estuvieran / estuviesen

PAST PARTICIPLE   estado
GERUND   estando
IMPERATIVE (tú) está (te), (vosotros) estad, (usted) esté, (ustedes) estén

haber * (to have)

*mainly used as an auxiliary verb

PRESENT	IMPERFECT	PRETERITE	FUTURE
he	había	hube	habré
has	habías	hubiste	habrás
ha	había	hubo	habrá
hemos	habíamos	hubimos	habremos
habéis	habíais	hubisteis	habréis
han	habían	hubieron	habrán

CONDITIONAL	PRESENT SUBJUNCTIVE	IMPERFECT SUBJUNCTIVE
habría	haya	hubiera / hubiese
habrías	hayas	hubieras / hubieses
habría	haya	hubiera / hubiese
habríamos	hayamos	hubiéramos / hubiésemos
habríais	hayáis	hubierais / hubieseis
habrían	hayan	hubieran / hubiesen

PAST PARTICIPLE   habido
GERUND   habiendo

hacer (to do, make)

PRESENT	IMPERFECT	PRETERITE	FUTURE
hago	hacía	hice	haré
haces	hacías	hiciste	harás
hace	hacía	hizo	hará
hacemos	hacíamos	hicimos	haremos
hacéis	hacíais	hicisteis	haréis
hacen	hacían	hicieron	harán

CONDITIONAL	PRESENT SUBJUNCTIVE	IMPERFECT SUBJUNCTIVE
haría	haga	hiciera / hiciese
harías	hagas	hicieras / hicieses
haría	haga	hiciera / hiciese
haríamos	hagamos	hiciéramos / hiciésemos
haríais	hagáis	hicierais / hiciéseis
harían	hagan	hicieran / hiciesen

PAST PARTICIPLE   hecho
GERUND   haciendo
IMPERATIVE (tú) haz, (vosotros) haced, (usted) haga, (ustedes) hagan

ir (*to go*)

PRESENT	IMPERFECT	PRETERITE	FUTURE
voy	iba	fui	iré
vas	ibas	fuiste	irás
va	iba	fue	irá
vamos	íbamos	fuimos	iremos
vais	ibais	fuisteis	iréis
van	iban	fueron	irán

CONDITIONAL	PRESENT SUBJUNCTIVE	IMPERFECT SUBJUNCTIVE
iría	vaya	fuera / fuese
irías	vayas	fueras / fueses
iría	vaya	fuera / fuese
iríamos	vayamos	fuéramos / fuésemos
iríais	vayáis	fuerais / fueseis
irían	vayan	fueran / fuesen

PAST PARTICIPLE ido
GERUND yendo
IMPERATIVE (tú) ve, (vosotros) id, (usted) vaya, (ustedes) vayan

poder (*to be able*)

PRESENT	IMPERFECT	PRETERITE	FUTURE
puedo	podía	pude	podré
puedes	podías	pudiste	podrás
puede	podía	pudo	podrá
podemos	podíamos	pudimos	podremos
podéis	podíais	pudisteis	podréis
pueden	podían	pudieron	podrán

CONDITIONAL	PRESENT SUBJUNCTIVE	IMPERFECT SUBJUNCTIVE
podría	pueda	pudiera / pudiese
podrías	puedas	pudieras / pudieses
podría	pueda	pudiera / pudiese
podríamos	podamos	pudiéramos / pudiésemos
podríais	podáis	pudierais / pudieseis
podrían	puedan	pudieran / pudiesen

PAST PARTICIPLE podido
GERUND pudiendo

poner (*to put*)

PRESENT	IMPERFECT	PRETERITE	FUTURE
pongo	ponía	puse	pondré
pones	ponías	pusiste	pondrás
pone	ponía	puso	pondrá
ponemos	poníamos	pusimos	pondremos
ponéis	poníais	pusisteis	pondréis
ponen	ponían	pusieron	pondrán

CONDITIONAL	PRESENT SUBJUNCTIVE	IMPERFECT SUBJUNCTIVE
pondría	ponga	pusiera / pusiese
pondrías	pongas	pusieras / pusieses
pondría	ponga	pusiera / pusiese
pondríamos	pongamos	pusiéramos / pusiésemos
pondríais	pongáis	pusierais / pusieseis
pondrían	pongan	pusieran / pusiesen

PAST PARTICIPLE   puesto
GERUND   poniendo
IMPERATIVE (tú) pon, (vosotros) poned, (usted) ponga, (ustedes) pongan

querer (to want)

PRESENT	IMPERFECT	PRETERITE	FUTURE
quiero	quería	quise	querré
quieres	querías	quisiste	querrás
quiere	quería	quiso	querrá
queremos	queríamos	quisimos	querremos
queréis	queríais	quisisteis	querréis
quieren	querían	quisieron	querrán

CONDITIONAL	PRESENT SUBJUNCTIVE	IMPERFECT SUBJUNCTIVE
querría	quiera	quisiera / quisiese
querrías	quieras	quisieras / quisieses
querría	quiera	quisiera / quisiese
querríamos	queramos	quisiéramos / quisiésemos
querríais	queráis	quisierais / quisieseis
querrían	quieran	quisieran / quisiesen

PAST PARTICIPLE   querido
GERUND   queriendo
IMPERATIVE (tú) quiere, (vosotros) quered, (usted) quiera, (ustedes) quieran

saber (to know)

PRESENT	IMPERFECT	PRETERITE	FUTURE
sé	sabía	supe	sabré
sabes	sabías	supiste	sabrás
sabe	sabía	supo	sabrá
sabemos	sabíamos	supimos	sabremos
sabéis	sabíais	supisteis	sabréis
saben	sabían	supieron	sabrán

CONDITIONAL	PRESENT SUBJUNCTIVE	IMPERFECT SUBJUNCTIVE
sabría	sepa	supiera / supiese
sabrías	sepas	supieras / supieses
sabría	sepa	supiera / supiese
sabríamos	sepamos	supiéramos / supiésemos
sabríais	sepáis	supierais / supieseis
sabrían	sepan	supieran / supiesen

PAST PARTICIPLE sabido
GERUND sabiendo
IMPERATIVE (tú) sabe, (vosotros) sabed, (usted) sepa, (ustedes) sepan

ser (*to be*)

PRESENT	IMPERFECT	PRETERITE	FUTURE
soy	era	fui	seré
eres	eras	fuiste	serás
es	era	fue	será
somos	éramos	fuimos	seremos
sois	erais	fuisteis	seréis
son	eran	fueron	serán

CONDITIONAL	PRESENT SUBJUNCTIVE	IMPERFECT SUBJUNCTIVE
sería	sea	fuera / fuese
serías	seas	fueras / fueses
sería	sea	fuera / fuese
seríamos	seamos	fuéramos / fuésemos
seríais	seáis	fuerais / fueseis
serían	sean	fueran / fuesen

PAST PARTICIPLE sido
GERUND siendo
IMPERATIVE (tú) sé, (vosotros) sed, (usted) sea, (ustedes) sean

tener (to have)

PRESENT	IMPERFECT	PRETERITE	FUTURE
tengo	tenía	tuve	tendré
tienes	tenías	tuviste	tendrás
tiene	tenía	tuvo	tendrá
tenemos	teníamos	tuvimos	tendremos
tenéis	teníais	tuvisteis	tendréis
tienen	tenían	tuvieron	tendrán

CONDITIONAL	PRESENT SUBJUNCTIVE	IMPERFECT SUBJUNCTIVE
tendría	tenga	tuviera / tuviese
tendrías	tengas	tuvieras / tuvieses
tendría	tenga	tuviera / tuviese
tendríamos	tengamos	tuviéramos / tuviésemos
tendríais	tengáis	tuvierais / tuvieseis
tendrían	tengan	tuvieran / tuviesen

PAST PARTICIPLE   tenido
GERUND   teniendo
IMPERATIVE (tú) ten, (vosotros) tened, (usted) tenga, (ustedes) tengan

traer (to bring)

PRESENT	IMPERFECT	PRETERITE	FUTURE
traigo	traía	traje	traeré
traes	traías	trajiste	traerás
trae	traía	trajo	traerá
traemos	traíamos	trajimos	traeremos
traéis	traíais	trajisteis	traeréis
traen	traían	trajeron	traerán

CONDITIONAL	PRESENT SUBJUNCTIVE	IMPERFECT SUBJUNCTIVE
traería	traiga	trajera / trajese
traerías	traigas	trajeras / trajeses
traería	traiga	trajera / trajese
traeríamos	traigamos	trajéramos / trajésemos
traeríais	traigáis	trajerais / trajeseis
traerían	traigan	trajeran / trajesen

PAST PARTICIPLE   traído
GERUND   trayendo
IMPERATIVE (tú) trae, (vosotros) traed, (usted) traiga, (ustedes) traigan

venir (to come)

PRESENT	IMPERFECT	PRETERITE	FUTURE
vengo	venía	vine	vendré
vienes	venías	viniste	vendrás
viene	venía	vino	vendrá
venimos	veníamos	vinimos	vendremos
venís	veníais	vinisteis	vendréis
vienen	venían	vinieron	vendrán

CONDITIONAL	PRESENT SUBJUNCTIVE	IMPERFECT SUBJUNCTIVE
vendría	venga	viniera / viniese
vendrías	vengas	vinieras / vinieses
vendría	venga	viniera / viniese
vendríamos	vengamos	viniéramos / viniésemos
vendríais	vengáis	vinierais / vinieseis
vendrían	vengan	vinieran / viniesen

PAST PARTICIPLE   venido
GERUND   viniendo
IMPERATIVE (tú) ven, (vosotros) venid, (usted) venga, (ustedes) vengan

Key to exercises

3.4.1
la abuela, la tía, la compañera, la madre, la hermana, la vecina, la mujer, la señora, la prima, la nuera, la amiga, la española, la colombiana, la nicaragüense, la pakistaní

3.4.2
1 camionera 2 taxista 3 intérprete 4 traductora
5 farmacéutica 6 cocinero 7 periodista 8 dependiente
9 profesor 10 fontanero

3.4.3
el libro (*book*), la mesa (*table*), el cuaderno (*notebook*), el bolígrafo (*ballpoint pen*), la cartera (*wallet*), la ventana (*window*), el clima (*climate*), el gimnasio (*gym*), la taza (*cup*), el vaso (*drinking glass*), el teléfono (*phone*), la radio (*radio*), la naranja (*orange*), el rosa (*pink*), el sofá (*sofa*), la moto (*motorcycle*), la tortilla (*omelette*)

3.4.4
los chocolates, las fresas (*strawberries*), los lunes (*Mondays*), los pasteles (*cakes*), las galletas (*biscuits*), las ensaladas (*salads*), los quesos (*cheeses*), los panes (*loaves of bread*), los árboles (*trees*), los camiones (*lorries*), los bares (*bars*), las tías (*aunts*), los maridos (*husbands*), las madres (*mothers*), las ciudades (*cities*), los martes (*Tuesdays*)

3.4.5
Quiero . . . dos helados (*ice creams*), dos cafés, dos hamburguesas, dos refrescos (*soft drinks*), dos zumos (*fruit juices*), dos vinos (*glasses of wine*), dos tés (*teas*), dos tortillas (*omelettes*), dos bocadillos (*sandwiches – baguette style*), dos pasteles (*cakes*)

3.6.1
MS: paraguas, jabalí, rey, viernes, abuelo, mono, pakistaní, programa, pijama
FS: agua, crema, princesa, pakistaní, madre, nuera, radio, crisis, ciudad, mano
MPL: menús, días, ratones, viernes, primos, padres, sofás, vecinos
FPL: patatas, amigas, fotos, mujeres, motos, jirafas, crisis

3.6.2
tardes (f pl)	apartamento (m sing)	anuncio (m sing)	salón (m sing)
cocina (f sing)	comedor (m sing)	dormitorios (m pl)	terrazas (f pl)
televisión (f sing)	lavadora (f sing)	lavavajillas (m sing)	personas (f pl)
muebles (m pl)	playa (f sing)	coche (m sing)	piscina (f sing)
jardines (m pl)	minutos (m pl)		

4.4.1
el aceite, los huevos, el vinagre, la sal, el queso, el jamón, las patatas fritas, el pastel, el pan, los tomates, las sardinas, el paquete, las cajas

4.4.2
1 el, la 2 el 3 el, la 4 el, la 5 el (los) 6 los, la 7 el, la 8 los, del 9 la, el 10 los

4.4.3
1 La señora 2 la cabeza 3 La gente 4 El abuelo 5 La hermana 6 la casa, los padres 7 El Madrid, el Barcelona 8 none 9 El padre 10 el señor 11 none 12 El doctor 13 none 14 El niño, la escuela 15 la universidad 16 El español

4.6.1
1 **La** cerveza es barata; quiero cerveza 2 **El** médico viene ahora; Pedro es médico 3 me encanta **la** música; escucho música 4 **Los** idiomas son útiles; estudio idiomas 5 hago ejercicio; me encanta **el** ejercicio 6 no tengo dinero; no tengo **el** dinero que me diste 7 tenemos pollo para comer; **El** pollo está bueno 8 Comemos fruta para postre; Nos gusta mucho **la** fruta.

4.6.2

1. La paella es el plato nacional de España.
2. La familia es importante para los niños.
3. El vino español es bueno.
4. El ejercicio es bueno para la salud.
5. La sociedad española es diferente ahora.
6. La naturaleza está en peligro.
7. La educación es importante.
8. La universidad es cara.
9. El alcohol puede ser malo para la salud.
10. El desayuno está incluido en el precio.

5.5.1

1 una 2 un 3 un 4 una 5 unas 6 un 7 un 8 unas 9 un
10 unos 11 un 12 unos

5.5.2

1. Quiero una lata de atún.
2. Quiero una caja de galletas.
3. Quiero un litro de agua mineral.
4. Quiero una docena de huevos.
5. Póngame un cuarto de queso.
6. Deme un paquete de patatas fritas.
7. Quiero un bote de mermelada.
8. Deme una botella de vino blanco.
9. Quiero media docena de pasteles.
10. Póngame medio kilo de tomates.
11. Quiero un kilo de sardinas.
12. Deme medio litro de aceite.

5.7.1

1 una comunidad 2 una iglesia 3 none 4 un pintor 5 una
zona 6 unas avenidas 7 un estadio 8 none

5.7.2

1. What a nice skirt!
2. I'd like half a kilo of ham.
3. It's a lie!
4. He / she is a student.
5. Are you Colombian?
6. She is studying to become a teacher.
7. Ali is a Muslim.
8. I'd like half a dozen eggs.
9. What a pity!
10. Juan is looking for work (*or* a job).
11. Maria can't find any work (*or* a job).
12. You shouldn't go out without an umbrella.
13. He doesn't have a car, he has a motorbike.
14. Ana always wears trousers.
15. What a coincidence!

6.5.1

M: delgado, alto, feo, malo, conservador, bonito, guapo,
moreno
F: baja, simpática, pequeña, alta, rubia, delgada, guapa
M/F: verde, azul, naranja, grande, marrón, circular, gris,
optimista, débil, cosmopolita

6.5.2

delgado > delgados	alta > altas	moreno > morenos
baja > bajas	feo > feos	guapa > guapas
alto > altos	malo > malos	marrón > marrones
azul > azules	rubia > rubias	circular > circulares
naranja > naranjas	conservador > conservadores	gris > grises
grande > grandes	bonito > bonitos	optimista > optimistas
simpática > simpáticas	delgada > delgadas	débil > débiles
pequeña > pequeñas	guapo > guapos	cosmopolita > cosmopolitas

6.5.3

1 irlandesa 2 egipcio 3 peruano 4 boliviana
5 guatemalteca 6 japonesa 7 mexicano 8 marroquí
9 griego 10 brasileña 11 uruguayo 12 ecuatoriana

6.7.1

1. Mi padre ha perdido una bufanda roja, muy larga, de lana.
2. Mi primo ha perdido una cartera marrón mediana, de piel.
3. Mi hermana ha perdido un bolso transparente grande, de
   plástico.
4. Mi abuela ha perdido unas gafas de sol doradas, grandes,
   de metal dorado.
5. Mi prima ha perdido una pulsera pequeña de plata.
6. Mi hermano ha perdido una bolsa negra muy grande, de
   tela.
7. Mi tía ha perdido unos guantes azul marino, pequeños,
   de piel.
8. Mi madre ha perdido unos pendientes largos de oro.

6.7.2

Sopa de pollo	Vino de la casa
Zumo de tomate	Pastel de queso
Chuleta de cordero	Estofado de ternera
Sopa de pescado	Tarta de manzana
Helado de fresa	Salsa de tomate

7.4.1
verde fuerte pueblo coche balcón caliente malo guapo grande puente calor cielo amor

7.4.2
pequeñito, azulito, despacito, lentito, blandito, redondito, cuadradito, blanquito, pobrecito, viejecito, prontito, deprisita, cuidadito, fresquito

7.4.3
little house – casita
big house – casona
little book – librito
big book – librote
horrible house – casucha
big dog – perrazo
little dog – perrito
little window – ventanilla
horrible town – pueblucho
little table – mesita
teaspoon – cucharita
little child – niñito/ita
big man –grandote

8.9.1
1. El coche es más rápido que la bicicleta.
2. El autobús es menos caro que el tren.
3. La bicicleta es más lenta que la moto.
4. El tren es más cómodo que el autobús.
5. El autobús es menos rápido que el avión.
6. El tren es tan barato como el autobús.

8.9.2
1 peor 2 mayor 3 mejor 4 menor 5 peores 6 mayor
7 mayor, menores 8 mejores

8.9.3
1 tantos 2 tantas 3 tanto 4 tantas 5 tanta 6 tanta

8.9.4
1. Mi hermano es mayor que mi hermana.
2. Tu casa es más grande que la mía.
3. Él siempre llega más tarde que tú.
4. Mi paella es tan buena como la de mi madre.
5. Él tiene tanto dinero como tú.
6. Fernando trabaja menos que Pepe.
7. Ana estudia más que yo.
8. Luis tiene tantos libros como Julia.
9. Hablo español mejor que mi hermana.

10. Juan está peor que la semana pasada.
11. El chico es como su madre.
12. Este abrigo es igual que el mío.

8.9.5
1 buenísimo 2 carísimos 3 viejísimo 4 altísimo
5 estrechísimas 6 guapísima

8.11.1
1 tan 2 tantos 3 mejor 4 tan 5 más 6 más 7 menos
8 menos 9 más 10 tantas

8.11.2
1 inferior 2 óptimas 3 máxima 4 superiores 5 anterior
6 posterior 7 pésima 8 mínimo

9.7.1
1 yo 2 tú 3 ellos / ellas / ustedes 4 nosotros/as
5 vosotros/as 6 él / ella / usted

9.7.2
1 la, la 2 lo, lo 3 los, los 4 las, las

9.7.3
1 lo / le 2 la 3 los / les 4 la 5 las 6 lo / le

9.7.4
1. ¿Me traes un regalo?
2. ¿Le regalas el libro?
3. ¿Les das la comida?
4. ¿Les sacas las entradas?
5. ¿Le compras el reloj?
6. ¿Os comprará la guitarra?
7. ¿Nos entregarás el paquete?
8. ¿Me escribirás un email?

9.7.5
1 ¿Me lo traes? 2 ¿Se lo regalas? 3 ¿Se la das? 4 ¿Se las sacas? 5 ¿Se lo compras? 6 ¿Os la comprará? 7 ¿Nos lo entregarás? 8 ¿Me lo escribirás?

9.7.6
1. Sí, quiero comprarlo.
2. Sí, estoy arreglándola.
3. Sí, quiero escribirles.
4. Sí, estoy pintándola.
5. Sí, quiero cerrarlas.
6. Sí, vengo a verla.
7. Sí, estoy comiéndolas.
8. Sí, quiero llamarlas.

9.10.1

1 Regálaselo. 2 Cómprasela. 3 Dáselos. 4 Cómpraselas.
5 Préstaselo. 6 Regálaselos. 7 Cómprasela.

9.10.2

1. Se lo recomiendo.
2. Se la traigo.
3. Os la digo.
4. ¿Te lo compras?
5. Me la compro.
6. ¿Te lo pruebas?
7. ¿Se la pides?
8. ¿Nos lo compramos?

10.6.1

1 me levanto 2 se acuestan 3 se baña 4 se visten 5 nos
despertamos 6 te duchas 7 me arreglo 8 nos acostamos

10.6.2

1 bañándome 2 levantarse 3 arreglándonos 4 os vestís
5 ducharme 6 lavándose 7 bañamos

11.6.1

1. No, no quiero ésta, prefiero aquélla.
2. No, no quiero éstos, prefiero aquéllas.
3. No, no quiero éste, prefiero aquél.
4. No, no quiero éstas, prefiero aquéllas.
5. No, no quiero esto, prefiero aquello.

11.6.2

1. Quisiera aquellas naranjas.
2. Prefiero estas manzanas.
3. Prefiere esos plátanos, no aquéllos.
4. ¿Qué es esto? Esto es un reloj.
5. Quisiéramos aquel pastel.
6. Me puedes dar estas manzanas, no ésas (or: aquéllas).
7. No quiero esos melocotones, prefiero estos.
8. ¿Cómo se llama eso?
9. ¿Cómo se dice esto?

11.8.1

1 esa 2 esta 3 ésa, aquel 4 ese 5 aquél, estos 6 Estos
7 éstos, ésos 8 Ésos 9 ésos, esto 10 esto 11 este 12 éste
13 éste 14 este, aquél, Aquel, éste 15 aquél

12.7.1

1 mi apartamento 2 su casa 3 sus maletas 4 sus hijos
5 nuestros coches 6 su hija 7 sus casas 8 vuestro
coche

12.7.2

1 el mío 2 la suya 3 las suyas 4 los suyos 5 los nuestros
6 la suya 7 las suyas 8 el vuestro

12.7.3

1. Sí, el apartamento es mío.
2. Sí, las bolsas son nuestras.
3. Sí, los coches son nuestros.
4. Sí, la maleta es vuestra.
5. Sí, el libro es tuyo.
6. Sí, la casa es suya.
7. Sí, el coche es nuestro.
8. Sí, las fotos son nuestras.

12.9.1

1 El mío también. 2 La nuestra también. 3 Los nuestros
también. 4 El tuyo también. 5 La suya también. 6 Las
nuestras también. 7 El tuyo también. 8 Los vuestros
también.

12.9.2

1. Este bolígrafo es mío.
2. ¿Es esta cartera la suya?
3. ¿Es este paraguas el suyo?
4. ¿Estos pendientes son suyos?
5. Este coche no es el nuestro.
6. Estas maletas son vuestras.
7. La casa de Antonio es muy bonita.
8. Encontré tu bolso, pero no puedo encontrar el mío.
9. Tengo las mías, pero no tengo las suyas.
10. El padre de Isabel es amigo mío.

13.4.1

1. Juan es el chico que lleva la camiseta amarilla.
2. Isabel es la chica que lleva el jersey verde.
3. Carlos es el chico que lleva la camisa blanca.
4. Elena es la chica que lleva los vaqueros negros.

13.4.2

1. El profesor que tiene Isabel es excelente. (*Isabel's teacher is excellent.*)
2. El chico con quien sale Ana es amigo mío. (*The boy Ana is going out with is my friend.*)
3. Las uvas que compré en el mercado son buenísimas. (*The grapes I bought in the market are very good.*)
4. Los amigos de quienes te hablé llegan hoy. (*The friends I told you about are arriving today.*)
5. Esta chica es la que limpia la oficina. (*This girl is the one who cleans the office.*)
6. Ésta es la casa donde vive Juan. (*This is the house where Juan lives.*)

13.6.1

1 es el que 2 es la que 3 son los que 4 son las que 5 es el que 6 es la que 7 son las que 8 son las que 9 es el que 10 son los que

13.6.2

1 con las que 2 al que 3 a los que 4 de la que 5 para el que 6 a los que

13.6.3

1 con las cuales 2 al cual 3 a los cuales 4 de la cual 5 para el cual 6 a los cuales

14.4.1

1. ¿Quién es usted?
2. ¿Cuál es su nombre?
3. ¿Cómo está?
4. ¿De dónde es, señor González?
5. ¿Dónde vive usted?
6. ¿Cuál es su dirección?
7. ¿Cuántos años tiene?
8. ¿Por qué trabaja en esta empresa?
9. ¿Cuánto (dinero) gana?
10. ¿Cuándo llega a la oficina?
11. ¿Qué quiere tomar?

14.4.2

1 Cómo 2 Quién 3 De dónde 4 Dónde 5 Qué 6 Qué
7 Cuál 8 Quién 9 Dónde 10 Cuántos

14.4.3

1. ¿Qué libros compras?
2. ¿Quiénes estudian español?
3. ¿Cuántos pasteles quiere?
4. ¿Cuáles son más bonitos?
5. ¿Cuántas pizzas compras?
6. ¿Qué abrigos quieres?
7. ¿Quiénes viven en Madrid?
8. ¿Cuánto cuestan las chaquetas?
9. ¿De quiénes hablas?

14.6.1

1. ¿Qué horario tiene el Bus turístico?
2. ¿A qué hora sale el Bus por la mañana?
3. ¿Cuándo termina el Bus por la tarde?
4. ¿Cuántas horas para el Bus a mediodía?
5. ¿Cuánto dura el itinerario por la ciudad?
6. ¿De dónde sale el bus turístico?
7. ¿Dónde se pueden comprar los billetes?
8. ¿Cuánto cuesta el billete?
9. ¿Cuántas paradas hay en el centro?

14.6.2

1. ¿Qué hiciste?
2. ¿Adónde fuiste?
3. ¿Por qué tuviste el día libre?
4. ¿A qué hora te levantaste?
5. ¿Cuánto tiempo estudiaste?
6. ¿Cuándo fuiste de compras?
7. ¿Cuántas cosas compraste?
8. ¿Con quién fuiste al cine?
9. ¿Qué tal lo pasaste?
10. ¿Cuál prefieres . . . ?

15.4.1

1. ¡Cuánto trabajo tiene!
2. ¡Qué caro es el bolso!
3. ¡Cómo juega el equipo! / ¡Qué bien juega el equipo!
4. ¡Cuántos libros tienes!
5. ¡Cuánto estudia Luis!
6. ¡Qué difícil es el examen!
7. ¡Cuántas cosas tienes!
8. ¡Qué grande es la casa!

15.4.2

1. What a lot of work he has!
2. How expensive the bag is!
3. How well the team plays!
4. What a lot of books you have!
5. Luis studies so much!
6. How difficult the exam is!
7. What a lot of things you have!
8. The house is so big!

16.4.1

1
A: ¿Tienes <u>muchos</u> amigos en el pueblo?
B: No, tengo <u>pocos</u> amigos. ¿Y tú? Tienes <u>algún</u> amigo en la ciudad?
A: No tengo <u>ningún</u> amigo. Este pueblo es <u>demasiado</u> pequeño y <u>bastante</u> aburrido.
2
A: ¿Te gusta <u>algún</u> vestido?
B: No me gusta <u>ninguno</u>.
A: ¿Te gusta <u>alguna</u> chaqueta?
B: No, no me gusta <u>ninguna</u>. Además esta tienda es <u>demasiado</u> cara.
A: Pues vamos a otra. Hay una tienda <u>bastante</u> barata <u>muy</u> cerca.
3
A: Tengo <u>demasiado</u> trabajo y <u>demasiados</u> problemas.
B: Pues yo no tengo <u>tanto</u> trabajo esta semana. Si quieres te ayudo con <u>algo</u>.
A: Muchas gracias, pero tengo que hacerlo <u>todo</u> yo solo.

16.4.2

1 algo 2 algún 3 mucha 4 algunas 5 alguna 6 ninguna
7 bastante 8 otro

16.6.1

1 alguien, nadie 2 algunas, ningunas 3 algo, nada 4 algo,
nada 5 algunos, algunos 6 algún, alguno 7 alguien, nadie
8 alguna, ninguna

16.6.2

1 nada, nada 2 nadie, nadie 3 nada, nada 4 alguien, nadie
5 nadie, alguien 6 alguien, nadie 7 nadie, alguien 8 algo,
nada

16.6.3

1 cada 2 varios 3 cierta 4 varias 5 cualquier
6 cualquiera 7 cada 8 cualquier

17.6.1

1 128   3 515   5 402
2 249   4 78   6 2010

17.6.2

a 723 > Setecientos veintitrés
b 45 > cuarenta y cinco
c 28 > veintiocho
d 259 > doscientos cincuenta y nueve
e 178 > ciento setenta y ocho
f 17 > diecisiete
g 349 > trescientos cuarenta y nueve
h 586 > quinientos ochenta y seis
i 215 > doscientos quince
j 176 > ciento setenta y seis

17.6.3

a Son las doce menos cuarto de la mañana.
b Son las dos y media de la tarde.
c Son las diez y cinco de la noche.
d Son las cinco menos diez de la tarde.
e Son las siete y media de la tarde.
f Son las seis y veinte de la mañana.
g Son las cuatro menos veinticinco de la tarde.
h Son las siete y media de la mañana.
i Son las cuatro y cuarto de la mañana.
j Es la una menos cuarto de la tarde.

17.6.4

1. El tren sale a las tres y media de la tarde.
2. La tienda abre a las diez y cinco de la mañana.
3. La película empieza a las siete y cuarto de la tarde.
4. El autobús llega a las cuatro y veinticinco de la tarde.
5. Como a las doce y cuarto del mediodía.

17.6.5

1 mañana por la mañana 2 anoche 3 una hora y media
4 pasado mañana 5 la semana que viene / la semana
próxima 6 tres cuartos de hora 7 media hora 8 de / desde
las tres a las cinco 9 dos veces a la semana 10 cada día

17.8.1

a 1.843.576 > un millón, ochocientos cuarenta y tres mil,
  quinientos setenta y seis
b 5.345.707 > cinco millones, trescientos cuarenta y cinco
  mil, setecientos siete
c 3.830.748 > tres millones, ochocientos treinta mil,
  setecientos cuarenta y ocho
d 87.570 > ochenta y siete mil, quinientos setenta
e 92.000 > noventa y dos mil
f 8.789.507 > ocho millones, setecientos ochenta y nueve
  mil, quinientos siete.
g 7.000 > siete mil
h 65.135.946 > sesenta y cinco millones, ciento treinta y
  cinco mil, novecientos cuarenta y seis

18.5.1

fácilmente	próximamente	últimamente
difícilmente	especialmente	frecuentemente
tranquilamente	normalmente	anteriormente
lentamente	simplemente	descuidadamente
exactamente	inmediatamente	

18.5.2

1. cerca / lejos (place) / muy (quantity)
2. siempre (time) / muy (quantity) / bien (mood)
3. mal (mood) / mucho (quantity)
4. hoy (time)
5. muy (quantity) / temprano (time) / rápidamente (mode)
6. despacio (mode)
7. siempre (time), lejos (place)
8. mañana (time)
9. pronto (time), tarde (time)
10. luego (time), ahora (time)

18.5.3

1. I live next to the university but before, I used to live very
   far away.
2. The boy always does his homework very well.
3. My brother is not well, his head aches a lot.
4. My parents are coming to lunch today.
5. Juan gets up very early and leaves the house quickly.
6. Every day they walk slowly/stroll through the park.
7. Juan says that he always arrives late to class because he
   lives far away.
8. My sister will come to see me tomorrow.

9. Leave home early because you are going to arrive late at the office.

10. Phone me later because I'm busy at the moment.

18.5.4

1 alguna vez 2 nunca 3 alguna vez 4 nunca 5 nunca (also: alguna vez) 6 alguna vez

18.5.5

1 ya 2 aún 3 aún 4 ya 5 ya 6 ya

18.7.1

anteriormente, últimamente, inmediatamente, simultáneamente, definitivamente, continuamente, instantáneamente, repetidamente, repentinamente, frecuentemente, mensualmente, estupendamente, totalmente, dolorosamente, afortunadamente, desgraciadamente, lamentablemente,

19.4.1

1. No, no quiero café.
2. No, no juego al fútbol.
3. No, no quiero salir contigo.
4. No, Ana no viene a la fiesta.
5. No, no tomamos más cerveza.
6. No, no me gustan las patatas asadas.
7. No, no voy a comprar el billete esta tarde.
8. No, no tengo mucho trabajo.

19.4.2

1. No sale nunca de casa.
2. No compra nadie en esta tienda.
3. No aprobará el examen ninguno.
4. No iré a la playa este año tampoco.
5. No me apetece nada estos días.
6. No hablamos nunca de trabajo.

19.4.3

1 ni 2 tampoco 3 nada 4 nunca 5 jamás / nunca 6 nadie

19.6.1

1 no, ni, tampoco 2 nunca 3 no, ninguna 4 no, nadie 5 ni, ni 6 no, nada 7 no, nada, tampoco 8 no, nada

19.6.2

1. de ningún modo	no way, absolutely not
2. de ninguna manera	no way, absolutely not.
3. claro que no	of course not
4. nada más	no more/ nothing else
5. eso sí que no	not that
6. en absoluto	absolutely not
7. casi nada	almost nothing
8. nada de eso	none of that
9. ¡que no!	of course not!
10. ni hablar	not at all
11. en mi vida	never in my life
12. ¡qué va!	of course not

20.6.1

1 a 2 con 3 en 4 al 5 en 6 con 7 a 8 con, en 9 en 10 al, en 11 desde, hasta (de, a)

20.6.2

1 para 2 para 3 para, por 4 por, por 5 por 6 por, por 7 para, para 8 para, para

20.6.3

Restaurant:
Pollo asado con patatas fritas
Chuleta de ternera
Bistec a la pimienta
Vino tinto de la casa
Cerveza sin alcohol

Hotel:
Quiero reservar una habitación para el día quince.
Quiero una habitación con vistas a la playa.
Hay piscina para niños.
¿Puede despertarme por la mañana?
La cena es a las nueve de la noche.

20.6.4

1 con 2 de 3 para 4 a 5 sin 6 para 7 sobre, de 8 en 9 para 10 por, con

20.6.5

1. El libro trata de un actor famoso.
2. Juan se sentó a la mesa con nosotros.
3. Yo voy a trabajar a pie.
4. Quiero cambiar de coche.
5. La película acaba de empezar.
6. El profesor se queja de los estudiantes.
7. Juan está aprendiendo a cocinar.
8. Empecé a trabajar hace dos años.
9. Llegaremos a casa hacia las dos de la tarde.
10. Quiero cambiar este abrigo por otro.

20.6.6

1 para 2 por 3 por, por 4 por 5 para 6 para 7 por 8 para 9 para 10 para 11 por 12 para

21.4.1

1. Vine con Ana e Isabel.
2. Trabajo en una tienda y estudio por las noches.

3. Llegaré esta tarde o mañana por la tarde.

4. No quiero tomar primer plato ni postre.

5. Me gusta este abrigo pero es muy caro.

6. No estoy enfadado sino triste.

7. El profesor dice que hay clase mañana.

8. No vamos al parque porque está lloviendo.

9. No sé si prefieres éste u otro más barato.

21.4.2

Pepe me dijo que este pueblo es muy bonito y muy tranquilo y que podemos ir a la playa o a la montaña en poco tiempo porque está muy cerca de las dos. A mí me gusta la playa pero mi marido prefiere la montaña, pero mis hijos este año no quieren ir de vacaciones (ni) a la playa ni a la montaña, sino al extranjero. Dicen que quieren visitar Italia e Inglaterra. Tambien van a viajar por Alemania y Holanda, u otros países del norte de Europa.

21.6.1

1 pues 2 menos 3 excepto 4 por lo tanto 5 sin embargo 6 a pesar de 7 no obstante 8 aunque

22.3.1

1

A: ¿Quieres ir al cine conmigo hoy? / ¿Quieres ir al cine hoy conmigo?

B: No me gusta el cine. / El cine no me gusta.

A: ¿Quieres jugar a las cartas?

B: Sí, me gusta jugar a las cartas.

2

A: ¿Quieres jugar al fútbol?

B: No me gusta el fútbol. / El fútbol no me gusta.

A: ¿Prefieres escuchar música?

B: Sí, bueno, me gusta la música. / Bueno, sí, me gusta la música.

22.3.2

1.¿Vais vosotros de compras esta tarde? / ¿Vais de compras vosotros esta tarde? / ¿Vais de compras esta tarde vosotros?

2. ¿Vendrán ellos por la mañana?

3. ¿Fuiste tú a la playa?

4. ¿Compró ella mucha ropa en esta tienda? / ¿Compró mucha ropa ella en esta tienda?

5. ¿Tienes tú un apartamento en la playa?

6. ¿Vendrán tus padres mañana? / ¿Vendrán mañana tus padres?

24.4.1

1 vengo 2 juegas 3 es 4 sé 5 conduces 6 oigo 7 va 8 pido 9 digo

24.4.2

soy; pones; empezáis; prefieren; juego; comemos; sales; vais; eres; vuelvo; duermen; encuentras; seguimos; traduzco; conducimos; repiten; hago; venís; digo; vienes; estáis; doy

24.6.1

1 comemos 2 vuelve 3 nos levantamos, desayunamos 4 cenáis 5 salen 6 nos acostamos 7 tomáis 8 meriendan

24.6.2

1. Yo hago la cama. I make the bed.

2. Nosotros ponemos la mesa. We lay the table.

3. Vosotras quitáis la mesa. You (more than one) clear the table.

4. Ellos friegan los platos. They wash up the plates.

5. Mi madre friega el suelo. My mother washes the floor.

6. Tú limpias el polvo. You dust.

7. Él pasa la aspiradora. He vacuums.

8. Vosotros plancháis la ropa. You (more than one) iron the clothes.

9. Nosotros barremos la cocina. We sweep the kitchen.

10. Yo saco la basura. I take out the rubbish.

25.4.1

1 te levantas 2 nos despertamos 3 se acuestan 4 os vestís 5 se lava 6 se bañan 7 me peino 8 te cambias 9 nos arreglamos

26.7.1

1 le gusta el teatro 2 te gustan las revistas 3 me gustan los deportes 4 les gusta ver la televisión 5 nos gusta jugar al fútbol 6 le gustan las películas cómicas 7 le gusta el cine 8 os gusta ir de excursión 9 les gustan los pasteles

26.7.2

1. A mí me encantan las canciones románticas.

2. A mis amigos les gusta salir a cenar.

3. A mi amiga Ana le gusta bailar.

4. A mis hermanas les encanta la música clásica.

5. ¿A vosotros os gustan las películas de misterio?

6. A ti te encantan los libros de historia.

7. A nosotros no nos gusta la televisión.

8. A mi madre le interesa el arte.

9. A mí no me importa trabajar el fin de semana.

26.9.1

Arturo: ¿Te **gustaría / apetece** ir a cenar a algún restaurante?

Carmen: No, no me **apetece**. No me **gusta** comer en los restaurantes,.

Arturo: ¿Te **gustaría** cenar en casa?

Carmen: Sí, me **gustaría / apetece** más cenar en casa.

Arturo: ¿Qué te **gustaría / apetece** cenar?

Carmen: Me **apetece** mucho pasta con salsa de carne. ¡Me **encanta** la pasta!

Arturo: Pero la pasta me **da / causa** dolor de estómago.

Carmen: Pues, no sé . . . ¿Te **apetece** un poco de jamón serrano y queso?

Arturo: No, el jamón por la noche me **da** mucha sed y el queso me **produce / causa** pesadillas.

Carmen: ¿Te **apetece** más una paella?

Arturo: Sí, no me **importaría** cenar una paella. Es lo que más me **apetece** en este momento.

Carmen: Pero por la noche te **sienta** mal. Mejor no.

26.9.2

1 A él lo que más le gusta son las patatas fritas. 2 A nosotros lo que más nos gusta es el pescado. 3 A mí lo que más me gusta es el café solo. 4 A ti lo que más te gusta es la verdura. 5 A vosotros lo que más os gusta es la fruta. 6 A ella lo que más le gusta son las naranjas. 7 A mí lo que más me gusta es el chocolate. 8 A vosotros lo que más os gusta es la tortilla de patata.

27.6.1

1 estoy 2 está 3 estás 4 está 5 estamos 6 están 7 está 8 estás 9 está 10 estáis

27.6.2

1 es, es 2 es, es 3 está 4 está 5 está 6 es 7 es, es 8 está 9 está, está 10 es, es 11 está, es 12 está

27.6.3

1 es 2 es 3 está 4 es 5 está 6 estamos 7 es 8 son 9 es 10 es 11 son 12 están 13 son 14 estoy 15 es

27.6.4

1. La puerta está abierta. (está sucia)
2. El café está frío.
3. El pueblo está destruido. (es interesante)
4. El árbol está muerto. (está destruido)
5. La pelota es redonda.
6. La taza está vacía. (está sucia)
7. El documental es interesante.
8. La camisa está sucia.
9. Este plato está roto.
10. La televisión está encendida.

27.8.1

1 está 2 es 3 es 4 está 5 estoy, es 6 es 7 es 8 estoy, está

27.8.2

1 es 2 está 3 está 4 es 5 es (or está, if the speaker means that Pedro is feeling weak rather than actually weak) 6 está 7 es 8 está 9 es 10 está 11 es 12 está 13 es 14 está

27.8.3

1 era; estaba 2 estaba 3 era 4 era 5 estaba 6 estaba 7 éramos 8 eran 9 estaba 10 era; era

28.4.1

1 voy a comprar 2 va a estudiar 3 va a trabajar 4 vamos a viajar 5 van a escribir 6 vais a ir 7 van a limpiar 8 voy a comer 9 vamos a desayunar 10 va a vender

28.4.2

1 compraré 2 estudiará 3 trabajará 4 viajaremos 5 escribirán 6 iréis 7 limpiarán 8 comeré 9 desayunaremos 10 venderá

28.4.3

1 podrás 2 querrás 3 haremos 4 pondrá 5 saldré 6 vendrán 7 tendrás 8 dirá 9 habrá 10 cabrá 11 sabré

28.4.4

1 tendrán 2 podremos 3 saldréis 4 vendré 5 harán 6 querréis 7 pondremos 8 sabré 9 querrán 10 habrá 11 cabrá 12 diré

29.4.1

1 pisó 2 empezó 3 llegó 4 entraron 5 formaron

29.4.2

1. Me levanté a las 8 de la mañana.
2. Fui al centro de la ciudad.
3. Fui de compras y (después) fui al cine.
4. Compré muchas cosas.
5. Fui (al cine) con mi hermano.
6. Cené en casa, salí a un club y bailé hasta las 3 de la mañana / la madrugada.
7. Me acosté a las 4 de la mañana / la madrugada.
8. Lo pasé muy bien.

29.4.3

1 llovió 2 estuve, hizo 3 fui, hizo 4 estuve, vi 5 fuiste, fui 6 nevó

29.4.4

1 fuimos 2 estuvieron 3 visitasteis, fuisteis, visitamos
4 hicimos, estuvimos 5 alquilaron, montaron, estuvieron
6 salieron, fueron, vieron

29.6.1

Teresa tuvo un día aburrido. Estuvo enferma por la mañana
y se quedó en casa. Estuvo en la cama toda la mañana y
leyó un libro. Después se levantó, comió un poco y se
acostó otra vez. Durmió la siesta hasta las seis. Por la tarde
se vistió y fue a casa de su amiga Carmen. Llegó a su casa y
cenó con ella. Después volvió a casa y se acostó pronto.

29.6.2

1 llegaron, llegué 2 traje, trajeron 3 vinieron, dieron
4 estuvo, murió 5 cayó, rompió 6 vi, viste 7 bebió,
conduje 8 pudimos, hizo 9 caí, pedí, oyó 10 dije, creyó

30.4.1

1 me levantaba 2 desayunaba 3 iba 4 nadaba 5 tomaba
6 comía 7 dormía 8 salía 9 cenaba 10 me acostaba

30.4.2

1 iban, van 2 comía, come (or tomaba, toma) 3 tenían,
tienen 4 bebías, bebes (or tomabas, tomas) 5 estabais,
estáis 6 trabajaba, trabaja 7 vivíamos, vivimos 8 iba, voy

30.4.3

1 había 2 era 3 tenía 4 estaba 5 era 6 había 7 tenía
8 estaba

30.8.1

1 tocaba, entré 2 limpiaba, vinieron 3 corría, me caí
4 cruzábamos, vimos 5 hablaba, llegó 6 veía, llamó
7 viajaba, se puso 8 preparaba, volvió

30.8.2

1 vivía, conocía, vivo, conozco 2 era, trabaja 3 era,
practicaba, practico 4 nadabas, nadaste 5 íbamos, fuimos
6 vivían, fueron 7 iba, fui 8 jugábamos, jugamos

31.4.1

1 has visitado, he visitado 2 habéis estado, hemos estado
3 has comido, he comido 4 habéis probado, hemos
probado 5 han ido, han ido 6 has estudiado, he estudiado
7 habéis comprado, hemos comprado 8 han bebido, han
bebido

31.4.2

1 hemos comido 2 han escrito 3 habéis conocido 4 has
enviado 5 ha roto 6 ha dicho 7 han hablado 8 hemos
visto 9 he hecho 10 hemos ido 11 he vuelto

31.6.1

1. Me he quemado con la plancha.
2. Me he cortado con un cuchillo.
3. Me he dado un golpe en la cabeza.
4. Me he roto el brazo y no puedo escribir.
5. He tomado el sol demasiado y me escuece la espalda.
6. Me he torcido el tobillo y no puedo andar.
7. Me han salido unos granos por toda la cara.

31.6.2

1. I've burnt myself with the iron.
2. I've cut myself with a knife.
3. I've bumped myself on the head.
4. I've broken my arm and I can't write.
5. I've sunbathed too much and my back is burning.
6. I've twisted my ankle and I can't walk.
7. I've come out in spots all over my face.

31.6.3

1 se ha roto 2 se han acostado 3 nos hemos bañado
4 me he torcido 5 se ha roto 6 se ha cortado 7 me he
duchado 8 te has roto 9 me he roto 10 se ha dado

32.4.1

1. ¿Te gustaría venir al cine conmigo?
2. Me encantaría ir al cine contigo.
3. ¿Te interesaría visitar el museo?
4. Me gustaría visitar el museo.
5. ¿Podrías abrir la puerta, por favor?
6. ¿Querrías vivir aquí?

32.4.2

1 comeríamos, tenemos 2 te escribiría, tiene 3 vendrían,
es 4 compraría, tengo 5 podríamos, preferimos 6 se
pondría, está 7 tendrías, gastas 8 sabría, estudio

32.6.1

1 deberías 2 compraría 3 sería 4 tendrías 5 haría
6 tendríais 7 deberíamos 8 deberían

32.6.2

1 vendríamos 2 tendrías 3 cuidaríamos 4 saldría
5 pondrías 6 sería

32.6.3

1 iría 2 cenaríamos 3 aprobarías 4 viajaría 5 estarías
6 compraríais 7 vivirías 8 tendrían

33.4.1

1 terminar 2 comprender 3 comprar 4 vivir 5 poner,
comer 6 dirigir

33.6.1

1. d El libro es difícil de encontrar
2. h Hacer deporte es bueno para la salud
3. j Compró el billete una semana antes de viajar.
4. e Fuimos de compras al salir de la oficina.
5. i Fue a casa de su madre para celebrar su cumpleaños.
6. a La casa que compré aún está por terminar.
7. f Tiene que estudiar otro año antes de terminar la carrera.
8. b Se puso enfermo después de comer el pescado.
9. g No podemos limpiar sin ordenar las cosas antes.
10. c Juan fue con sus amigos a sacar entradas para el teatro.

33.6.2

1. The book is hard to find.
2. Doing sport is good for your health.
3. He bought the ticket a week before travelling.
4. We went shopping when we left the office.
5. He went to his mother's house to celebrate her birthday.
6. The house I bought is still to be finished.
7. He has to study another year before finishing the course.
8. He became ill after eating the fish.
9. We can't clean without tidying the things first.
10. Juan went with his friends to buy tickets for the theatre.

34.5.1

1 estamos estudiando 2 está trabajando 3 está haciendo
4 estamos terminando 5 está desayunando 6 estamos comiendo 7 estoy tomando 8 estamos jugando 9 está bebiendo 10 estoy escribiendo

34.5.2

1 está comiéndola 2 estoy leyéndolo 3 están terminándolos 4 estoy planchándola 5 estamos fregándolos 6 estoy limpiándolo 7 están bañándose 8 está dándolos 9 estoy haciéndola 10 estoy escuchándolas

34.7.1

1. Sí, estoy comprándoselos.
2. Sí, estamos preparándosela.
3. Sí, estan escribiéndoselos.
4. Sí, estoy preparándotelos.
5. Sí, estoy dándosela.
6. Sí, estoy leyéndoselo.
7. Sí, estamos comprándoselo.
8. Sí, estoy buscándotelo.
9. Sí, estamos preparándoosla.
10. Sí, estoy haciéndotelo.

35.4.1

1. Ya hemos comprado el pan. 2. Ya hemos terminado el trabajo. 3. Ya he estudiado. 4. Ya han salido. 5. Ya he comido. 6. Ya hemos paseado.

35.4.2

1 cubierto, llovido 2 hecho, acostado 3 dicho, engañado
4 abierto, oído 5 caído, roto 6 puesto, pasado 7 vuelto, empezado 8 visto, gustado 9 muerto, puesto

35.6.1

1 pintado 2 hecha 3 encontrados 4 invitada 5 vistos
6 puesta 7 examinados 8 expuestos 9 comprada
10 devuelto

35.6.2

1. This picture was painted by Goya.
2. This sculpture was done (made) by a French sculptor.
3. The papers were found in a taxi.
4. María wasn't invited to the wedding.
5. The thieves were seen in a suburb in the outskirts.
6. The woman was set free (lit: placed at liberty).
7. The students were tried (lit: examined) by a court.
8. The paintings were exhibited in the national museum.
9. The house has been bought by a family with children.
10. The parcel was returned because you weren't at home.

36.5.1

1 habían cenado 2 había terminado 3 había empezado
4 había comido 5 había vendido 6 habían escapado
7 había abierto

36.5.2

1. habrá terminado	future perfect
2. había terminado	pluperfect
3. habrías sacado	past conditional
4. habremos terminado	future perfect
5. han cenado	present perfect
6. había llegado	pluperfect
7. habrán limpiado	future perfect
8. he salido	present perfect

36.5.3

1. Teresa will have finished her exams by now.
2. The programme had finished when I put the television on.
3. If you had studied you would have got good results.
4. When the boss gets here we will have finished the project.
5. My brothers and sisters haven't had dinner yet.
6. When the accident happened I hadn't arrived.

7. When we arrive they will already have cleaned the apartment.
8. I haven't left the house for a week.

37.4.1
1 toma 2 escribe 3 coma 4 pase 5 habla 6 compra
7 abra 8 mande 9 vende 10 suba

37.4.2
1 tomad 2 escribid 3 coman 4 pasen 5 hablad
6 comprad 7 abran 8 manden 9 vended 10 suban

37.4.3
1 pon 2 ven 3 sal 4 ve 5 ten 6 haz 7 di 8 sé

37.6.1
1 siéntese 2 levántate 3 dame 4 ponte 5 vete 6 lavaos
7 llámala 8 abróchense 9 daos

37.6.2
1 cómpramelo 2 dánosla 3 cómeselo 4 cóbraselos
5 pásamelas 6 póngasela 7 tómatelas 8 véndamelo
9 bebéoslos 10 préstenmelos

38.4.1
1 pongas 2 viaje 3 vayamos 4 contaminen 5 deje
6 ahorren 7 haya 8 uses

38.4.2
1 Es mejor que estudies. 2 Te recomiendo que pruebes
3 Es importante que vayas. 4 Es mejor que compres.
5 Te aconsejo que te des. 6 Es importante que escribas.
7 Te recomiendo que tomes. 8 Es mejor que vengas. 9 Te
aconsejo que te pongas. 10 Es mejor que cojas.

38.4.3
1 Es necesario que estudies. 2 Es necesario que leas.
3 Es necesario que tengas. 4 Es necesario que hagas.
5 Es necesario que organices 6 Es necesario que pases.
7 Es necesario que practiques. 8 Es necesario que aprendas.

38.4.4
1. Yo quiero ir de vacaciones.
2. Yo quiero que mi hermano compre una moto.
3. Yo quiero que mi padre venga a verme.
4. Yo quiero aprobar los exámenes.
5. Yo quiero que mis amigos aprueben los exámenes también.
6. Yo quiero dar una fiesta.
7. Yo quiero que mi madre me regale una moto.
8. Yo quiero que tú vengas a mi fiesta.
9. Yo quiero que mis amigos traigan muchos regalos.
10. Yo quiero salir a dar una vuelta.

38.4.5
1 A: ¿Qué opinas de la ciudad?
B: Yo creo que está limpia.
A: Yo no creo que esté limpia.

2 A: ¿Qué opinas de este libro?
B: Yo creo que es interesante.
A: Yo no creo que sea interesante.

3 A: ¿Qué opinas de este tema?
B: Yo creo que es fácil de entender.
A: Yo no creo que sea fácil de entender.

38.4.6
1 te levantes 2 salir 3 vaya 4 llegar 5 vengas 6 vienes
7 practicar 8 practiquen 9 salir 10 salgas

39.5.1
1. Me dijo que no comprara ese coche.
2. Me dijo que no bebiera tanto café.
3. Me dijo que no discutiera siempre con los amigos.
4. Me dijo que no usara el coche para todo.
5. Me dijo que no comiera demasiados pasteles.
6. Me dijo que no abriera la puerta a personas extrañas.
7. Me dijo que no entrara a la oficina.
8. Me dijo que no escribiera tan mal.

39.5.2
1 viajara 2 fuéramos 3 contaminaran 4 dejara
5 ahorráramos 6 hubiera 7 usaras

39.5.3
1 fueran 2 llamaran 3 me visitaran 4 pusieras 5 me
regalaran 6 hiciera 7 me invitaras

39.5.4
1 te hayas levantado 2 haya salido 3 haya ido 4 haya
llegado 5 hayan ido 6 haya practicado 7 haya salido
8 hayáis empezado 9 hayamos tomado 10 hayan visto

40.3.1
1. En París llueve.
2. En Londres hacía / hizo niebla.
3. En Dublín hará frío.
4. En Moscú nevará.
5. En Roma hacía / hizo viento.
6. En Barcelona hace calor.
7. En Madrid hará sol.
8. En Berlín estaba cubierto.
9. En Atenas hay tormentas.

40.3.2

1. En París hará viento.
2. En Londres lloverá.
3. En Dublín estará cubierto.
4. En Moscú hará mucho frío.
5. En Roma hará sol.
6. En Barcelona habrá tormentas.
7. En Madrid habrá niebla.
8. En Berlín nevará.
9. En Atenas hará calor.

40.5.1

1 falta 2 faltan 3 faltan 4 falta 5 faltan

40.5.2

1 hay 2 hace 3 falta 4 hay que 5 hace falta 6 es tarde
7 es pronto 8 es mejor 9 hace 10 faltan 11 son 12 es
importante

41.4.1

1 se acuestan 2 se fue 3 me pongo 4 te bebes 5 nos
hablamos 6 os ponéis 7 se conocen 8 me cambio

41.6.1

1 se ríe 2 creerte 3 se corta 4 me marcho 5 se
divorciaron 6 quejándote 7 nos comimos 8 te hiciste 9 os
olvidasteis 10 ponerte 11 hacerme

41.6.2

1. The baby laughs a lot.
2. You shouldn't believe everything he tells you.
3. Elena has her hair cut at the hairdresser's.
4. I'm going to the countryside with my sister.
5. My parents were divorced last year.
6. You're always complaining about everything.
7. We ate all the food yesterday.
8. Last year you became a mechanic, didn't you?
9. You have forgotten to do the exercises this morning, haven't you?
10. You shouldn't get upset about that.
11. I'm going to make myself a dress for my sister's wedding.

41.6.3

1 me aburro 2 se encuentran 3 (me como) 4 none
5 (me comí) 6 none 7 me quedaré 8 se casan
9 (se han comprado) 10 none 11 os cambiáis 12 none

42.3.1

1. No tengo hambre porque acabo de comer.
2. María no terminó el curso y ha vuelto a empezar.
3. Mis amigos y yo vamos a estudiar español.

4. Enrique y yo fuimos de compras cuando terminamos de trabajar.
5. Isabel no puede ponerse al teléfono porque está durmiendo.
6. María llegó, dejó sus maletas y volvió a salir.
7. Llegas tarde, el tren acaba de salir.
8. Cuando tenía cinco años empecé a tocar el piano.

42.3.2

1. I'm not hungry. I've just finished eating.
2. Maria didn't finish the course and has started again.
3. My friends and I are going to study Spanish.
4. Enrique and I went shopping when we finished work.
5. Isabel can't come to the phone because she's sleeping.
6. Maria arrived, left her suitcases and went out again.
7. You're late, the train has just left.
8. When I was five I started to play the piano.

42.5.1

1 pone 2 quedamos 3 llegué 4 continúan 5 dejamos 6
para 7 quedaron 8 seguimos 9 pongo 10 llevan

42.5.2

1. My mother always cleans the house until midday.
2. My cousin and I stay talking until very late.
3. I didn't get to finish the exam because it was very long.
4. My parents continue to live in the same house after forty years.
5. Pedro and I stopped going out together a month ago.
6. The boy doesn't let us sleep, he never stops crying.
7. Juan and Luis arranged to meet at the entrance to the cinema.
8. We are still living in Seville.
9. I'll start working right now.
10. My friends have been living in London for three years.

43.4.1

1. Juan sabe nadar muy bien.
2. Pepe debe trabajar más.
3. Tengo que levantarme muy pronto mañana.
4. Hay que cortar la hierba del jardín.
5. No quiero estudiar el año próximo.
6. Nosotros no podemos correr tan rápido.
7. Tú deberías comer menos.
8. Ana tuvo que quedarse en casa ayer.
9. ¿Podréis encontrarnos en la puerta del cine?
10. El tren debe de llevar retraso.

43.4.2

1. Juan can swim very well.
2. Pepe should work more.

3. I have to get up very early tomorrow.

4. We need to cut the grass in the garden.

5. I don't want to study next year.

6. We can't run so fast.

7. You should eat less.

8. Ana had to stay at home yesterday.

9. Can you meet us at the cinema entrance?

10. The train must be late.

44.3.1

1 Derribaron 2 Plantaron 3 Instalaron 4 Pusieron
5 Abrieron 6 Hicieron

44.3.2

1 Se desayuna 2 Se come 3 Se toma 4 Se merienda 5 Se cena 6 Se sale

44.3.3

1 se diseñó 2 se fabricaron 3 se celebró 4 se organizó
5 se suspendieron 6 se construyó 7 se cancelaron

44.3.4

1 fue diseñado 2 fueron fabricados 3 fue celebrado 4 fue organizada 5 fueron suspendidos 6 fue construida 7 fueron cancelados

44.3.5

1. Se vende esta casa.

2. Se alquila este apartamento.

3. Se prohíbe el ruido.

4. No se permite / Se prohíbe jugar a la pelota.

5. No se puede / debe hablar en clase.

6. Se prohíbe el paso / No se puede pasar.

7. Se tiene que pagar con dinero solamente.

Index